GOD'S STATESMAN

*The Life and Work of Dr John Owen*

# GOD'S STATESMAN

*The Life and Work of John Owen*

Pastor, Educator, Theologian

by

PETER TOON
M.A., B.D., M.Th., Th.D.
*Tutor in Religious Studies, Edgehill College,
Ormskirk, Lancashire*

WIPF & STOCK · Eugene, Oregon

Wipf and Stock Publishers
199 W 8th Ave, Suite 3
Eugene, OR 97401

God's Statesman
The Life and Work of John Owen
By Toon, Peter
Copyright©1971 by Toon, Peter
ISBN 13: 978-1-5326-4387-3
Publication date 12/1/2017
Previously published by The Paternoster Press, 1971

## CONTENTS

|        | Preface                                   | vii |
|--------|-------------------------------------------|-----|
| I.     | The Years of Preparation                  | 1   |
| II.    | Extending Service                         | 25  |
| III.   | Dean and Vice-Chancellor                  | 50  |
| IV.    | Ecclesiastical Statesman                  | 80  |
| V.     | Changing Responsibilities                 | 103 |
| VI.    | Protestant Nonconformist                  | 123 |
| VII.   | Pastor and Theologian                     | 150 |
| VIII.  | Epilogue                                  | 173 |
|        | Appendix I. List of Owen's Books.         | 179 |
|        |     II. Epitaph by Thomas Gilbert. | 182 |
|        | List of Abbreviations                     | 184 |
|        | Comparative Chronological Table of Events | 185 |
|        | Select Bibliography                       | 188 |
|        | Index of Subjects and Places              | 196 |
|        | Index of Personal Names                   | 198 |

# PREFACE

THIS BOOK IS AN ATTEMPT TO PRODUCE A STUDY OF THE LIFE, CAREER and basic teaching of a man into whose innermost thoughts and feelings it is difficult if not impossible to enter. Not one of John Owen's diaries has been preserved; and since the extant letters in which he lays bare his soul are very few, and recorded, personal reactions of others to him are brief and scarce, this study necessarily lacks many of those personal touches which have helped to establish biography as an important part of English literature. Nevertheless it is my sincere hope that this study will satisfy the current need for a fuller life of Owen.[1]

The organisation of the chapters is dictated mainly by the availability of material and most of this relates to the years 1651 to 1660. Chapters I and II are essentially chronological in form, describing the life of Owen from 1616 to 1651 and examining the formative influences which helped to shape his character. They are in fact an improved version of the introductory chapters of my edition of *The Correspondence of John Owen* (1970). Chapters III and IV deal with the years 1651 to 1658 from two different angles. One investigates his work at Oxford whilst the other is concerned with his contribution to religious affairs on a national level. The next chapter describes his efforts between the death of Oliver Cromwell and the restoration of Charles II to preserve the liberties of the Congregational churches. Chapters VI and VII are parallel in that both look at the years 1660 to 1683 from two different angles; the first examines his efforts to gain toleration for Nonconformists and the other looks at his work as a pastor and theologian. The last chapter takes the form of an epilogue.

If there is any merit in my work it is due in large part to the inspiration supplied by Dr Geoffrey Nuttall and the kind help and criticisms of Dr Brian Quintrell, Dr Barrie White, Dr John Mason, Dr Charles Webster, Dr E. W. Ives, Dr J. I. Packer, Mr E. G. W. Bill, Mr C. H. T. Parry, the Rev Alan Beesley, Mrs Sarah Cook, Dr B. S. Capp, and Mr B. H. Mudditt.

The British Museum, the Bodleian Library, the Libraries of the University of Durham, the University of Liverpool, New College, London, Christ Church, Oxford, Edge Hill College, Ormskirk, and Lambeth Palace, London, gave me excellent service. Last, but not least,

---

[1] Earlier biographies of Owen are described in the Epilogue, chap. viii.

my wife, who has endured for over four years the experience of my intense commitment to the life and times of John Owen, deserves a special word of thanks.

All books cited in footnotes are published in London unless otherwise indicated.

PETER TOON

CHAPTER I

THE YEARS OF PREPARATION

WHEN, ON THE 29TH APRIL 1646, JOHN OWEN, THEN A YOUNG MAN of thirty years of age, preached before the House of Commons in St Margaret's Church, Westminster, it may be said that he had achieved national recognition as a preacher and theologian.[1] He called upon Parliament to provide for the propagation of the Gospel of Christ in all parts of Britain and, when the sermon was printed, he added an appendix which contained advice for the settlement of religion in the nation. Here were two themes that were to occupy his attention for the rest of his life. From that day onward his fame and influence steadily grew. The explanation and account of this growth will occupy our attention in subsequent chapters; in this chapter we must examine the experiences of the first thirty years of his life which contributed to his development into the Independent divine who spoke with such conviction before the Commons on that fast-day in 1646.

It was in the thirteenth year of the reign of James I in England, the year in which William Shakespeare died, that John Owen came into the world.[2] Though he could not know it, he was born into a country which, from a political and religious standpoint, was far from happy. There was tension between the King and his subjects. Since February 1611, except for the two months in 1614 when the "Addled Parliament" expressed the anger but demonstrated the impotence of the electoral classes, public affairs were abandoned to the chance intrigues of the Court, which morally was far from healthy. Owen's parents, like most Puritans, must have been scandalized by news they received from London of favour shown by James to papists and to immoral nobles.[3] No doubt John's father, the Reverend Henry Owen, shared with fellow clergy grave misgivings about the behaviour of his earthly sovereign and his chief advisers.[4] Little did he or they realise that under the next monarch, Charles I, matters would get worse and many members of the puritan

---

[1] The sermon is printed in *Works*, VIII, pp. 1ff.
[2] Despite much effort (as I pointed out in *Correspondence*, pp. 3-4) I have not been able to ascertain the place of his birth.
[3] The poisoning of Sir Thomas Overbury and the sinister events which surrounded it were especially disgusting. Cf. Godfrey Davies, *The Early Stuarts, 1603-1660*, Oxford, 1959, pp. 16ff.
[4] Henry Owen was of Welsh blood, had studied at Oxford and then taught in a school at Stokenchurch, Bucks, before going to Stadham. Anthony Wood, *Athenae Oxonienses*, ed. Philip Bliss, 1813-20, IV, col. 97.

brotherhood of preachers would emigrate.[1] This however was a long time ahead. In 1616 baby John had only one brother, William, born four years earlier, but in the next few years his mother gave birth to at least three more children. These were two boys and a girl, all of whom survived the precarious years of infancy, which at that time claimed so many infants for an early grave.[2] This meant that he had the happy and stabilising experience of growing up as a member of a family.

After 1616 the family lived in the parsonage at Stadham (now Stadhampton), a small village five miles from Oxford. The origins of the parish church here went back into the eleventh century, from which time until the dissolution of the monasteries by Henry VIII it was controlled by Dorchester Abbey. From 1607 the living at Stadham was granted to the D'Oyley's, who owned the neighbouring Manor at Chislehampton and the gift of the living there. So the two parishes were served by the one curate.[3] Furthermore, the two villages could claim a puritan tradition. In 1604, John D'Oyley persuaded Robert Harris, who later became President of Trinity College, to live and preach at Chislehampton whilst Oxford was affected by the plague. D'Oyley's wife, Ursula, was a woman well versed in Calvinist divinity and a sister of Sir Anthony Cope of Hanwell, who went to the Tower in 1586-7 for his determined but unsuccessful efforts to reform the Book of Common Prayer. Walter Chaundler, the curate before Henry Owen, was known as "a faithful minister and a zealous preacher of God's Word."[4] So the arrival of John Owen's father meant that the existing puritan tradition was to be strengthened and enlarged.

Within the parsonage the children were taught to pray, to read the Bible and to obey the commandments. Each day they sat with the servants listening to their father expound a portion of Holy Scripture and pray for the country, the parish and for each of them individually. At their mother's knee they learned psalms and other portions of the Bible. As each Lord's Day came along they knew that it was a day of rest and worship for the whole community, the squire, the yeomen and

---

[1] See Perry Miller, *Orthodoxy in Massachusetts*, Boston, Mass , 1933.

[2] The names of the two boys were Henry and Philemon. Henry became a major in the Lord Protector's regiment (C. Firth & G. Davies, *The Regimental History of Cromwell's Army*, Oxford, 1940, p. 594) and outlived his brother John. Philemon became a captain in the army that went to Ireland in 1649 and was killed there (*C.J.*, VII, p. 39). I cannot trace the Christian name of his sister who married a Mr Singleton (*C.R.* s.v. John Singleton). His mother's name (if the widow who survived Henry Owen was his first wife) was Hester and she married the Rev. John Hartcliffe. See *Correspondence*, p. 9.

[3] For a description of Stadham see the *Victoria County History of Oxfordshire*, ed. R. B. Pugh, 1962, VII, pp. 81ff. For the D'Oyley family see W. D. D'Oyley Bayley, *A Biographical Account of the House of D'Oyley*, 1845, and for Cope see *D.N.B.* s.v. his grandfather of the same name.

[4] This statement is from the parish register and is quoted in the *Vict. Hist. Of Oxfordshire*, VII, p. 83. Chaundler was buried at Stadhampton on March 7 1615 and in 1618 one of the parishioners, who had greatly esteemed him, erected a tomb for him, which is still in the churchyard.

the labourers. Religious observance, though important, was not the only activity of the parsonage. The children had to learn to read and write as well as help with the manual chores. For their recreation they probably joined children from the village and made use of the open countryside, the haystacks and the farm animals to have fun. In his voluminous writings, John made no reference to his mother or his brothers and sister. There is, however, one brief but telling reference to his father, whom he certainly admired. "I was bred up from my infancy," he wrote in 1657, "under the care of my father, who was a nonconformist all his days, and a painful labourer in the vineyard of the Lord."[1] Obviously Henry Owen did not wear certain prescribed ecclesiastical vestments (e.g. the surplice) and he also omitted those parts of the Prayer Book which he believed were contrary to the teaching of Holy Scripture and the Genevan, Calvinist tradition. He was able to do this at Stadham only because he had the support of the D'Oyley family who must have protected him from the ecclesiastical authorities. Apart from his puritan approach to worship, Henry Owen seems also to have been a faithful pastor who taught his parishioners the fundamentals of the Faith, visited the sick and dying and engaged in prayer to God for the salvation of all their souls. We may thus perhaps attribute to the influence of his father the genesis of many of Owen's later emphases, characteristics and opinions. His insistence that Holy Scripture is the only authority for faith, worship and conduct, his Calvinist theology, his opposition to ceremonial in worship, his understanding of the pastoral office, his deep conviction of God's providential dealings with the British people and his personal search for communion and fellowship with God through Christ may all have had their origin in the home and church at Stadham.

John was perhaps about ten years old when he was sent with his elder brother, William, to the small grammar school run by Edward Sylvester in a house in the parish of All Saints, Oxford.[2] William Chillingworth, author of the classic *The Religion of Protestants a Safe Way to Salvation* (1638), and Henry Wilkinson, who was to become the Lady Margaret Professor of Divinity and a Canon of Christ Church, had been scholars there a few years earlier.[3] The fees for the two sons of Henry Owen were paid by his brother (or brother-in-law) who lived in Wales. In Sylvester's school they gained the rudiments of grammar, Latin, and literature as a preparation for the undergraduate course in the University, Queen's College being chosen as the place where the boys were to pursue their studies.[4] The reasons for the choice are not

[1] *Works*, XIII, p. 224.
[2] Anthony Wood briefly mentions Sylvester in *Fasti Oxonienses*, ed. Philip Bliss, 1815, p.34.
[3] For Chillingworth and Wilkinson see *D.N.B.*
[4] The most recent history of Queen's is R. H. Hodgkin, *Six Centuries of an Oxford College*, Oxford, 1949.

known: perhaps Henry Owen or a relative had studied there, or perhaps the boys' father knew Christopher Potter, the new Provost, who in earlier years had enjoyed the reputation of being a Puritan.[1] At least one point in favour of Queen's, we may reflect, was that it had once provided shelter for John Wyclif, the Biblical reformer, for whom Henry Owen would have had a high regard. .

From the Diary kept by Thomas Crosfield, a Fellow of Queen's, we are able to catch a glimpse of student life at this time.[2] On many mornings there was a Latin sermon in the College Chapel at 6.a.m. followed by breakfast. Lectures, tutorials and disputations, all conducted in Latin, took up the hours to dinner at 10.a.m. After the meal there was time for recreation before more lectures and disputations were held. After Chapel in the afternoon there was time for private study and consultation with a tutor. The regular routine was interrupted by such things as Holy Days when Holy Communion in the Chapel was compulsory. The two great social occasions, when relatives and former students came to the College, were the Act in July and Founder's Day in August. On the 15th August (the *obit* of Queen Philippa) many "old boys" returned to meet former friends and to enjoy the pleasures of wine and merriment. On the Monday after 7 July came the climax of the academic year, the *Comitia*, commonly known as the Act. Oxford was filled with visitors for the celebrations of the weekend. They began with Vesperies on the Saturday which involved public lectures and disputations followed by a formal supper in each faculty. Special sermons were preached on the Sunday. On the Monday morning those who were due to graduate or to take part in the public academic exercises assembled at 9.a.m. for Holy Communion at St Mary's Church. After this service they went in solemn procession to the place where the exercises were to take place. When all was completed, and the degrees of doctor conferred, the Vice-Chancellor addressed the audience in Latin to give them his impression of the highlights of the year now completed. Associated with the public disputation in philosophy was the custom of *terrae-filius*, the elected wag of the students, who was given licence to act stupidly and speak provocatively for the entertainment of onlookers. With his puritan training Owen may have viewed the festivities in both July and August with some horror, even if he actually was obliged to join in them with the other students. Indeed, it was probably a combination of what he had experienced whilst at Queen's and that which he was to experience in 1653-4 which made him try to reform the festivities which closed the academic year when he was Vice-Chancellor.

[1] For Potter see *D.N.B*. In his youth he had been a follower of the puritan Provost, Henry Airay, a noted opponent of William Laud.
[2] *The Diary of Thomas Crosfield*, ed. F. S. Boas, 1935.

John entered Queen's at the tender age of twelve years but this was not exceptional at that time. His name was entered into the Buttery-Book, which meant he would be served with meals. However, he did not matriculate until the 4th November 1631 when he was fifteen. The ceremony of matriculation, usually conducted in the presence of the Vice-Chancellor, involved subscription to the Articles of the Church. He graduated Bachelor of Arts on the 11th June 1632, the same day that his brother, William, also graduated.[1] To secure this degree, they had to be in residence for sixteen terms or four years, to attend specified lectures in the Public Schools of the University and to perform prescribed academic exercises. The course in Liberal Arts included the study of grammar and rhetoric in the first year, logic and moral philosophy in the second, geometry and Greek with more philosophy in the third and fourth. The academic exercises, which were central to the whole educational system at Oxford, were the disputations or the formal organised debates, which were developed in the medieval universities as a means of resolving questions left in doubt by the best authorities or as a way of reconciling conflicting opinions. A controversial point from logic or philosophy was put into the form of a question and then the debate proceeded in three stages. A participant, called the respondent, offered an answer or an interpretation of the question. Next, several opponents stated contradictory propositions and attacked flaws in the respondent's argumentation. Finally, the moderator, who presided over the proceedings, summed up the arguments on each side, called attention to matters that had been overlooked and then bestowed praise or blame as due and gave his decision. John and William would have watched disputations in their first two years but in the latter part of the course they would have taken part in them. The purpose of these exercises was to develop the art of thinking logically and exploring all sides of a problem. In John's case they certainly succeeded in doing this. Apart from the academic work, which for an intelligent boy was not over-demanding, John found time for physical exercises and was fond of throwing the javelin and doing the long jump. This suggests that he had a robust constitution, a fact which later portraits confirm.[2]

The degree of Bachelor of Arts did not signify in the 1630s the completion of a complete course of study. Rather it signified the attainment of a sufficient standard to pursue higher studies for the degree of Master of Arts, which was considered to be a degree in the full sense of the word. John was fortunate in having the gifted Aristotelian scholar,

[1] J. R. Magrath, *The Queen's College*, Oxford, 1921, pp. 270ff. lists some of Owen's fellow students but none of those listed seem to have played an important part in his later life.
[2] Asty, p. iii. Asty's *Memoir* may be regarded as a reliable source since he relied for most of his information on Sir John Hartopp who from 1662 was a close friend of Owen. For details of existing portraits see chap. VIII, p. 176. n. 3.

Thomas Barlow, later Bishop of Lincoln, with whom he was to enjoy a life-time friendship, as his tutor for this course.[1] From Barlow he imbibed "a full draught of Oxford learning at a time when the streams of controversy were in tumultuous conflict." For, as Mark Curtis has shown, "the work of College tutors was definitely in the seventeenth century the most important influence on a scholar's education."[2] The M.A. course lasted for three years and involved the listening to public lectures in geometry, metaphysics, ancient history, Greek, Hebrew, and astronomy, together with the usual round of disputations. As a review of the style and contents of Owen's later books reveals, he was able to build upon and develop (though not always to the ease of his readers) this basic training in ancient languages, literature and philosophy. Indeed, so great was his zeal for knowledge at this time that he often allowed himself only four hours of sleep each night. His health was affected, and in later life, when he was often on a sick-bed, he regretted these hours of rest that he had missed as a youth. One of his recreational activities was playing the flute. He was taught by Thomas Wilson, whom twenty years later he appointed the Oxford professor of Music.

On the 27th April 1635 both John and William received the degree of M.A. John was only nineteen, but this was not an exceptional age for a degree at the time. Soon afterwards they were ordained deacons by John Bancroft, Bishop of Oxford, in Christ Church.[3] Still in receipt of an allowance from his Welsh uncle, John (and perhaps William also) began the seven-year course for the degree of Bachelor of Divinity. This gave him a splendid opportunity to begin to read widely in both British and Continental authors, an activity, we may note, that he kept up until his death nearly fifty years later. The two basic areas of divinity which had already attracted his attention, and which now would do so far more, were the continuing controversy between Protestants and Roman Catholics and the growth of Arminian doctrine in Holland and in the Church of England. Since we shall have cause to refer to the Arminian controversy in Holland when describing Owen's first book, we need here only refer to the so-called "Arminianism" of the High-Church theologians of the Church of England (e.g. Lancelot Andrewes, John Cosin, Richard Montague, Richard Neile and William Laud) whose influence was particularly felt at Oxford in the 1630s. Naturally their understanding of grace and free-will, like that of modern Anglo-Catholics, fitted in with their doctrine of the Church, its ministry and

[1] For Barlow see *D.N.B.*
[2] M. H. Curtis, *Oxford and Cambridge in Transition*, Oxford, 1959, p. 107. The quotation in the previous sentence is from *The Register of the Visitors . . . 1647–1658*, ed. M. Burrows, 1881, p. xxix.
[3] For Bancroft see *D.N.B.* The dates of the ordinations are not known for the lists for these years have not been preserved.

sacraments. Against the majority of English churchmen they denied that the Pope was Antichrist and that the Papacy was under God's condemnation. For them the Roman Church, along with the Orthodox Churches, was part of the Catholic Church and its ministry was a valid ministry. They contended that in the Catholic Church of which the Church of England was part the grace of God was channelled to the faithful by means of the lawful ministry and its administration of the Word and Sacraments. Necessarily such a position reduced the need to stress the sovereign, free grace of God and put greater emphasis on man's part within the process of salvation. The faithful had to avail themselves of the sacraments and the ministry had faithfully to administer them. God's grace came through the human, ecclesiastical system and those who would be saved had to accept salvation by this means.

From the Provost of his own College, as well as from many of the Fellows, Owen heard preaching and catechising which, whilst ascribing salvation ultimately to God, nevertheless allowed man, through the exercise of his freewill, some part in the redemptive process. He saw and experienced the emphasis on the sacraments as a primary source of grace and on ceremonial in worship as a supposed expression of beauty and order. Provost Potter revived in the College Chapel practices which his predecessors had regarded as papistical. Tutors and students were required to bow to the holy table and at the mention of the name of Jesus, to wear full ecclesiastical robes, and to stand for the reading of the Gospel and the recital of the Creed. Sometimes incense was burned and the Chapel was beautified at a cost of £2,800, money which had been saved in the College chest.[1]

What was happening in his own College was also taking place in others. At Christ Church, for example, under Brian Duppa, the inside of the Cathedral was renovated and beautified, the singing of the *Venite*, *Te Deum* and *Benedictus* was improved, grace was sung after meals by the chaplains, greater use was made of the organ and organist, and "caps" instead of "hats" were required to be worn for worship. And the doctrine from the pulpit was made to harmonise with the emphasis on beauty and orderliness.[2] Indeed, since Owen had entered the University, a growing high-Church influence had made itself felt, inspired primarily by William Laud, who in 1630 became Chancellor of Oxford and three years later Archbishop of Canterbury.[3] No doubt his influence was behind the actions of Potter and Duppa. Also, in 1628 Charles I had forbidden debates over such controversial subjects as

[1] Hodgkin, *op. cit.*, pp. 72ff.
[2] H. L. Thompson, *Christ Church*, 1900, pp. 61–3. For the state of the University see Anthony Wood, *The History and Antiquities of the University of Oxford*, ed. John Gutch, Oxford, 1796, II, pp. 368ff. and C. E. Mallet, *A History of the University of Oxford*, 1924, II, pp. 303ff.
[3] For Laud see H. R. Trevor-Roper, *Archbishop Laud*, new ed. 1962.

divine election and predestination.¹ To the Calvinists at Oxford this was seen as "a Jesuitical plot to subvert the Gospel."² But to Laud it was a ruling which he believed would work in such a way that the "unhappy differences likely to rend the Church . . . might sleep first and die after."³ And, at least on the surface, the issues between the old Calvinists and the new Laudians did virtually sleep. Yet they were kept alive by the faithful and resolute stand for their beliefs by such men as John Prideaux, the Regius Professor, John Wilkinson and Christopher Rogers, both Heads of Halls, as well as by the infrequent theological eruptions from such men as Thomas Hill.⁴ Laud, however, saw to it that those who disturbed the peace were punished, especially those who voiced Calvinist notions. Furthermore, he appointed as his Vice-Chancellors men who shared his doctinal views.⁵

Outside the confines of Oxford the opposition to Arminian and high-Church theology (which most Calvinists saw as necessarily linked) was much stronger. In Parliament, for example, Francis Rous made a concerted attack against Richard Montague, the Bishop of Chichester (later of Norwich).⁶ A reading of the debates in the Commons of that year reveals that a majority of the members assumed that Arminianism was a branch of popery, or, at least, a helpmeet to it, that its propagation was a selling out of the Church to foreign domination, that the Church of England was a Calvinist and Reformed Church, and that those who were seeking to destroy the legal religion of England were also the instigators of the destruction of English liberties and property. Defence of Calvinism also came from the learned William Twisse and the energetic William Prynne.⁷ Quite rightly Owen quickly perceived that the central point at issue was the doctrine of predestination. For the Calvinist it guaranteed the free, unmerited grace of God, eliminated all human merit in salvation, and ensured the preservation of a reformed attitude to both the ministry and the sacraments. For the high-Church Arminian the same doctrine seemed to make man less than human, to deny human freewill and autonomy, and to make the "apostolic" ministry

---

¹ Cf. Curtis, *op. cit.*, pp. 172–3.
² At least this is what Peter Heylyn reports in his *Cyprianus Anglicus*, 1671, p. 178.
³ Laud, *Historical Account of Chancellorship*, in *The Works of William Laud*, ed. J. H. Parker, Oxford, 1853, V, p. 5.
⁴ Wood, *History . . . of the University*, II, pp. 372ff. In 1631 Hill of Hart Hall publicly denounced Arminian doctrine and was made to recant publicly upon his knees.
⁵ Between 1630 and 1640 the Vice-Chancellors were: William Smyth (Warden of Wadham), Brian Duppa (Dean of Christ Church), Robert Pinke (Warden of New College), Richard Baylie (President of St John's) and Accepted Frewen (President of Magdalen).
⁶ *Commons Debates for 1629*, ed. Wallace Notestein and Frances Relf, Minneapolis, 1921, pp. 12–13, 15–16, 33–34. For Montague and his connections with Laud see Trevor-Roper, *op. cit.*, pp. 73ff.
⁷ For Twisse and Prynne see D.N.B. Twisse wrote *Vindicae Gratiae*, Amsterdam, 1632, and Prynne, *Anti-Arminianisme*, 1630.

of the Church as well as the Eucharist unimportant or even redundant.[1]

While we have no contemporary account of Owen's feelings concerning the dominance of high-Church theology at Oxford in the 1630s, we do know that his first book in 1643 was a defence of the doctrine of predestination and that in his sermon to Parliament in 1646 he severely criticised the innovations of Archbishop Laud.[2] As he saw the situation the "paintings, crossings, crucifixes, bowings, altars, tapers, wafers, organs, anthems, litany, rails, images, copes and vestments" were "but Roman varnish, an Italian dress" for devotions, introduced to lead men into the clutches of Antichrist. The *Laudian* emphasis on "the divinity of Episcopacy, auricular confession" and such-like was an attempt to make the Articles of Religion "speak good Roman Catholic" and thus lead England back into the arms of the Pope. Owen did not feel that he could remain in a College where such things were encouraged and so, after consultation with his father and others, he decided that Oxford was no place for him, at least for the time being.

As he considered the situation, the thought must have crossed his mind that, had he been at Cambridge instead of Oxford, there would have been no need to leave the University. Though Laud had his friends in Peterhouse, where Arminianism triumphed under Matthew Wren and John Cosin, Calvinism and Puritanism remained in the ascendant in most Colleges. The intention of the Archbishop to visit Cambridge as metropolitan never materialised and so Laudianism never gained that wide acceptance that it enjoyed in Oxford. Owen, however, did not leave Queen's until 1637. This meant that he was probably present on the 22nd June at the solemn convocation in St Mary's when the Statutes for the University were published and then subscribed by Heads of Houses. The inspiration behind the completion of the new Code was the Chancellor. Not even his severest critic could have reasonably denied the need for a revision, since the old Statutes were imperfect and confused: perhaps a puritan Chancellor, whilst agreeing with most of the new academic and disciplinary measures, would have made such matters as the taking of oaths and the wearing of full ecclesiastical or academic robes as optional rather than compulsory. As it was, the Statutes had the effect for four or five years of creating and continuing in the University that uniformity and order on which Laud placed so much emphasis.[3] Twenty years later, when he was ruling the University in very different conditions, Owen expressed his feelings about the Statutes

---

[1] It seems to me that C.H. & K.G. George, *The Protestant Mind of the English Reformation, 1570–1640*, Princeton, 1961, minimises by careful use of quotations the basic differences of doctrine that existed in the English Church. J. P. F. New, *Anglican and Puritan: the basis of their opposition*, 1964, is more reliable but there is still room for a careful theological study of the period.

[2] *Works*, VIII, p. 28.

[3] Mallet, *op. cit.*, II, pp. 314ff. There is an English translation in *Oxford University Statutes*, tr. G. R. M. Ward, 1845, I.

in a letter to Henry Cromwell. He maintained that they were "framed to the road of studies of former days" and not "expedient for the promotion of the good ends of godliness and literature."[1]

Two months after the publication of the Statutes, the King and Queen freely chose to visit Oxford and, as it were, consecrate the achievements of Laud.[2] This visit perhaps provided Owen with his first and last opportunity to see Charles I until he witnessed his execution thirteen years later at Whitehall. The royal couple lodged in Christ Church Deanery and watched several plays in the great Hall. In the Cathedral they were no doubt pleased to hear a sermon from one of the proctors which demonstrated the royal authority over all Englishmen, including Puritans, Papists and Anabaptists. Then the royal party left Oxford, not to return again until the 29th October 1642 when the City and University became a royal fortress in the civil war.

Owen did not go far from Oxford. Probably through his father's help, he became chaplain and tutor in the household of Sir Robert Dormer at the Manor House in the hamlet of Ascot in the parish of Great Milton. The Dormer family owned property, including two water mills, in Stadham, which was only three miles from their home, and in 1633 Sir Robert had been given permission to erect a pew near the pulpit in Stadham Church.[3] Taking a chaplaincy was of course a common puritan way both of avoiding clashes with the hierarchy of the Church and of continuing theological reading. Owen probably read services from the Prayer Book and preached in the private chapel, which had been built on to the side of the house at Ascot. Also, since he was so near to his father, we may presume that he also took services at Chislehampton or Stadham. But he did not stay long with the Dormer family. He moved some twenty miles nearer London to be chaplain in the home of John, Lord Lovelace, the second Baron, and his wife Anne, the daughter and heiress of Thomas Wentworth, first Earl of Cleveland.[4] Just why Owen left Ascot for Hurley is not clear. Perhaps pressure from the Bishop of Oxford upon Sir Robert, who was not legally entitled to have a chaplain, or even economic factors played some part in the decision.

With Lord Lovelace Owen had more security; being a nobleman his Lordship was allowed to keep a chaplain. Owen's employer was

[1] *Correspondence*, No. 52, p. 100.

[2] For a description of the visit see Mallet, *op. cit.*, pp. 341ff. and Trevor-Roper, *op. cit.*, pp. 287ff. Professor Trevor-Roper singles out for special mention as outstanding achievements of Laud at Oxford not only the Statutes but also the building of the Canterbury Quadrangle at St John's and the establishment of the chair of Arabic.

[3] For the history of Ascot with references to Sir Robert see *Vict. History of Oxfordshire*, VII, pp. 117ff.

[4] For Lovelace see *D.N.B.* s.v. his son of the same name. It is mistakenly stated there that Owen was the tutor to the young John from 1640 to 1650. As the boy was born in 1638 it is impossible that Owen was his tutor 1641-2. For the house at Hurley see *Vict. County History of Berkshire*, ed. W. Page & P. H. Ditchfield, 1923, III, p. 155.

probably one of the many Englishmen who was a firm Protestant and had no special love for Archbishop Laud and his religion. So, presumably, Owen was allowed to read services and to preach dressed in the minimum ecclesiastical dress. His Lordship was more interested in the character and ability of his chaplain than in his attire. Both men must have been deeply troubled by the news that came from Scotland, and must have felt that the attempt to force the Prayer Book upon the Scots was a tactless move by the King and Archbishop. They were also probably in agreement with the majority in the Short and then Long Parliaments who believed that the power of the bishops had to be restricted and the liberties of Englishmen restored. Nevertheless, as the hostility between the Long Parliament and Charles I became more obvious during 1641-2, the sympathies of Lord Lovelace gradually moved towards his King. This did not mean that he was becoming a Laudian in religion; rather, it signified that he believed that the demands of Parliament were now too radical.[1]

Parliament's demands are clearly highlighted in the *Grand Remonstrance* which was sent to Charles I in November 1641. It petitioned His Royal Highness to be

> graciously pleased to concur with the humble desires of your people in a parliamentary way, for the preserving the peace and safety of the kingdom from the malicious designs of the Popish party:—
> For depriving the Bishops of their votes in Parliament, and abridging their immoderate power usurped over the Clergy and your other good subjects, which have been perniciously abused to the hazard of religion, and great prejudice and oppression to the laws of the kingdom and just liberty of your people.
> For the taking away such oppressions in religion, Church government and discipline, as have been brought in and fomented by them.
> For uniting all your loyal subjects together as join in the same fundamental truths against the Papists, by removing some oppressive and unnecessary ceremonies by which divers weak consciences have been scrupled and seem to be divided from the rest, and for due execution of those good laws which have been made for securing the liberty of your subjects.

Owen's later attitude would seem to indicate that he would have been wholeheartedly in favour of this petition. But perhaps the later declaration from Westminster made on the 27th May 1642 stating that the King, seduced by wicked counsellors, was making war on Parliament, would have seemed to him, as it must have done to Lord Lovelace, to be a provocative gesture. At about this time his Lordship began to follow the example of other noblemen and began to persuade his tenants and neighbours to be ready to fight for the King in what he believed would be a short war. In June 1642 he signed the declaration in favour of

[1] For the political background see C. V. Wedgwood, *The King's War, 1641-1647*, 1958.

Charles.[1] During this period, Owen remained quietly at his task continuing his theological reading and anxiously awaiting news of national affairs. In August he heard how the King had raised the royal standard at Nottingham and proclaimed the Commons and its army traitors. Two months later came news of the battle of Edgehill between the armies of the King and the Earl of Essex. This was followed by the expected news that His Majesty had been given a royal welcome by the University of Oxford. Perhaps Owen saw some of the royalist forces as they moved towards London on what was to be an unsuccessful march or as they returned to make Oxford the seat of the Court. By autumn 1642 both Lord Lovelace and his chaplain realised that the war would not end as quickly as they had previously thought. His Lordship's sympathies were with the King but those of his chaplain were not so clear. Owen's religious convictions led him to sympathy with the Presbyterian preachers of London who at this time were wholly behind the stated aims of Parliament, but certain family pressures (e.g., that of his Welsh uncle and benefactor) pushed him in the opposite direction. Eventually he made up his mind to go to London, where he had relatives. This move cost him the friendship and financial support of his uncle and must have seemed to him at this time only the better of two poor alternatives.[2]

Owen soon came to believe, however, that the move to London was providential. Not only did it bring him into contact with the leading clerical defenders of the cause of Parliament, those puritan preachers who saw the conflict between the King and Parliament in terms of that battle of Christ against antichrist which they believed was portrayed in such vivid terms and symbols in the Book of Revelation.[3] It also provided the scene for an experience he could never forget. By 1642 he was convinced that the only source of authority in religion was Holy Scripture; he wholeheartedly accepted the doctrines of orthodox Calvinism and knew how and why these differed from the doctrines of Lutheranism, Arminianism and Roman Catholicism; but he had not yet experienced that personal, spiritual assurance of the Holy Spirit witnessing to his own spirit that he was a child of God. He knew that much of the literature of the Puritan brotherhood of preachers had concerned itself with the need for this sense of the reality of salvation.[4] Happily, Owen found what his soul desired in St Mary's Church, Aldermanbury. One Sunday, Asty informs us, he went with his cousin

[1] See *D.N.B.* s.v. John Lovelace and Wedgwood, *op. cit.*, pp. 95ff.

[2] The loss of financial support by his uncle is mentioned in both the anonymous *Life of Owen* (1720) and by Asty. I cannot determine the identity of the uncle.

[3] To this period in Owen's life we may perhaps attribute the beginnings of his serious reading of the standard books on prophecy and eschatology—e.g. the works of Brightman, Mede and Alsted. Cf. *Puritans, the Millennium and the Future of Israel: Puritan Eschatology, 1600–1660*, ed. Peter Toon, 1970.

[4] Cf. William Haller, *The Rise of Puritanism*, 1957, pp. 83ff.

to hear the famous Presbyterian, Edmund Calamy, who was rector of the parish.[1] On arrival they were told that Calamy could not preach and that a country preacher (whose name Owen never ascertained) was to deputise. Though his cousin pressed him to leave and go to hear Arthur Jackson at nearby St Michael's, Owen decided to remain at St Mary's. The preacher took as his text Matthew 8:26, "Why are ye fearful, O ye of little faith?" It proved to be a message which Owen needed to hear and accept. An unknown preacher was the means God used to speak to him. The great preacher Charles Spurgeon was to have a similar experience over two centuries later when he experienced conversion through the ministry of an illiterate preacher who substituted at the last minute for the preacher who had been engaged to speak. Owen's doubts, fears and worries as to whether he was truly regenerate and born anew of the Holy Spirit were removed as he felt himself liberated and knew he was an adopted son of God. This spiritual experience cannot really be over-rated for it gave Owen the inward conviction that he was a true child of God, chosen in Christ before the foundation of the world, that God loved him and had a loving purpose for him, and that his God was the living God. In practical terms this meant that he would now see everything that happened to him and to the Church of Christ in terms of the providence and predestination of God; it meant also that he would strive to ensure that church people received both the doctrines of the Gospel and the inward presence of the Holy Spirit in their hearts. So began his great interest in the work of the Holy Spirit which came to fruition thirty years later in the monumental study of the Holy Spirit, *A Discourse Concerning the Holy Spirit.*

Both before and after this encounter with God, Owen was working on his first book. It was to be polemical in character since this was the way that young men made a name for themselves, just as young scholars do today in Continental Universities. Earlier we noted that he read widely in the Arminian controversy. In Holland after the publishing of the Arminians' *Remonstrance* (1610) and the consequent debates which reached their climax at the Synod of Dort (1618), this had resolved itself into five basic questions:— whether the human will is free or in bondage to sin; whether or not the saving grace of God is irresistible; whether or not God chose some to salvation before He made the world; whether Christ died only for the elect or for the whole human race; and whether it is possible for the regenerate believer to fall from grace.[2] The Arminians (Remonstrants) held that the will was free, that God's grace may be resisted, that God did not arbitrarily choose some to salvation, that Christ died for all the world and that a Christian may

[1] Asty, p.v.
[2] For the theology of Jacobus Arminius see Carl Bangs, *Arminius: A study in the Dutch Reformation,* Nashville, 1971. For the Arminian controversy in Holland see A. W. Harrison, *The Beginnings of Arminianism,* 1926.

fall from grace. Owen's defence of the limited extent of the atonement of Christ was to come in 1647 and of the final perseverance of the saints in 1654. In 1642 he confined himself to the doctrines of predestination and the extent of human freewill since he felt that these were the areas in which high-Church theology and Laudianism had made the greatest impact in England. Like the majority of his contemporaries Owen called the theology of the Dutch Remonstrants and the theology of the English high-Churchmen "Arminianism." Of course people in the seventeenth century were well aware that, whilst the doctrines of grace were similar amongst these two groups, in other matters—the doctrine of the Church and sacraments for example—they were poles apart.[1] His book was published in April 1643 with the title: *A Display of Arminianism: being a discovery of the old Pelagian idol, free-will, with the new goddess, contingency, advancing themselves into the throne of God in heaven to the prejudice of His grace, providence and supreme dominion over the children of men.*[2] Modern scholarship has clearly shown that there is a great difference between the Pelagianism which horrified Augustine of Hippo in the fifth century and the Arminianism of the Dutch Remonstrants.[3] The latter were genuinely trying to recover what they believed to be the original emphases of the Reformation which they felt had been somewhat hardened in the development of Reformed divinity. Pristine Arminianism had a far superior doctrine of grace to Pelagianism but in that both systems of doctrine denied the absolute predestination of God, Owen, together with most of the puritan brotherhood of preachers, saw a clear link between them, and therefore felt justified in calling both Dutch Arminianism and English high-Church theology by the term "Pelagianism."

Owen dedicated the book (presumably with their permission) to the "Lords and Gentlemen of the Committee for Religion," which had been set up in March 1640 by the House of Lords to examine innovations in doctrine introduced into the Church. His aim was obviously to be noticed! He told the committee of his deep horror on hearing about the massacre in November 1641 of several thousand English Protestants in Ireland. News of this massacre, often in exaggerated form, had had a tremendous effect on the English and served to strengthen Parliament's intention to rid England of traces of popery. Owen also went on in the dedication to argue that the Church of England could "not wrap in her

---

[1] There were few genuinely "Arminian" English theologians amongst Puritans and moderate Anglicans in the 1640's. John Goodwin, with whom Owen engaged in controversy in 1654, was one of the very few Puritan Arminians. In the 1630's and 1640's the majority of English theologians were Calvinistic: even after 1662 an Arminian Protestant Dissenter was still a rare type!
[2] In *Works*, X., pp. 2ff.
[3] For Augustine and Pelagianism see Peter Brown, *Augustine of Hippo*, 1967, Pt. IV., and for Arminianism see Bangs, *op. cit.*, pp. 332ff.

communion Augustine and Pelagius, Calvin and Arminius." In his "Epistle to the Christian Reader" he wrote:

> The fates of our Church having of late devolved the government thereof into the hands of men tainted with this poison, Arminianism became backed with the powerful arguments of praise and preferment and quickly prevailed to beat poor naked truth into a corner. It is high time, then, for the lovers of the old way to oppose this innovation.

This of course was written at the beginning of the war when the men whom Laud and Charles I had put in positions of power in the Church and Universities were still entrenched even though their days were numbered. Owen's sense of outrage at Laudian policy is well conveyed in his further remark that "had a poor Puritan offended against half as many canons as they opposed articles [i.e. 39 Articles] he had forfeited his livelihood." Owen's book was no masterpiece but it was a thorough defence of the Calvinist doctrine of the bondage of the will to sin and of the absolute predestination of God, with His sovereign right to elect unto salvation whom He would and to give the grace of faith and repentance to whom He would. Lacking any literary elegance and showing clear signs of his Aristotelian education, this was nevertheless the first of a long line of books in which he resolutely defended the central core of orthodox Calvinism.[1] The question as to whether Owen was fair to Arminianism cannot be dealt with here. To him it was a system of doctrine that ran contrary to the Reformed Confessions of Faith and thus contrary to the true mind of Protestantism. And, as was noted above, he was trying to make his name as a scholar by scoring polemical points.

Owen did not spend all his time in 1642–3 with his relatives in London. On two occasions, in December 1642 and July 1643, he visited Scot's Hall in the parish of Smeeth, near Ashford, Kent, as the guest of Sir Edward and Lady Scott.[2] In all probability the reason for these visits was his friendship with the son of Lady Scott by her first marriage, Thomas Westrow, whom he had known at Oxford when they were students together at Queen's. Of Westrow Owen had the highest opinion: he told Thomas' stepfather that "his judgement to discern the differences of these times, and his valour in prosecuting what he is resolved to be just and lawful, place him among the number of those very few to whom it is given to know aright the causes of things and vigorously to execute

---

[1] The term Calvinism is not used in this book to describe the theology of Calvin himself but rather that of the Reformed Churches as expressed by such divines as Beza, Zanchius, Perkins, Ames etc. and systematised in the Westminster Confession of Faith of 1648.

[2] Sir Edward Scott was the fifth son and eventual heir of Sir Thomas Scott (died 1611). He was Sheriff of Kent in 1625 and M.P. for Hythe in 1627. His third wife (née Mary Aldersley) whom he married in 1639 had been married first to Thomas Westrow of London and then to Sir Norton Knatchbull of Mersham.

holy and laudable designs." If asked, Westrow would probably have described Owen in glowing terms also for after he became the M.P. for Hythe he nominated his friend as a preacher for the fast-day in April 1646. While the two young men discussed the state of the nation and of the war, they were probably joined at times by Sir Edward and by Thomas Rooke, a kinsman of Sir Edward. Rooke lived at the house and was the treasurer in Shepway for the collection for Parliament organised by the County Committee.[1] Both Sir Edward and Rooke would have been busily engaged in the hasty moves to prepare the defence of their area when, late in 1642, the royalist, Sir William Brockman of Beachborough near Hythe, endeavoured to raise a rebellion in the county. The King sent him a commission of array and, at the same time, the Earl of Thanet was despatched with a regiment through Sussex to support him. In Shepway, Owen informs us, there was general fear of an "invasion of a potent enemy," by which presumably he meant the Earl. But the revolt quickly collapsed; Brockman was arrested and the Earl surrendered.[2]

During Owen's second visit to Scot's Hall, the County Committee was administering the Covenant with only moderate success. This "Sacred Vow and Covenant" had been taken on June 6 by members of Parliament.[3] A few weeks later the Committee of Kent was ordered to administer it to every person of age in the county. It was to be taken in parish churches and those taking it had to affirm their belief "that the forces raised by the two Houses of Parliament were raised and continued for their just defence . . . against the forces raised by the King without their consent." One of the effects of this activity at the local level was to cause many who had previously been uncommitted in the national conflict to affirm their support for the King. Rebellion broke out at Sevenoaks. To Owen those who rebelled were "a rude, godless, multitude;" yet, we must remember, they were led by gentry from some of the oldest families of Kent, and the men who prepared to fight under them were descendants of the men who in previous centuries had marched on London under leaders of the stature of Sir Thomas Wyatt. At first the cause of Parliament in the county seemed hopeless, but, within a month, the Kentish Rebellion had been suppressed by the intervention of parliamentary forces from outside the county. While the victory of arms went to Parliament, many of the clergy and gentry never did take the Covenant and they also continued to use

---

[1] I cannot ascertain any details about Rooke. However, his complete series of 29 account books from 1644-1651 have survived. Alan Everitt, *The Community of Kent and the Great Rebellion*, Leicester, 1966, p. 159.

[2] For a brief description of this revolt and the Kentish Rebellion of six months later see Everitt, *op. cit.*, pp. 187ff. Owen's brief comments about Westrow and the insurrections are in the dedicatory letter to Sir Edward in *Works*, XIII, p. 3.

[3] S. R. Gardiner, *History of the Great Civil War*, 1893, I, p. 149.

the Prayer Book. Perhaps it was this general lack of Puritanism in Shepway that made Owen reject the offer of a parish living there made to him by Sir Edward.[1] He chose instead to go to Essex which had a long and honourable tradition of Presbyterianism and Puritanism.

When Owen returned to London he was offered by Parliament the living at Fordham.[2] The village was about five miles from Colchester and the parish church was situated in a commanding position on higher ground than the rest of the parish. As this part of Essex has little stone the church, like the large houses in the area, had to be constructed of what was available locally, which meant flint and pebble-rubble. However, the church had some Roman brick at the base of the tower. John Alsop, the rector since 1633, and also a chaplain to Archbishop Laud (who was now in the Tower of London) was sequestered because of his desertion of the parish.[3] A note at the top of a page in the parish register reads: "John Owen, Pastor, Anno.Dom. July:16:1643."[4] The word "pastor" is significant suggesting that Owen did not think of his calling as that of a "vicar" or "rector," but rather as the pastor of the faithful in the parish and evangelist to the rest. The date, the 16th July, was probably the day on which he was authorised to begin his ministry but as he was in Kent in July he could not have begun there until August.

It is quite possible that Owen's visit to Scot's Hall in July was connected with his marriage, which occurred about this time. According to his earliest biography he married a Miss Rooke. She was probably a relative of Thomas Rooke of Smeeth and may have been the daughter of William Rooke, a clothier whose business had been in Coggeshall (which was quite near Fordham) until his death in 1622. In his will, Rooke made provision for his very young daughter, Mary, who, it would seem, married John Owen in late 1643.[5] The baptism of their first child is recorded in the parish register: "John, the sonne of John Owen, pastor of the church at Much Fordham and Mary his wife was baptized, Dec. 20, 1644."

When Alsop was in residence the parish church would have been suitably adorned for High-Church worship and the parishioners would have received no evangelical teaching. To rectify this Owen went around the village, whose houses were constructed mainly of lath-and-plaster or weather-boarding, teaching both young and old the basic doctrines

---

[1] This information is also in the dedicatory letter to Sir Edward.
[2] For the history of Fordham see Mary Gunary, *The Story of Fordham*, Fordham, 1954, and H. Smith, *The Ecclesiastical History of Essex*, Colchester, 1930, p. 310. The living was worth £116 per annum.
[3] For Alsop see *Walker Revised*, ed. A. G. Matthews, Oxford, 1948, p. 145.
[4] The Rev. Hugh Barber, rector of Fordham, kindly sent me photocopies of the appropriate pages from the parish register, which is still kept in the church. Inside the church there is a plaque giving a summary of the life of Owen.
[5] *The Life of Owen*, 1720, p. xxxiv. Rooke's will is in the Essex Record Office: ref. D/ACW. 9/99.

of Protestantism from two catechisms which he himself composed and then published in 1645.[1] One was for young people and the other for adults. Like his father he tried to be a "painful labourer" in the vineyard of the Lord. Nevertheless, despite his endeavours, there were, to use his own words, still those in the parish who "walked disorderly . . . little labouring to acquaint themselves with the mystery of godliness," and these he tried to convert. For his faithful hearers he also wrote a little book entitled, *The Duty of Pastors and People Distinguished* (1644)[2] in which he gave advice "for the increasing of divine knowledge in themselves and others." His counsel included explanations of the attitude they should adopt toward their minister and teacher and the way they should approach Christian worship. From the preface to this book we also get some insight into his thinking concerning church polity. He was in favour of a system that was "presbyterian or synodical, in opposition to prelatical or diocesan on the one hand and that which is commonly called independent or congregational on the other." Like many middle-of-the-road Puritans he hated prelacy, which, with the London authors of the Root and Branch Petition, he believed was wholly contrary to God's Word, but at the same time he feared "the democracy" of Congregationalism. He wanted something between the two extremes; that is, "between the valley of democratical confusion and the precipitous rock of hierarchical tyranny." One contemporary described him as a "moderate and learned Presbyterian."[3]

His days, however, as a moderate Presbyterian were soon to end. In London the Westminster Assembly of divines was in session and within its learned membership differences of opinion over church government were being voiced. In 1643 five of the divines, with whom Owen was later to become friendly, published *An Apologeticall Narration*,[4] in which they explained their adherence to the Congregational way (that is, the doctrine that to a gathered church of committed Christians Christ gives His authority for the group to appoint officers and admit and exclude members), and their reasons for dissenting from the Presbyterian

---

[1] They were entitled *Two Short Catechisms wherein the Principles of the Doctrine of Christ are unfolded and explained*, and are in *Works*, I, pp. 463ff. Owen, it seems, also used his theological learning in the investigation of Samuel Cock, Rector of St Giles, Colchester, who was accused before the Essex Committee of teaching error. See *Correspondence*, p. 15, and T. W. Davids, *Annals of Evangelical Nonconformity in Essex*, 1863, p. 324.

[2] *Works*, XIII, pp. 2ff.

[3] William Bartlet, *A Model of the Primative Congregational Way*, 1647, p. 23. Cf. G. F. Nuttall, *Visible Saints*, Oxford, 1957, p. 54.

[4] For a facsimile edition of this tract with notes see *An Apologeticall Narration*, ed. R. S. Paul, Philadelphia, 1963. The five men were Thomas Goodwin, Philip Nye, Sidrach Simpson, Jeremiah Burroughs and William Bridge, whose careers are described by Paul. See also *C.R.* for Goodwin, Nye and Bridge. For a description of the Westminster Assembly see S. W. Carruthers, *The Everyday Work of the Westminster Assembly*, Philadelphia, 1943. Two recent studies of aspects of the work of the divines are J. B. Rogers, *Scripture in the Westminster Confession*, Kampen, 1966, and J. R. De Witt, *Jus Divinum: the Westminster Assembly and the Divine Right of Church Government*, Kampen, 1969.

views of the majority of the members of the Assembly. Two of the dissenting brethren also commended the *Keyes of the Kingdom of Heaven* (1644) by John Cotton, who had influenced them in their views on church polity, and who was now minister of the First Church of Boston, Massachusetts.[1] Owen acquired both these books and also others which defended the Presbyterian polity and studied them with diligence.

Meanwhile rumours reached Fordham that Alsop, who had fled to the Continent, was dead. This meant that the patrons of the living, Sir John Lucas, who owned the Manor of Great Fordham, and a young boy named William Abell, had the right to nominate a successor.[2] Owen, therefore, made preparations to move. The last entry he made in the parish register was the record of a baptism on the 28th December 1645, although he does not seem to have vacated the parsonage until about Easter 1646. Whilst he was seeking God's guidance as to where should be his next sphere of service, he received an invitation to preach before the House of Commons on April 29. His name had been put forward by his friend Thomas Westrow and by Sir Peter Wentworth, the M.P. for Tamworth.[3] Three years earlier the Long Parliament had begun the custom of a regular fast-day on the last Wednesday of each month.[4] In time of war these days of prayer and preaching were a means of renewing and propagating the conviction that, in its just demands, God was on the side of Parliament and against the King and his evil advisers. Its cause was His cause. And, through the printing of the sermons, the message was made known to a much wider audience than that which sat in St Margaret's Church.

In general it may be said that underlying the sermons from 1643 to 1646 were five major themes. First, God governs the destinies of individuals and nations and thus England is the continual object of His care and providence. Second, this divine care for England is such that, to all intents and purposes, the nation may be termed an "elect nation." Third, because of the Solemn League and Covenant, England is in a covenant relationship both to Scotland and to God. This means that the nation has solemn responsibilities; her people must repent and seek further reformation of the Church and of their lives. Fourth, the period of civil strife being experienced is part of a time of divine shaking which will lead either to a glorious reformation such as England has not known before or to further divine judgement. Fifth, God promises a glorious

---

[1] The two were Goodwin and Nye. A recent biography of Cotton is Larzer Ziff, *The Career of John Cotton*, Princeton, 1962.

[2] For John Lucas who was made a Baron in 1645 by the King see the *D.N.B.* s.v. Sir Charles Lucas his brother.

[3] For Westrow and Wentworth see D. H. Pennington & D. Brunton, *Members of the Long Parliament*, 1954.

[4] For studies of these fast-day sermons see H. R. Trevor-Roper, "The Fast Sermons," in *Religion, the Reformation and Social Change*, 1967, and J. F. Wilson, *Pulpit in Parliament*, Princeton, 1969.

future for His Church in the world, when the Turks and the Papacy will be no more and when all antichristian doctrine and ceremonies will be removed from the churches of Europe.

Owen accepted all these themes. His only quarrel with the Presbyterian preachers was, as we shall see, over the question of the toleration of orthodox Calvinists who were not Presbyterians. The time at which he addressed the Commons is significant. General Fairfax had just completed the reduction of Cornwall and was soon to take Oxford. The New Model Army had effectively dealt with the armies of Charles I and the Civil War was virtually at an end. To the young divine, the victories of the New Model Army were inspired and even predestined by God. Two years later, using imagery drawn from the description of theophanies in the Old Testament, he said that "God came from Naseby (the scene of a great victory in June 1645) and the Holy One from the West. 'His glory covered the heavens and the earth was full of His praise'."[1] The ascendancy of the New Model on the field of battle had meant the rise to prominence (but not to a majority) in Parliament of the Independents, which in turn meant that from 1646 a growing number of preachers who were not doctrinaire Presbyterians or members of the Westminster Assembly were invited to officiate at the fast-days.[2] In March, Hugh Peter, the army chaplain and known Independent, had preached at the day of thanksgiving for the reduction of royalist opposition in Cornwall.[3] So Owen's appearance was part of this new phase. And he was, as it were, by his participation, declaring his allegiance, at least in general principles, to the aims of the Independents in the Commons and the dissenting brethren in the Assembly of divines. What were these principles will become clear as we examine the printed version of Owen's sermon.

*A Vision of Unchangeable Free Mercy*, with its appended tracts, provides us with basic information concerning Owen's theological doctrine and how he related this to the sweep of contemporary events, government policies and religious toleration.[4] It contains no specific references to

[1] *Works*, VIII, p. 88.

[2] Many articles have been written in recent years (Cf. e.g. *Past and Present* for 1970 and 1971) on the identity of the Independents in the 1640's ,and the debate continues. I use the term to describe those who did not favour either a strict episcopal or strict presbyterian church government and who were in favour of some form of limited toleration. It is sometimes but not always synonymous with Congregationalists.

[3] A recent biography of Peter is R. P. Stearns, *The Strenuous Puritan, Hugh Peter, 1598–1660*, Urbana, 1954.

[4] *Works*, VIII, pp. 3ff. His fellow preacher was James Nalton. Wilson, *op. cit.*, p. 87. In a Latin dedication, Owen spoke of the Long Parliament in glowing terms:— "To the most noble Senate, the most renowned Assembly of England; most deservedly celebrated throughout the whole world, and to be held in everlasting remembrance by all the inhabitants of this island; for strenuously and faithfully asserting the rights of Englishmen; for recovering the liberty of their country, almost ruined by the base attempts of some; for administering justice boldly, equally, moderately and impartially; for dissolving the power of a hierarchical tyranny in ecclesiastical affairs, and abolishing the popish, newly-invented,

battles or political events; rather, it deals with generalities and basic principles. After a suitable explanation of his text, Acts 16:9, Owen emphasised that God had exercised His sovereignty in history by causing the Gospel of Christ to be preached in some lands and not in others. "The sending of the Gospel to any nation," he explained, "is of the mere free grace and good pleasure of God." But perhaps the young divine went too far in his claim that one could see in recent history a clear imprint or reflection of the eternal counsel of God. Success in war, and even liberty for the preaching of the Gospel, are not necessarily signs of the divine favour.[1] Christianity has often fared best under a persecuting régime. But Owen, believing he could read at least part of the intricacy of the divine purpose in recent English history, felt obliged to warn that unless Parliament made full use of the current opportunities to honour Christ and propagate the Gospel, God would again cause the nation to revert to spiritual darkness. This had happened twice in the past. The light of the Gospel had been put out by the invading Saxons in the fifth century and by Archbishop Laud in the 1630s. For the policies of the latter Owen had nothing but contempt. However, God was now wanting to bless England once more. "The reformation of England," he prophesied, "shall be more glorious than of any nation in the world, being carried on neither by might or power, but only by the Spirit of the Lord of hosts." Parliament should therefore observe the divine intention with regard to the future. It should provide for the preaching of the Gospel in the dark corners of the land now that victory of arms had been assured. Owen closed with an appeal:

O that you would labour to let all parts of the kingdom taste of the sweetness of your successes, in carrying to them the Gospel of the Lord Jesus: that the

antichristian rites; for restoring the privileges of the Christian people; for enjoying the powerful protection of the Most High in all these, and in innumerable other things in council and war, at home and abroad: To the illustrious, honourable, select Gentlemen of the Commons in Parliament assembled, the Discourse, humble indeed in its pretensions, but being preached before them by their desire, is now by their command published." Here we find Owen echoing the ideological "trinity" of the English Revolution: pure religion, liberty and property. This is intermingled with the strong belief in God's help and encouragement. Cf. Christopher Hill, *God's Englishman: Oliver Cromwell and the English Revolution*, 1970, pp. 211ff.

[1] It is possible that Owen's words in 1646 (when he was but 30!) were capable of being interpreted in terms of the belief that success in war necessarily means that the victors enjoy of God's favour. Much later in his life (1670) he wrote the following summary of his mature thoughts on this matter: "A cause is good or bad before it hath success one way or another; and that which hath not warrant in itself can never obtain any from its success. The rule of the goodness of any public cause is the eternal law of reason, with the just legal rights and interests of men. If these make not a cause good, success will never mend it. But when a cause on these grounds is so indeed, or is really judged such by them that are engaged in it, not to take notice of the providence of God in prospering men in the pursuit of it, is to exclude all thoughts of Him and His providence from having any concern in the government of the world." *Works*, XVI, p. 269. If he really believed this in 1646 then his position was that the success in war against Charles merely confirmed the righteous cause of Parliament.

doctrine of the Gospel might make way for the discipline of the Gospel, without which it will be a very skeleton!

His use of the word "discipline" would not have raised many eyebrows at this point of time since the need for its implementation at the parish level in the reorganisation of the National Church was generally agreed both in the Westminster Assembly and by a Committee of Parliament.

The appendix to the sermon is interesting for what it contains concerning Owen's views on church government and religious toleration, and for the light it throws on the troubled state of the Essex clergy and churches. In "A Short Defensative" (which is the preface to the longer "Country Essay") Owen wrote of the existence of dissension and bitterness in the county. This piece of information comes as somewhat of a surprise to the reader after the lofty words and ideals of the sermon itself. In both public and private, ministers were calling each other by a variety of "odious appellations" because of their differing views about church organisation and toleration of dissenters. Strict Presbyterians and Independents were forgetting Paul's teaching in I Corinthians 13 concerning charity. What Owen wrote thus reveals to what extent the Puritan movement, which had such a proud history in Essex, had been fragmented by the pressures of war and the liberty that accompanied it. His paragraphs also show that he was deeply troubled about this situation which brought dishonour to Christ; and he desperately hoped to be able to pacify his brethren. He believed that the situation was being aggravated by the efforts of some Presbyterians to produce signatures for petitions to be sent to Westminster. These petitions called for the full implementation of Presbyterian discipline at the parish level within the framework of the recent legislation for a Presbyterian National Church.[1]

In London both the Westminster Assembly and the City authorities had petitioned Parliament to authorise that church discipline in the parishes be wholly exercised by the minister and lay elders as in Scotland or Geneva without the help or the interference of a body of lay commissioners appointed by Parliament.[2] Owen had refused to sign any petition

---

[1] The legislation consisted of two ordinances. The first, of August 1645, established London as a test area with 12 classes and with lay elders to be appointed by a board of triers, composed of both clergy and godly citizens. The second, of March 1646, established the presbyterian government as that of the Established Church of England and the disputed issue of the exclusion of the spiritually unfit from Holy Communion was vested in the local eldership with the right of appeal to a Committee of Parliament. Cf. W. K. Jordan, *The Development of Religious Toleration in England, 1640–1660*, 1938, pp. 70 and 80. A petition from Suffolk and Essex ministers was presented to the House of Lords on 29 May 1646. This called for the rigid system of lay elders at the parish level with full powers in co-operation with the minister to exclude people from Communion and discipline them. L.J., VIII, p. 388.

[2] W. A. Shaw, *A History of the English Church, 1640–1660*, 1900, II, pp. 292ff. and Jordan, *op. cit.*, pp. 80ff.

and he supplied four reasons to justify his action. First, he was sure that the existence of many moral evils in the parishes was not simply explained (as the petitions suggested) by the lack of strong presbyterian discipline. Second, Parliament had already in August 1645 established the English Church as Presbyterian and this was all that was really required since it allowed a measure of liberty at the local level. Third, the origin of the request for the signing of petitions, not to mention the drafting of them, was "distant and unseen" (certain ministers in London?) and such petitions tended to undermine the authority of "our noble Parliament." Fourth, in Owen's own words:

> A particular form of church discipline is usually, in such petitions, either directly expressed or evidently pointed at and directed unto as that alone which our covenant engageth us to embrace . . . Now, truly to suppose that our covenant did tie us up absolutely to any one formerly-known way of church discipline—the words formally engaging us into a disquisition out of the Word of that which is agreeable to the mind and will of God—is to me such a childish, ridiculous, selfish conceit, as I believe no knowing men will once entertain, unless prejudice, begotten by their peculiar interest, hath disturbed their intellectuals. For my part, I know no church government in the world already established amongst any sort of men of the truth and necessity whereof I am convinced in all particulars; especially if I may take their practice to be the best interpreter of their maxims.

The covenant to which he referred was the Solemn League and Covenant which he had taken and which from 1643 bound England and Scotland together in a civil and religious bond. Into the article on religion the English negotiators had persuaded the Scots to add the words "according to the Word of God" to qualify the type of church organisation to be erected in England. Obviously Owen did not interpret the implications of the article in the same way as the dogmatic Presbyterians who wanted the Scottish model to be followed.

The aim of the "Country Essay" was to propose plans for an accommodation between Presbyterians, Independents and others within the context of the existing ecclesiastical legislation. Coming from a young, little-known preacher, this proposal was a rather audacious move. He began by admitting that Essex had "a rich supply of able, godly, orthodox, peace-loving pastors," many parishioners who knew not the power of godliness, and a few souls in most parishes who were "inclined to separation" because of the unsatisfactory state of the parish churches. Then he proposed that each parish minister should continue the normal round of preaching and catechising, seeking to bring reformation to his parish. His novel suggestion was that the "visible saints" from each parish within areas of not more than 100 square miles (10 x 10) should meet at least once a month for fellowship and form themselves into a gathered church. When gathered, they should elect their local ministers as their pastor, teacher, and ruling elders. Concerning the actual membership of this gathered church Owen wrote:

> Let the rules of admission into this society and fellowship be scriptural, and the things required in the members only such as all godly men affirm to be necessary for every one that will partake of the ordinances with profit and comfort—special care being taken that none be excluded who have the least breathings of soul in sincerity after Jesus Christ.

He expected that the members of this church would also attend the services of their own parishes.

The second part of the "Country Essay" deals with the subject of toleration.[1] Owen found that though the word was much used few attempted to define its meaning. Among "the contestors," he wrote, "few on the one side or the other clearly and distinctly define what they mean by toleration." For Presbyterians it implied a "universal, uncontrolled licence" to men to teach and do what they liked with regard to religion and morals. Owen's own position was to the left of the Presbyterians and to the right of the Separatists and Sectarians. He was firmly of the opinion that heretics as well as dissenters from the Established Church should not be punished merely because they were so, but only if they caused a public disturbance or were openly licentious. Their doctrinal errors should be countered by reasonable argument and spiritual weapons not by the power of the sword. He believed that a study of Church history revealed that persecution and punishment of heretics achieved no lasting good but rather led to tyranny. So he did not want to see either the Parliament or the Church launch into a persecution of any people with erroneous views who were not causing any civil disturbance.

As far as is known, Owen's proposals for a peaceful solution to the problems of Essex never got off the ground. Nevertheless, they do provide an important indication of the way in which his mind was moving. Since writing *The Duty of Pastors* in 1644, when he called himself a Presbyterian, he had moved rapidly in the direction of the Congregational way, stimulated by a careful study of John Cotton's book and by his own assessment of the problems which a hard-line Presbyterianism had caused and would cause. But, as yet, he had not taken the step of gathering a church of "visible saints" in his own parish. That was to come later. At this stage we gain the impression that the thirty-year old divine was quietly confident that what he had to say was valuable and that it had important consequences for the future of his country.

[1] See Jordan, *op. cit.*, for a full discussion of the whole issue of toleration. Since the rise to fame and power of the New Model Army the question of toleration had been hotly debated not only amongst the soldiers but also in Parliament and by the Westminster Assembly.

CHAPTER II

## EXTENDING SERVICE

WHEN THE *Vision of Unchangeable Free Mercy* APPEARED IN PRINT in May 1646, John Owen was described on the title-page as the "minister of the Gospel at Coggeshall." This small town, then a prosperous centre of the wool and cloth industry, is situated on the banks of the River Blackwater and stands on the line of the old Roman military road (Stane Street) built to connect St Albans (Verulamium) and Colchester (Camulodunum). A church, with the rare dedication to "St Peter ad Vincula," existed in the twelfth century but it was not until the fifteenth century that it was rebuilt to become one of the larger and finer churches of the Eastern Counties.[1] Probably many of the wool merchants and their workers who worshipped in the church also used the facilities of the "Woolpack," an inn situated next door to the church. For many years before Owen's arrival the people of Coggeshall had enjoyed as vicars a series of able Calvinist divines. For the first eight years of the seventeenth century the church was served by two friends, both Cambridge Puritans. From 1600 to 1606 the vicar was Thomas Stoughton and from 1606 to 1608 it was Ralph Cudworth, whose widow married Dr Stoughton, and whose son, Ralph, became one of the famous Cambridge Platonists.[2] Following Cudworth came the long ministry of thirty years of John Dod, the elder. During part of this period his son, Nehemiah, assisted him as curate. On the 9th November 1635 John Dod was reported as saying that the bubonic plague was in the land as God's judgement on "the mixture of religion that is commanded in the church."[3] With such sentiments he was obviously not a Laudian! Owen's immediate predecessor was Obadiah Sedgwick. He was presented to the living on the 6th July 1639 by Robert Rich, the second Earl of Warwick, who was a noted opponent of Laudianism and Arminianism, and generally regarded as a Presbyterian.[4] Sedgwick, who was a member of the Westminster Assembly of divines, and a licenser of the press, moved in 1646 to St Paul's, Covent Garden, London. So Owen came to a town that was accustomed to a high

[1] On the 16th Sept. 1940 the church was badly damaged by a bomb. The Tower, Nave and North Aisle have since been rebuilt.
[2] For Ralph Cudworth Jnr see *D.N.B.*
[3] Smith, *Ecclesiastical History of Essex*, pp. 56-7. Two of Nehemiah's sons, John and Robert, were at Oxford in the 1650s. Both became Nonconformists and are in *C.R.*
[4] For Rich and Sedgwick see *D.N.B.*

standard of preaching and to evangelical theology. That Owen maintained this high standard is obvious since Asty informs us that as many as 2,000 people crowded into the church each Lord's Day to hear the young divine expound the Bible.[1]

Worship in the church was centred on the Word of God and on free prayer. This was possible because the Book of Common Prayer had been set aside in 1644 by Parliament and the Directory for Public Worship brought in to replace it. Beginning with a solemn call to worship, followed by a prayer acknowledging the majesty of God and the sinfulness of man, the service proceeded with the singing of psalms and the public reading of Holy Scripture. Then perhaps another psalm was sung before the long prayer that preceded the sermon was uttered. This prayer began with a full confession of sin and a plea for divine grace and forgiveness. It continued by beseeching God for the conversion of the Jews, the fall of Antichrist (the Pope), and the hastening of the second coming of Jesus Christ; for deliverance of the distressed churches abroad from the tyranny of Roman Catholicism and from the cruel blasphemies of the Turk and for blessing upon the Church in Britain. Then came prayers of intercession for the King, Queen and Prince as well as for the Queen of Bohemia and the Elector Palatine of the Rhine. Also the divine blessing was asked for those in positions of authority in England, for Parliament, the judges, magistrates, nobles and gentry. Following this long prayer which would have taken anything from ten to twenty minutes, the people listened to a sermon which would have taken at least one hour. This contained the exposition of one or more principles of the Faith from the Word with suitable application to the needs and hearts of the hearers. Finally the worship closed with a prayer that the divine Word would bear fruit in repentant and obedient souls.

Owen believed that he was "directed by the providence of the Most High" to Coggeshall where, we learn, he had been "sought by the people of God." Since Coggeshall had been a centre for Separatism in Essex it is just possible that Owen's sympathy for Congregationalism, evident as we have seen in his appendix to *A Vision of Free Mercy*, was a factor in making him popular with some parishioners. This, however, did not prevent him from using the first opportunity to express in print his thanks to the patron of the living for admitting him. He expressed his gratitude in the dedication of *Salus Electorum, Sanguis Jesu: or the Death of Death in the Death of Christ* (1647)[2] to the Earl. This treatise, though not particularly easy to read because of Owen's heavy style and Aristotelian methodology, is filled with much theological learning. It defended the orthodox Calvinist doctrine that the death of Christ was intended in God's sovereign will to be a redemption of the elect only, not of the world in general. Being a noted opponent of

[1] Asty, p. vii.     [2] *Works*, X, pp. 140ff.

Arminianism of both the Dutch and English variety the Earl would have approved this teaching. He would also have agreed with Owen's attack upon the new doctrines from the Protestant Academy of Saumur, set forth in the writings of Cameron, Amyraut and Daillé. This "new Methodism" was a kind of half-way house between orthodox Calvinism and Arminianism although it claimed to be restoring the original emphases and principles of the Reformed Faith.[1] Against all innovations Owen's position was clear. Those upon whom God set His love before the creation of the world were the ones, and the only ones, for whom Christ died. The book has a commendation by two Presbyterians, Stanley Gower and Richard Byfield, both members of the Westminster Assembly. They describe Owen's work as "pulling down the rotten house of Arminianism upon the head of those Philistines who would uphold it."

Before the publication of his exposition of the limited atonement of Christ, Owen had finally adopted the Congregational way. In a rare autobiographical statement in a book published in 1657 he told his readers how he finally came to this position. Up to 1643 he had not examined the doctrine of the Church to a greater depth than "an opposition to Episcopacy and ceremonies" necessitated. But, as he explained:

> Not long after (the publication of *The Duty of Pastors*) I set myself seriously to inquire into the controversies then warmly agitated in these nations. Of the Congregational way I was not acquainted with any one person, minister or other; nor had I, to my knowledge, seen any more than one in my whole life. My acquaintance lay wholly with ministers and people of the Presbyterian way. But sundry books being published on either side, I perused and compared them with the Scripture and with one another according as I received ability from God. After a general view of them, as was my manner in other controversies, I fixed on one to take under peculiar consideration and examination, which seemed most methodically and strongly to maintain that which was contrary, as I thought, to my present persuasion. This was Mr Cotton's book of the *Keys*. The examination and confutation hereof, merely for my own particular satisfaction, with what diligence and sincerity I was able, I engaged in. What progress I made in that undertaking I can manifest unto any by the discourses on that subject and animadversions on that book yet abiding by me. In the pursuit and management of this work, quite beside and contrary to my expectation, at a time and season wherein I could expect nothing on that account but ruin in this world, without the knowledge or advice of, or conference with, any one person of that judgement, I was prevailed on to receive that and those principles which I had thought to have set myself in an opposition unto.[2]

[1] For a recent study of this theology see B. G. Armstrong, *Calvinism and the Amyraut Heresy*, Madison, Wisconsin, 1969.
[2] *Works*. XIII, p. 223.

Another decisive moment, virtually as important for the future as his spiritual experience in St Mary's, Aldermanbury, had arrived in his life. True to his character he immediately acted on his new principles and gathered a church within the parish of St Peter's, Coggeshall. A Congregational church claiming its origins to this point in time still worships in the town. In practical terms Owen's new ecclesiastical position meant that he continued to hold the statutory Sunday services for the whole parish based on the Directory and at a different time of the day or on a weekday those who were visible saints met for mutual edification. Only to this gathered church would he have administered the Holy Communion. For the benefit of his parishioners and for any others who were interested he explained the principles of the Congregational way in simple terms in *Eshcol, a Cluster of the Fruits of Canaan . . . Or, Rules of Direction for the walking of the Saints* (1648).[1] This eminently practical book, often reprinted in the seventeenth century, contained rules for the relationship of members of the gathered church to each other and to the pastor. Each rule is established by a body of evidence from Scripture and by a general explanation. As Goold remarks in his editorial comments "for once Owen is the master of the art of condensation." We may illustrate this point by giving his rules to preserve Christian fellowship.

1. Affectionate, sincere love in all things, without dissimulation towards one another, like that which Christ bare to His Church.
2. Continual prayer for the prosperous state of the Church, in God's protection towards it.
3. Earnest striving and contending in all lawful ways, by doing and suffering, for the purity of the ordinances, honour, liberty, and privileges of the congregation, being jointly assistant against all opposers and common adversaries.
4. Sedulous care and endeavouring for the preservation of unity, both in particular and in general.
5. Separation and sequestration from the world and men of the world, with all ways of false worship, until we have apparently a people dwelling alone, not reckoned among the nations.
6. Frequent spiritual communication for edification, according to gifts received.
7. Mutually to bear with each other's infirmities, weakness, tenderness, failings, in meekness, patience, pity, and with assistance.
8. Tender and affectionate participation with one another in their several states and conditions—bearing each other's burdens.
9. Free contribution and communication of temporal things to them that are poor indeed, suitable to their necessities, wants, and afflictions.
10. To mark diligently and avoid carefully all causes and causers of divisions; especially to shun seducers, false teachers, and broachers of heresies and errors, contrary to the form of wholesome words.

[1] *Works*, XIII, pp. 52ff.

EXTENDING SERVICE 29

11. Cheerfully to undergo the lot and portion of the whole church in prosperity and affliction and not to draw back upon any occasion whatever.
12. In church affairs to make no difference of persons, but to condescend to the meanest persons and services for the use of the brethren.
13. If any be in distress, persecution, or affliction the whole church is to be humbled and to be earnest in prayer in their behalf.
14. Vigilant watchfulness over each other's conversation, attended with mutual admonition in case of disorderly walking, with rendering an account to the church if the party offending be not prevailed with.
15. Exemplary walking in all holiness and godliness of conversation to the glory of the gospel, edification of the church and conviction of them that are without.

When Owen met his fellow ministers he sought to convince them of the truth he had recently found and how in the parish situation the Congregational ideal could work. On the 31st March 1648, for example, he was present at a ministerial meeting in Colchester. The purpose was to suggest to the government how the recent ordinance of Parliament "for the speedy and effectual settling of the presbyterian government" in Essex could be achieved.[1] (As yet the classical system was operative only in London and Lancashire.)[2] Ralph Josselin, the minister at Earls Colne, was present and later wrote in his Diary a brief but revealing comment on Owen's attitude: "We had much discourse concerning falling into practice, and, in the first place, seeing that elders are to be chosen, by whom it shall be done; the Parliament proposeth by the people who have taken the Covenant; others, as Mr Owen, conceived this too broad, and would have first a separation made in our parishes, and that by the minister and those godly that join unto him, and then proceed to choosing."[3] Here we see Owen making a valiant effort to fit the Congregational way into the proposed Presbyterian structures. Happily for him however the Presbyterian National Church never fully materialised in practice and he did not have to face the problem of reconciling his views with such an organisation.

It is not often realised that the adoption of the Congregational way was much more than the practice of a different form of church government. In the 1640s there were important implications in the fields of eschatology and religious toleration. The writings of the dissenting brethren of the Westminster Assembly and the leading divines of Massachusetts make it clear that the creation by them of gathered churches of visible saints was seen not only as an act of obedience to Christ, the Head of the Church, but also as an expression of hope for the future.

[1] See Smith, op. cit., p. 192 for more detail.
[2] Shaw, History of the English Church, 1640–1660, II, pp. 1–33.
[3] The Diary of Ralph Josselin, ed. E. Hockliffe, 1908, p. 48. A few days later Josselin signed the Testimony of the Ministers of Essex, which was a manifesto of orthodox Presbyterianism. Smith, op. cit., pp. 102ff. Owen refused to sign.

For in the millennium the purified Church militant would take the form of multitudes of gathered churches, enjoying fellowship with each other and with Christ. There were, it is true, a few Presbyterians (William Twisse, for example) who also looked forward to a millennial kingdom, but the majority of that group were content to hope for a great revival at the close of the age connected with the conversion of many Jews. The Congregationalists, however, to a man were millenarians of one kind or another and chiliasm was recognised by contemporaries as one of their peculiar doctrines.[1] Now Owen did not accept any doctrine merely because others taught it and so we may suggest that he gave much attention to the topic and studied especially the millenarian writings of John Cotton. The evidence of his writings, especially the sermons he preached to the Rump Parliament, which we shall examine below, clearly reveals the general lines of this thought. Though not explicitly millenarian, he often spoke of the latter-day glory of the Church of Christ on earth, which would follow the abolition of the power of both the Turks and the Papacy. As for religious toleration, we have already noted his views as they appeared in print in 1646. The logic of his doctrine of the Church demanded that he argue for freedom of organisation at the parish level and for some basic toleration of gathered churches, who taught orthodox Calvinism, outside the parish system. His brethren in Massachusetts, however, believing they alone had the true doctrine of the church, refused to tolerate others who differed from them and this became in time an embarrassment to him and his English colleagues.[2]

Soon after the meeting at Colchester to discuss the implementation of Presbyterianism in Essex a second civil war began. Charles I was not willing to make an effective compromise with the House of Commons and on the first day of May news reached London and Essex that in Pembroke a high-ranking army officer had been killed by neo-royalist rebels. This rebellion in Wales was followed by a Scottish invasion of England led by Hamilton and by scattered risings in many parts of England, especially in the heavily-taxed South-East. The army acted quickly. John Lambert went North to meet the Scots. Edmund Waller went West to Cornwall; Oliver Cromwell moved into Wales and Thomas Fairfax stayed in the London area. There was discontent all over the country caused in part by the bad harvest of 1647 and the current crippling taxation.[3] The area in which Owen lived was no exception. An army of both old and new royalists under the Earl of Norwich was at Braintree on the 11th June intending to march direct

---

[1] Cf. Wilson, *Pulpit in Parliament*, pp. 223–230, and Nuttall, *Visible Saints*, pp. 146ff.
[2] See *Correspondence*, pp. 145–6 for a letter on this issue.
[3] For a description of the second civil war and the siege of Colchester see S. R. Gardiner, *History of the Great Civil War*, 1891, III, pp. 391ff.

to Norfolk and Suffolk where help was expected from the gentry and where supplies by sea would be available. But, at the suggestion of Sir Charles Lucas, a tried and capable soldier with family connexions in Essex, they turned aside to seek to attract recruits from Colchester. On the night of the 11th there was much excitement at Coggeshall as Sir Thomas Honeywood, a member of the unpopular County Committee, waited with (in Owen's words) "a poor handful of unskilful men," of whom not more than three had ever fought in a war, to ambush the royalists. The latter, however, chose a different route and were eventually admitted into Colchester, taking with them some members of the County Committee whom they were holding captive. Not far behind them was General Fairfax who crossed the Thames at Tilbury and arrived with his army at Coggeshall on the 12th. During the next day he attacked Colchester hoping to achieve the same success there that he had recently enjoyed at Maidstone in Kent. This was not to be; he was repulsed and a long siege became necessary.[1] A few days later he was joined by Henry Ireton and the rest of the army who had successfully taken Canterbury on the 8th. Because of his known Independent principles, Owen was invited to minister to the soldiers who were now encamped outside Colchester. This work gave him the opportunity to have long conversations with the senior army officers as well as with many of the men; and friendships were hereby formed that were to last for many years. Writing after the siege, Owen said that he had had "the happiness for a short season to serve His Excellency (Lord Fairfax) in the service of Jesus Christ."[2] The parliamentary army did not actually gain entrance into Colchester until the 27th August at which time the County Committee was released and two of the leaders of the insurrection, Sir Charles Lucas and Sir George Lisle, were executed.

At the day of thanksgiving which followed the siege Owen was the preacher. He was also the speaker at another day of rejoicing held a few weeks later at Romford. Both sermons were from Habakkuk 3:1–9 and were printed as one treatise, *Ebenezer: a Memorial of the Deliverance of Essex County and Committee*.[3] The passage from the prophet contains a prayer which begins with a request to God to have mercy on the nation but it soon develops into a description of a theophany in which God visits the earth in judgement. From these verses Owen drew out twenty-one observations or principles which the supporters of Parliament could take to heart. These observations present an interesting combination of sound advice on prayer, faith and divine chastisement

---

[1] The dislocation of life locally is seen in the fact that Ralph Josselin had to take his wife and children to stay with Lady Honeywood for ten weeks. Smith, *op. cit.*, pp. 217–8.
[2] See his dedicatory epistle to Fairfax in *Ebenezer* (1648).
[3] *Works*, VIII, pp. 72ff.

in the life of the believer with an attempt to see in the events of the second civil war, especially in the siege of Colchester, the distinct providence of God. His first principle—"prayer is the believer's constant, sure retreat in an evil time"—no Christian would challenge. His fourteenth principle—"God's dealings with His enemies in the season of the Church's deliverance is of especial consideration"—is rather more speculative if taken out of its Old Testament context, where God supports Israel against her enemies. But Owen used this principle to introduce a long section in which he sought to explain just how God's sovereign providence had worked in local affairs first of all to allow the rebellion in Essex and then to crush it. Without any inhibitions he stated that God had caused the ruin of the royalist forces at Colchester. Under the twentieth principle he expounded his belief that God caused the second civil war to take place (that is, by His inscrutable provocation of the minds of the royalist leaders) in order to have the enemies of the Gospel finally defeated and to unite the saints in the common cause. Had God not caused the war then the persecution and tyranny of former days would have returned. Owen claimed that in the activities of the rebellious army led by the Earl of Norwich he could discern "sundry instances of how God mixed a perverse spirit of folly and error in all their counsels" in order eventually to engineer their defeat. Or, put another way, "God hath interposed in our quarrels from heaven." Owen's view of the Essex rebellion was necessarily biased since he understood everything in terms of God's judgement, chastisement or deliverance of His saints on earth. He did not think it important to consider what we may term "secondary causes"—excessive taxation, patriotism and fear of the future. For him God was so vitally concerned with every aspect of English life that he felt the need to explain any changes in that life in terms of God and His providence only. Needless to say Owen's views were in the main highly subjective even though he believed that they were wholly based on objective reality. It is always dangerous to try to see God's providence and judgements at work in the complex affairs of a nation or people, except that nation be the Jews of old.

Whilst Fairfax had been victorious in Kent and Essex, the other army commanders enjoyed success in the rest of the country and the royalist cause was soon in ruins. Meanwhile commissioners from both Houses of Parliament waited on the King at Newport, Isle of Wight, but made little progress in their discussions. From the army came a crescendo of calls for what they termed "impartial justice" on all offenders and on the 20th November *An Humble Remonstrance* was presented to the Commons, which, tactlessly, laid it aside.[1] In this document the army officers warned of the danger of continuing to negotiate with the King

[1] Gardiner, *op. cit.*, III, p. 508.

and expounded the justice and expediency of bringing him to trial. The draft of this document was the work of Henry Ireton, who, as we have noted, had come to be a personal friend of Owen at Colchester. So it is a distinct possibility that the soldier and the divine had discussed between themselves some of the ideas contained in this document. Just over two weeks after its presentation, members of Parliament found troops from the regiment of Colonel Pride around the Palace at Westminster, guarding the entrance to the Commons. Certain members who were known to be against the general aims of the army officers were prevented from entering. After this incident the purged Parliament acted speedily. The King was brought to Windsor in readiness for an early trial and on the 1st January 1649 the Commons declared it treason in the King to levy war on the Parliament and kingdom and a special high court of justice was set up. Thirty days later, by the will of a small minority of powerful men and without the general consent of the nation at large, Charles I was executed outside Inigo Jones's handsome Banqueting Hall in Whitehall. People everywhere were amazed.

At the monthly fast-day in December the Commons had been somewhat embarrassed by a sermon from Thomas Watson, a Presbyterian divine, who accused the members of making "religion a cloak for their ambition."[1] So when they made preparation for the next fast, due in the crucial month of January, they chose two men whose views were known to them and who could be expected to say the right things. One was John Cardell, minister at All Hallows in Lombard Street, London, and John Owen was the other. Sir Henry Mildmay of Essex, a member of the County Committee, was asked to pass on the invitation to the Coggeshall minister.

Since the execution of the King was to be on Wednesday, January 30, the fast-day was delayed for one day. Owen was in London to witness the dreadful ceremony and it was perhaps to the nights of January 28, 29 and 30 that he referred when he described his sermon as "a hasty conception and like Jonah's gourd the child of a night or two." But even if the discourse itself was prepared in a hurry the sentiments it contained were the result of several years of thought, observation and voluntary support of the Independent cause. Based on Jeremiah 15:19-20 and entitled in print *Righteous Zeal encouraged by Divine Protection*,[2] it compared ancient Judah in the time of Jeremiah the prophet with England in the seventeenth century. Because of the sins of King Manasseh and his people Jerusalem was destroyed and many of its inhabitants taken into exile. Likewise, God had judged England in the civil wars and in the execution of the King. To obtain God's favour for the future, those who

[1] Wilson, *op. cit.*, pp. 155-7.
[2] *Works*, VIII, pp. 128ff. On 21 July 1683 the University of Oxford condemned this sermon as pernicious and damnable. It was then publicly burned along with other books by Independents of this period.

ruled England must remove from the nation all traces of false worship, superstition and tyranny and wholeheartedly support religion based on Holy Scripture. Although there is nothing remarkable about the sermon itself it was an appropriate message in a difficult hour. The dedicatory letter to the "right honourable, the Commons of England" confirms, however, that Owen understood the removal of the King in eschatological and apocalyptic terms. "God Almighty having called you forth, right honourable," he wrote, "at His entrance to the rolling up of the nation's heavens like a scroll (Isaiah 34:4-5), to serve Him in your generation in the high places of Armageddon (Revelation 16:16), you shall be sure not to want experience of that opposition which is raised against the great work of the Lord, which generally swells most against the visible instruments thereof." It is perhaps not necessary to discuss, as nonconformist historians were prone to do in the nineteenth century, whether or not Owen condoned the execution, or whether or not he was able to refuse to preach on this occasion.[1] Had he not wished to preach he could have declined the invitation; there was no compulsion. And his subsequent actions and sermons make it perfectly clear that he believed God had condemned the house of Stuart (not kingship as such) for its support of false religion and tyranny, and that, on this basis, the execution was part of God's righteous judgement.

Attached to the printed sermon was an important tract with the title "Of Toleration: and the Duty of the Magistrate about Religion." As we have seen this topic had been exercising Owen's mind for over three years and now at a critical moment in the history of the nation, he hoped to influence any future religious settlement by potently presenting his own case which was essentially the same as what he expounded in 1646 and that of other men of the Congregational way.[2] He maintained that it was the duty of magistrates and churches to preserve the truth of God and oppose error by the spiritual sword and spiritual hammer of the Word of God and by proper use of church discipline. With many references to past history, he showed that persecution of people who hold erroneous opinions has never achieved any lasting good. Furthermore, he argued that the punishment of heretics is not required by God's Word unless they cause civil disorder. The duty of Parliament, being the supreme magistrate, is to provide for the preaching of the Gospel in the whole nation and to remove all antichristian worship. This meant retaining the organisation of the National Church into

[1] See e.g. Orme, pp. 67ff.
[2] Cf. for example the views of Thomas Goodwin and Jeremiah Burroughs as explained in Jordan, *Development of Religious Toleration* . . . *1640–1660*, pp. 347ff. Gardiner, *History of the Commonwealth and Protectorate*, 1903, I, p. 97 asserts that Owen's views resembled those of the *Agreement of the People* presented to Parliament by army officers. R. S. Paul, *The Lord Protector*, 1955, pp. 256–7 traces the similarities to a common cause. Henry Ireton and his fellow officers had the same ecclesiastical views as did Owen. Orme, pp. 72ff. ascribes too much originality to Owen's views on toleration.

parishes but in such a way that ministers holding different views on church polity could serve God's people in harmony. In conclusion he suggested that Parliament should organise and listen to a debate about religious toleration so that having heard contrary opinions it could make up its own mind in full knowledge of the facts. Though he did not specifically say so, Owen gave the impression that he would be prepared to participate in the debate against those of the Presbyterian school who wanted to have one form of religion in the whole number of parish churches with no dissenters of any kind. As far as we know this debate never took place although religious toleration was a topic often raised for discussion in the army.[1]

Owen obviously proved to be a popular preacher and in April he was back again in London to preach to the Commons. The fast-day was originally planned for March but it was postponed twice and was finally held on the 19th April. His text was Hebrews 12:2, "I shake not the earth only but also heaven." He entitled the sermon *The Shaking and Translating of Heaven and Earth*.[2] Quickly his hearers found out that he was not speaking of the conflagration of the universe. He explained that "heaven" referred not to the celestial regions but rather to the "political heights and glory" which men had framed for themselves. It meant "the grandeur and lustre of their dominions." Likewise, "the earth" did not mean the soil but the people who lived on the soil. So the explanation of the text was straightforward:

> The Lord Jesus Christ, by his mighty power, in these latter days, as antichristian tyranny draws to its period will so far shake and translate the political heights, governments and strength of the nations, as shall serve for the full bringing in of his own peaceable kingdom:— the nations so shaken become thereby a quiet habitation for the people of the Most High.

He then proceeded to expound this theme of the coming kingdom of Christ, preceded by the "fall of Babylon;" the overthrow of the political and religious power of the papacy, being clearly prophesied in Revelation 17, was certain. Those nations in Europe which traditionally had been the spheres in which the Roman Catholic Church enjoyed both spiritual and temporal power would rise up in revolt against Rome and remove from their midst all antichristian tyranny. Although Owen did not mention the fact, there were in Europe in this period a whole series of revolutions and this might have contributed to the strength of the interpretation of Revelation 17 amongst the Independents.[3] Apart from

---

[1] Whilst Owen was in London, Presbyterian ministers who opposed both the execution of the King and the proposals of the *Agreement of the People* composed and later published *The Essex Ministers Watchword*. Cf. Smith, *op. cit.*, p. 103.
[2] *Works*, VIII, pp. 244ff.
[3] Cf. R. B. Merriman, *Six Contemporaneous Revolutions*, 1938, and Christopher Hill, *Puritanism and Revolution*, 1965, pp. 132-3.

revolutions in Christendom he also spoke of the forthcoming destruction of the Turkish Empire and the conversion of the Jewish people to Christ. The whole tenor of the sermon reveals that Owen's mind was extremely excited by the events through which he was living because to him they were part of God's activity in the last days. Happily, he did not let his eschatological views overpower his understanding to the extent of becoming a Fifth Monarchist; but even so, his views were capable, in the minds of lesser men, of causing a wholly distorted view of politics and religion. A few years later he was accused by a Fifth Monarchy preacher of deserting the cause, which suggests that his views in 1649 were cherished by sectarian groups in London.[1]

Sitting amongst those who listened to this outline of future events and to the identification of the cause of Parliament with the cause of God was Oliver Cromwell. He himself was very interested in the interpretation of prophecy: writing to John Cotton in 1651 he asked the Massachusetts divine "What is the Lord a-doing? What prophecies are now fulfilling?"[2] So, naturally, he was deeply impressed with Owen's ability to relate those affairs in which he, as an army commander, had such a great stake to the will of God for the future of Christianity in Europe. Providentially (so both men came to believe) the soldier and the preacher met the next day.[3] Owen had called to pay his respects to General Fairfax at his home in Queen Street but was kept waiting. During this period Cromwell arrived with other officers. Seeing Owen, he walked over to him and, laying his hand upon the minister's shoulder, said, "Sir, you are the person I must be acquainted with." To this unexpected compliment the young divine answered, "That will be much more to my advantage than yours." Shortly afterwards, as they walked in the garden, Cromwell replied, "We shall soon see that," and then proceeded to tell him of his forthcoming expedition to Ireland in order to put down rebellion there and of his desire that he should accompany him as a chaplain and make a survey of the state and future prospects of Trinity College, Dublin. Owen was not ready to give an immediate answer and asked for time to consider the offer. The idea of leaving his church and parish was repugnant to him. He had not been back in Coggeshall for very long when a letter addressed to his church asking for his release arrived, and his brother, now Captain Philemon Owen, came to persuade him on Cromwell's behalf to accept the invitation to go to Ireland.[4] A request had virtually turned into a command

[1] For the views of the Fifth Monarchists see B. S. Capp, "Extreme Millenarianism" in *Puritans, the Millennium and the Future of Israel*, ed. P. Toon. The criticism of Owen is in the "Epistolary Perambulation" by John Rogers in *The Time of the End* (1657) by John Canne.
[2] *The Writings and Speeches of Oliver Cromwell*, ed. W. C. Abbott, Cambridge, Mass., 1937-47, II, p. 482.
[3] Asty, p. ix.
[4] The letter mentioned by Asty is no longer extant.

and so, after conferring with local ministers, Owen agreed to go. Once more he had taken what must have been a painful decision, but, like earlier momentous decisions, it was to have important consequences for his future and for that of many other people.

Before the expedition left London in July, Owen had to fulfil another preaching engagement in the City. On the 7th June in Christ Church, Newgate Street, he preached with Thomas Goodwin at a special day of thanksgiving held to commemorate the suppresion of the Leveller mutiny at Burford on the 15th May by Cromwell and Fairfax.[1] The origins of the Leveller party may be traced to the disappointment of some of the more radical supporters of Parliament in the Civil War at the way the victorious House of Commons was acting after the War. For example, it imprisoned people without trial and refused to receive petitions from ordinary people. Receiving support mainly from artisans in London and soldiers in the army the Levellers demanded that there be a new written constitution based on the sovereignty of the people and limiting the powers of Parliament. They also proposed reforms in education and in respect to the paying of tithes; but they were neither atheists nor anarchists. They merely wanted to take the revolution that step further than did the Independents and senior army officers. The mutiny at Burford was caused by frustration since they felt they were getting nowhere.

Owen spoke to the congregation of aldermen, M.P.'s and army officers from Psalm 76:5, "the stouthearted are spoiled, they have slept their sleep." He began by reaffirming a doctrine that he had often expounded—that the care of the churches and the ordinances of the Gospel lies "at the bottom of God's powerful actings and workings among the sons of men." His hearers were witnessing in their generation the glorious work of God in overthrowing ungodly tyranny. Even so, the defeat of the Levellers, when compared with the victory over the army of Charles Stuart, that agent of popery, was but an "appendix of good will for the confirming of the former work which God had wrought." They should view the recent uprising as a trial of their faith, since the Levellers were political radicals whose views if implemented would lead to the dethroning of the Gospel and the prevention of its propagation.

As we would expect, Owen's views were in harmony with those of the army leaders and he showed no sympathetic or careful understanding of the motivation or aims of this group of men, many of whom were guided by high ideals. Again, as with the royalists at Colchester, his evaluation of them was in terms of how he thought they would prohibit

[1] For the Leveller mutiny see Gardiner, *op. cit.*, I, pp. 30ff. A recent study of the Levellers is J. Frank, *The Levellers*, Cambridge, Massachusetts, 1955, but H. N. Brailsford, *The Levellers and the English Revolution*, (new edition ed. C. Hill), 1961, is still useful, and so is A. S. P. Woodhouse, *Puritanism and Liberty*, 1938.

the general propagation of the Gospel and the maintenance of the Christian ministry. And he condemned them in God's name for not fitting into his own attempts to understand God's will for England.

In the sermon there was one interesting and revealing question discussed the answer to which gives us interesting insights into Owen's mind. It was as follows: when God is shaking and changing the nations, and when governments are being overthrown, how can any nation be sure that its own government would not topple? Perhaps behind this question lay the public discussion about the legality of the Rump without the presence of the excluded members. Owen's answer was given in what he called six "scriptural principles." They were that God will not overthrow a government if He has honoured its undertakings for Him with success, if its members devote themselves wholly to His cause, if they subject their power to the power of Christ, if they are supported by the prayers of God's elect saints, if they courageously and sincerely fulfil the work of Christian magistracy, and if they have not the "qualifications of that power (Roman Catholicism) which in the latter days God hath promised to destroy." Whilst he did not say so, it appears that Owen believed that the government of England in 1649 fulfilled these principles and therefore could expect the continued blessings of God. No wonder he could condemn the Levellers.

The sermons in Christ Church were followed by a sumptuous feast in Grocers' Hall. This banquet was a farewell dinner for the army before it left for Ireland. Next day in the Commons, Owen and Goodwin were thanked for their sermons and invited to print them but neither of them did.[1] Also an Act was read for settling £100 on Owen for his help at the siege of Colchester, and there was discussion about the promotion of Goodwin and Owen to be Heads of Oxford Colleges.[2] Owen's advancement was necessarily delayed but Goodwin soon became the new President of Magdalen College. During the discussion of his future by the Commons, Owen was probably on his way back to Coggeshall to set his affairs in order before leaving for Ireland. He had to arrange for the care of his family as well as for the continued preaching of the Gospel at St Peter's.[3] By the 11th July he was back in London participating at Whitehall in the great prayer meeting which preceded the stately departure of the army. Cromwell, with Colonels Goffe and

---

[1] C.J., VI, p. 226. Goodwin and Owen chose not to print their sermons but that of Owen was preserved and first printed in 1721. See *Works*, IX, pp. 197ff.

[2] B. Whitelocke, *Memorials of English Affairs*, 1732, p. 406.

[3] It is possible that Constantine Jessop who had been minister at nearby Fyfield preached for him in his absence and acted as an assistant minister at other times. This is assumed on the List of vicars on the south wall of the church. During her stay at Coggeshall, Mary Owen had at least three children. Mary was baptised on 4 July 1647 but died three weeks later. Another Mary was baptised on 23 February 1650 and an Elizabeth on 10 February 1651. I am grateful to the County Archivist of Essex, Mr F. G. Emmison, for sending me photocopies of the relevant pages from the parish register.

Harrison, expounded relevant portions of Scripture concerning the judgement of God on the enemies of the Gospel and the expedition was commended to the protection and mercy of the Almighty.[1] Owen's thoughts as he joined the army probably centred on his task of ensuring as far as he was able that military action did not cloud the need for the propagation of the Gospel and the training of more preaching ministers in Trinity College.

Reaching Bristol by the 15th July, the army faced a long wait until the embarkation in mid-August. As the troops prepared to board ship at Milford Haven there came news of a victory in Ireland over the chief royalist adversary, the Earl of Ormonde, whose forces Colonel Michael Jones had routed at Rathmines. So at a time when the royalist forces needed to be at their greatest strength to resist Cromwell they had been decisively weakened. Nevertheless, they still held Drogheda, an important town on the banks of the Boyne and at a strategic point on the road from Dublin to Ulster. Anticipating success and believing that providence was already working on his behalf, Cromwell sailed on the 13th August and two days later arrived in Dublin, where he was greeted by the roar of cannon and a great crowd of people. They included no Roman Catholics since Colonel Jones had previously dispelled them from the city. A week after Cromwell's triumphant arrival, Ireton arrived with the rest of the army in eighty-four ships. The next few days were spent in organising resources and preparing to deal with the enemy in the North. The first task was to take Drogheda, some thirty miles from Dublin, but when the army marched out of Dublin at the end of August Owen did not go with it. This means that he did not witness the capture of Drogheda and the massacre of those who unsuccessfully had sought to defend it. Having no record of Owen's reaction to the news of the massacre, we must presume that he interpreted it in much the same way as did Cromwell.[2] That is, it was a necessary and indeed merciful policy, aimed at striking terror into the enemies and thereby preventing future bloodshed, and the possibility of a foreign invasion of Ireland. From the divine standpoint it was to be seen as a judgement upon those who were enemies of Christ and who were seeking to defend a monarchy and a religion that God had condemned. (As the Ireland of the twentieth century experiences the civil, religious and political aftermath of the English colonisation of Ireland, Christians now surely regret that God was made the excuse for policies that have led to war, slaughter, massacre and long resentment. Sadly we so very rarely learn from history.)

Whilst living in Dublin Castle, Owen concerned himself with preach-

---

[1] See *Writings and Speeches of Cromwell*, II, pp. 92ff.
[2] At least this is what his sermon *The Steadfastness of the Promises* noticed below would seem to indicate. For Cromwell's views see C. Hill, *God's Englishman*, pp. 112ff.

ing, which according to two contemporary testimonies was well received.¹ Apart from this he made a survey of Trinity College, now in its fifty-eighth year. It was in a bad state of repair and virtually devoid of both staff and students. Since it had included amongst its Provosts several famous Puritans, one of whom was the famous Presbyterian, Walter Travers, and amongst its graduates many learned men, of whom the greatest, Archbishop James Ussher, was still alive, Owen would have had a deep respect for this institution and would have longed for it to return to its former intellectual and numerical strength.² Ireland was much in need of preachers and Trinity had such an important role to play in the production of these men. Apart from his preaching and administrative duties, Owen also found time to write a short book, *Of the Death of Christ*, which was a reply to criticism of his earlier *Salus Electorum* made by Richard Baxter, the "reformed pastor" of Kidderminster, whose views on the atonement of Christ were similar to those of Amyraut. The fact that Owen felt it was a right use of his time to defend the doctrine of the limited atonement of Christ when there were so many things to do in the troubled country of Ireland reveals just how important the preservation of orthodox Calvinism was to him. Any compromise with Arminianism, and this is what he felt Baxter's views were, would lead people down the slippery slope to Arminianism itself, which, in turn, would lead either to popery or Socinianism. He finished the book on December 20 1649 and in its last paragraph he left a very brief description of his life in Dublin. "For the present," he wrote, "being by God's providence removed for a season from my native soil, attended with more than ordinary weakness and infirmities, separated from my library, burdened with manifold employments, with constant preaching to a numerous multitude of as thirsting a people after the Gospel as ever yet I conversed withal, it sufficeth me that I have obtained this mercy, briefly and plainly to vindicate the truth from mistakes."[3]

By the time he wrote this conclusion to his book the English army under Cromwell had captured Wexford, taken possession of Cork, temporarily abandoned the siege of Waterford and established winter quarters at Youghal. Owen did not remain to see the Spring campaign. He returned to London, intent, it would seem on pressing upon the Council of State the need to ensure that provision was made for the orderly preaching of the Gospel in Ireland. When he preached before the

[1] John Rogers, *Ohel or Bethshemesh*, 1653, bk. II, ch. vi, and see also Nuttall, *Visible Saints*, p. 73.
[2] For the early history of Trinity College see J. P. Mahaffy, *An Epoch in Irish History: Trinity College, Dublin, 1591–1660*, 1903. For Travers see S. J. Knox, *Walter Travers*, 1962, and for Ussher see R. B. Knox, *James Ussher*, Cardiff, 1967.
[3] *Works*, X, p. 479. Baxter's criticisms of Owen's theology were in an appendix to his *Aphorisms of Justification* (1649).

Commons on the last day of February 1650 this was his major theme. In the dedicatory letter printed in the published sermon he admitted that it was "a serious proposal for the advancement and propagation of the Gospel in another nation." The following quotation from near the end of *The Steadfastness of the Promises*[1] shows how Owen viewed the duty of the British government.

> God's work whereunto you are engaged is the propagating of the kingdom of Christ and the setting up of the standard of the Gospel. So far as you find God going on with your work, go you on with his. How is it that Jesus Christ is in Ireland only as a lion staining all his garments with the blood of his enemies; and none to hold him out as a Lamb sprinkled with his own blood to his friends? Is it the sovereignty and interest of England that is alone to be transacted there? For my part, I see no farther into the mystery of these things but that I could heartily rejoice that, innocent blood being expiated, the Irish might enjoy Ireland so long as the moon endureth, so that Jesus Christ might possess the Irish. But God having suffered those sworn vassals of the man of sin to break out into such ways of villainy as render them obnoxious unto vengeance, upon such rules of government amongst men as he hath appointed; is there, therefore, nothing to be done but to give a cup of blood into their hands? Doubtless the way whereby God will bring the followers after the beast to condign destruction for all their enmity to the Lord Jesus, will be by suffering them to run into such practices against men as shall righteously expose them to vengeance, according to acknowledged principles among the sons of men. But is this all? Hath he no further aim? Is not all this to make way for the Lord Jesus to take possession of his long since promised inheritance? And shall we stop at the first part? Is this to deal fairly with the Lord Jesus?—call him out to do battle and then keep away his crown? God hath been faithful in doing great things for you; be faithful in this one—do your utmost for the preaching of the Gospel in Ireland.

Following this eloquent appeal he exclaimed:

> I would that there were for the present one gospel preacher for every walled town in the English possession in Ireland . . . The tears and cries of the inhabitants of Dublin after the manifestations of Christ are ever in my view . . . If their being gospelless move not our hearts, it is hoped their importunate cries will disquiet our rest, and wrest help as a beggar doth an alms.

Perhaps some of those present recalled how that four years earlier he had made a similar plea for the propagation of the Gospel in the dark corners of England and Wales. This great concern that people should hear of and receive Christ reveals the true spirituality of Owen. At the height of military victory his first thoughts were to ensure that the enlargement of the kingdom of Christ was not ignored.

He was probably consulted at some stage in the composition of the

[1] *Works*, VIII, pp. 208ff.

"Act for the better advancement of the Gospel and Learning in Ireland" which went through the Commons on the 8th March.[1] By this the property of the late Archbishop of Dublin and the Dean and Chapter of St Patrick's Cathedral was vested in fifteen trustees. Apart from Owen these included Henry Ireton, Henry Cromwell (son of Oliver), Jonathan Goddard (physician to Oliver) and Jenkin Lloyd, Bursar of Jesus College, Oxford. The Act provided for the maintenance of Trinity College and also for the erecting of another College and a Free School. Neither of the latter seem to have been founded but efforts were made to make Trinity a great centre of Christian learning. Owen himself was consulted on various occasions concerning the College and it was probably he who suggested the name of Samuel Winter, a Yorkshire minister, as Provost.[2] Furthermore, it was perhaps in response to Owen's persuasive lobbying that Parliament resolved to send over six able ministers to Ireland, but the finding of suitable volunteers was to prove difficult.[3] Finally, as it were, to crown Owen's achievements of that cold March day, the Council of State announced that he was to be one of its official preachers at Whitehall with a salary of £200 a year. Gradually, it seemed, he was being weaned away from his first love, the pastoral office. He was provided with lodgings, probably those formerly occupied by the late Archbishop Laud, and required to offer prayers and Bible readings at the beginning of Council meetings and preach a weekly sermon on Fridays in Whitehall Chapel. This appointment in which he replaced Thomas Goodwin, who moved to Oxford, placed Owen at the very centre of the affairs of the Commonwealth and ensured that he knew the men who were deciding, under God, the future of the country. His acceptance of the appointment confirms what has already become clear; he was wholly committed to the new Republic and believed that he could influence its policies, especially in religious matters.

One of these policies was made clear on the 20th June, three weeks after the triumphant return of Cromwell to London. It was resolved that an English invasion of Scotland was the only means of preventing a Scottish invasion of England.[4] Six days later Parliament adopted the resolution without a dissentient vote. There was fear that the Scots would invade England both to restore the Stuart monarchy in the person of the young Charles and to establish Presbyterianism. Having decided on the necessity of the invasion, the next problem the Commons had to face was who should lead the invading army. Fairfax, being a moderate Presbyterian,

[1] For the Act see *Acts and Ordinances of the Interregnum, 1642–1660*, ed. C. H. Firth & R. S. Rait, 1911, II, p. 355.
[2] Mahaffy, *op. cit.*, pp. 295ff. For Winter, who was Provost from 1651–60, see C.R.
[3] Cf. the letters written by the Commissioners in Dublin to Owen asking for his held in finding preachers. *Correspondence*, No's 1 and 9, pp. 50 and 59.
[4] For the background of the decision to invade Scotland see Gardiner, *op. cit.*, I, chap's viii and ix.

was the obvious choice for he would have given a respectability and morality to the expedition by his very presence with the army. Unfortunately for the Council of State, Fairfax did not wholeheartedly see matters in its way and so, under pressure, he resigned his commission in the army, giving as his reason "disabilities both in body and mind," words that were capable of more than one interpretation. He was succeeded by Cromwell who now became the Captain-General and Commander-in-Chief of all the forces of the Commonwealth in England. Having a great respect for Fairfax, Owen must have been disappointed that he was leaving the army; but the cause was greater than any individual and being a firm friend and admirer of Cromwell and confident of his abilities and concern for the Gospel, he was no doubt happy that the expedition to Scotland was in the hands of such a brave and godly man.

When the army left London on the 28th June for the North, Cromwell had with him Charles Fleetwood as Lieutenant-General and John Lambert as Major-General. William Good and John Owen served as chaplains. Their route took them through Cambridge, York, Durham and Newcastle. In the latter town Owen visited the Congregational church and gave some help.[1] By the side of the river Tyne the army kept a fast and called upon God to bless its endeavours on His behalf. Owen was one of the five ministers who helped with the devotions. During the encampment at Newcastle, Cromwell and his advisers composed *A Declaration of the Army of England . . . to all that are Saints and Partakers of the Faith of God's Elect in Scotland*, which was to be sent on ahead to Edinburgh. This explained the English government's interpretation of the Solemn League and Covenant, the civil wars, the execution of Charles I and the actions of the young Charles. Since the English army was undertaking the invasion of Scotland in the "full assurance that their cause was just and righteous in the sight of God," they prayed that the true saints of God in Scotland would not oppose them. The theological assumptions of this *Declaration*, especially the claim to see God's hand at work against Charles I and his policies, were basically the same as those Owen made in his sermons to Parliament and to the Essex County Committee. These same assumptions were also clearly evident in the *Vindication of the Declaration* which was composed for Cromwell at Berwick, the next halting place, by several ministers of whom Owen was one.[2] In Berwick, the gateway to Scotland, Owen also preached on the Lord's Day, the 20th July. As the clergy of the country that was

[1] For the Scottish campaign see *Writings and Speeches of Cromwell*, II, pp. 260ff. Perhaps it was at this time that Owen's long and deep friendship with Fleetwood was born. For a reference to Owen's visit to the Congregational church see *Memoirs of Ambrose Barnes*, ed. W. H. D. Longstaffe, 1867.
[2] Cromwell stated that the *Vindication* was written by the ministers in the letter he later wrote to the General Assembly of the Kirk of Scotland, *Writings and Speeches*, II, p. 302.

about to be invaded were adamant in their divine-right presbyterianism, Owen chose to expound the Congregational understanding of the nature of the Church, the Body of Christ. He wanted to be sure that the soldiers knew what it was for which they were to fight.

After Cromwell had delivered a speech to his men telling them of the difficulties ahead, the army crossed the Tweed on the 22nd July and by Friday, the 26th, was at Dunbar, helping to unload provisions from the fleet. No resistance had been met as yet since all the men from the border counties had been ordered to leave their homes and go to the Scottish army, camped near Edinburgh. This army was not united for if it had been then it could probably have successfully defended the centre of Scotland in the days ahead. Its leader, David Leslie, an experienced soldier who had served under Gustavus Adolphus and who had fought with Cromwell at Marston Moor in the first civil war, had been given a very difficult task as commander since there was disagreement in Edinburgh as to whether or not "malignants" (i.e. those royalists who were not zealous for the Covenant) should be allowed to fight.[1] Eventually the zeal of the covenanting party triumphed and it was definitely ordered that the army should be purged. Meanwhile the opposing armies first confronted each other at Musselburgh, a few miles east of Edinburgh. Leslie had fortified the Edinburgh-Leith line and on the 29th some of his regiments were visited by Charles to whom, it seems, certain officers rashly promised that they would capture Cromwell. And this promise may have been the motive behind the attempt by Major-General Montgomery and the best cavalry to reach the English camp that night. They took Robert Lilburne's regiment by surprise and rushed towards Musselburgh. By this time the English army was aroused and a counter-attack by their horse scattered the Scots, who fled towards Edinburgh. They were intercepted by a party of English dragoons who killed some of them and took a number of prisoners. Owen witnessed some of these events and in a letter to John Lisle, a prominent member of the Council of State, he made reference to them. The letter was read out in the Commons but only a part of it has survived:[2]

> I dare not write the particulars of the fight, being assured that you have it from better hands: the issue, that they were repulsed by an handful, and an hundred and eighty taken prisoners; among them, Straughan's major himself reported to be slain: the whole party pursued to their works; four ministers came out with them, but being not known, received the lot of war, three of them killed and one taken.
>
> This was the party they most relyed upon, as being especially consecrated by the Kirk to this service.

[1] J. D. Douglas, *Light in the North: the Story of the Scottish Covenanters*, Exeter, 1964, pp. 34ff. For Leslie see the *D.N.B.*
[2] Part of Owen's letter is in (Sir W. Scott), *Original Memoirs written during the Civil War*, Edinburgh, 1806, pp. 244-5. Cf. *Writings and Speeches*, II, p. 301.

Their ministers told the people before our army came that they should not need to strike one stroke, but stand still, and they should see the sectaries destroyed.

Amongst the "better hands" who had sent a report of the fight was Cromwell.[1] He likewise referred to Colonel Strachan and his leader Major-General Montgomery as "two champions of the Kirk" on whom the Covenanters had placed great hopes.

Whilst the Scottish army was being purged of "malignants" and whilst the English soldiers were busy digging trenches in Musselburgh, Cromwell wrote what has become a famous letter to the General Assembly.[2] He asked the clergy of Scotland to reconsider their position and then went on to say:

> Your own guilt is too much for you to bear: bring not therefore upon yourselves the blood of innocent men, deceived with pretences of King and Covenant, from whose eyes you hide a better knowledge. I am persuaded that divers of you, who lead the people, have laboured to build yourselves in these things wherein you censure others, and established yourselves upon the Word of God. Is it therefore infallibly agreeable to the Word of God, all that you say? I beseech you, in the bowels of Christ, think it possible you may be mistaken.

Probably both Cromwell and the Covenanters were in part mistaken but for them to realise and accept this was to ask too much. The exchange of letters merely confirmed each side in its own convictions and the war continued. Owen, however, whose duties as preacher to the Council of State necessitated his return to London, left the scene of battle.

In Owen's absence, Cromwell achieved his crowning achievement in arms. This was at Dunbar on the 3rd September and he interpreted it as a miracle wrought by the Almighty. In practical terms it wrecked the Covenanters, weakened the power of Charles in Scotland and ensured the continuance of Independency in England. With the English army in Edinburgh and there hotly engaged in a battle of words with the stalwart Presbyterians, Cromwell felt the need not only of supplies of every kind for his men but also of competent Independent divines to combat the spiritual propaganda of the Scottish Kirk. So on the 13th September the Commons ordered that Joseph Caryl, a preacher in Westminster Abbey, and Edward Bowles, a preacher in York Minster, together with Owen, should go to Scotland.[3] For Owen this meant another long journey but happily it was not yet winter. By the 20th

---

[1] *Writings and Speeches*, II, pp. 299ff. In fact neither Strachan nor Montgomery were killed in this incident.
[2] *Writings and Speeches*, II, pp. 302-3.
[3] *C.J.*, VI, p. 468. For Caryl and Bowles see *C.R.*

October Caryl and Owen were in Edinburgh, for on that day Caryl preached before the Lord General and his officers.[1] The two ministers found that the Castle was still in Scottish hands and that Cromwell was seeking to intervene in the internal Scottish disputes to his own advantage. And, at least on one occasion, Owen himself preached before the General, taking as his theme, that which he had previously expounded at Berwick. The doctrine of the nature of the Church was currently much under discussion and so Owen once more expounded the New Testament ideal of the Body of Christ. Making one short treatise of the two sermons, Owen published it in Edinburgh so that both parties in the conflict could read it. Attached to *The Branch of the Lord the Beauty of Zion* was a dedicatory letter to Cromwell dated the 26th November.[2] In this the Congregational divine stated that his aim in joining the army was "to pour out a savour of the Gospel upon the sons of peace" in Scotland. Addressing himself particularly to the Lord General he wrote:

> I do present them to your excellency, not only because the rise of my call to this service, under God, was from you; but also, because in the carrying on of it I have received from you, in the weakness and temptations wherewith I am encompassed that daily spiritual refreshment and support—by inquiry into and discovery of the deep and hidden dispensations of God towards his secret ones—which my spirit is taught to value.

This suggests that the two men spent many hours together discussing the "deep things of God." Here probably was laid the foundation of the deep trust in each other's integrity which marked their relationship for the next six years.

Much of the rest of Owen's time was spent with the Scots seeking to persuade them of the folly of supporting the son of Charles I and of the need to establish Protestant Churches in which there was a measure of freedom so that men of differing churchmanship could effectively serve Christ together. One of the men to whom he talked was Alexander Jaffray, the Provost of Aberdeen. In his Diary, Jaffray wrote the following about his meetings with Owen and the grandees:[3]

> During the time of my being a prisoner, I had good opportunity of frequent conference with the Lord General, Lieutenant-General and Owen; by occasion of whose company, I had first made out unto me, not only some clear evidences of the Lord's controversy with the family and person of our King, but more particularly, the sinful mistake of the good men of this nation about the know-

---

[1] *Letters and Speeches*, II, p. 355.
[2] *Works*, VIII, p. 283.
[3] *The Diary of Alexander Jaffray*, ed. J. Barclay, 1833, pp. 58–9. The expression "grandees," though meaning persons of high rank and position, was used specifically in the Interregnum to describe the senior army officers.

ledge and mind of God as to the exercise of the magistrate's power in the matters of religion—what the due bounds and limits of it are. The mistake and ignorance of the mind of God in this matter—what evils hath it occasioned! Fearful scandals and blasphemies on the one hand and cruel persecution and bitterness among brethren on the other!

In fact the conversion of Jaffray, who had been taken prisoner at Dunbar, eventually found its fulfilment in his becoming a Quaker, a fact which could not have been very pleasing to Owen who, as we shall see, regarded the teaching of this sect with horror. The notion of the Lord's controversy with the family of Stuart, a theological idea much used by the Independents, was taken from the messages of the prophets of ancient Israel. They spoke at times of Jehovah's controversy with their King and nation.[1] It was easily adapted to the Stuart monarchy since preachers at this time were prone to describe England (or Britain) as enjoying a relationship with God similar to that enjoyed by the Israelites of old.[2] As we have noted, the general framework of this concept was in Owen's mind as he preached to the Commons on the day following the execution of Charles I. Though many would find such a viewpoint repugnant today, the army commanders throughout Scotland were of another mind. For example, Robert Lilburne, the commander at Hamilton, wrote to Cromwell to ask for "some of Mr Owen's sermons" to disperse amongst the Scots, who had expressed an interest in reading them.[3]

Edinburgh Castle surrendered on Christmas Eve 1650. This did not mean, however, that military activities were at an end or that Scottish resistance was completely broken. Charles II, who was crowned at Scone on the 1st January, and Leslie had yet to be overcome. So the army had still much to do when Owen set off once again on the long journey back to London. Here he remained until the 8th March when he was given permission by the Council "to repair into the country for six weeks."[4] Before he left London he heard that Oliver Cromwell had accepted the office of Chancellor of Oxford in succession to the Earl of Pembroke. This appointment must have made him feel that his own preferment to the University was soon to come. And whilst he was at Coggeshall with his family the Commons voted by a small majority to appoint him as the new Dean of Christ Church.[5] This fulfilled the intention of the House made on the eve of his departure for Ireland.

The small majority at Westminster reveals just how much uncertainty there was surrounding the appointment. The House had debated the

---

[1] E.g. Jeremiah 25:31, Hosea 4:12, 12:3, & Micah 6:2.
[2] For the idea of the elect nation see William Haller, *Foxe's Book of Martyrs and the Elect Nation*, 1967, and Wilson, op. cit., pp. 173ff.
[3] J. Nickolls, *Original Letters and Papers of State*, 1743, pp. 48–9.
[4] *C.S.P.D.* (1651), p. 74.
[5] *C.J.*, VI, p. 549.

possibility of allowing Edward Reynolds[1] to continue as Dean even though he had refused to take the Engagement, the promise to be faithful to the Commonwealth of England established without King or House of Lords.[2] Also it had studied the report from the Committee for the Universities in which it was stated that Joseph Caryl had refused to accept the office of Dean since he preferred to remain in London. The confusion and negotiations which took place at Oxford before Owen's appointment are seen in the contents of a series of letters which Robert Payne, an ejected Canon of Christ Church, wrote from Abingdon and Oxford to Gilbert Sheldon, the ejected Warden of All Souls and future Archbishop.[3] On the 11th November 1650 the news was that Philip Nye, the Congregational incumbent of Acton, Middlesex, and Stephen Marshall, who had preached so many times before the Commons, were being mentioned as the possible successors of Reynolds, who was objecting to taking the Engagement since it clashed with the previous commitment he had taken in the Covenant. By the 24th February it was anticipated that Caryl would take the appointment even though Reynolds was still living in the Dean's lodgings. Not until the 24th March was Payne able to inform his correspondent that "Owen, sometime scholar to Thomas Barlow of Queen's College is voted by the House . . . Dean of Christ Church and that Reynolds must certainly leave it after all the means he hath used to hold it." The day before this letter was written Ralph Josselin wrote in his Diary: "Mr Owen hath a place of great profit given unto him, viz. Dean of Christ Church."[4] Under normal conditions, and the 1650s were not so, the profit was about £800 a year.[5] According to Asty, the senior Students of Christ Church, glad that at least the uncertainty was over, wrote a letter to Owen expressing their great satisfaction with his appointment.[6]

Christ Church was therefore to have as its leader a clergyman of thirty-five years of age who was a personal friend of the new Chancellor. The new Dean believed as intensely in the righteousness of the parliamentary cause as Samuel Fell, the Dean whom Reynolds replaced in 1647, believed in the righteousness of the King's cause. Owen held that in opposing and then executing the King as well as in the invasion of Ireland and then Scotland the army had been doing the will of God. It had been

---

[1] For Reynolds see *D.N.B.* He had been Dean since 1647; before then he was a prominent member of the Westminster Assembly.

[2] The Engagement was a Declaration ordered by an Act of 2 Jan. 1650 to be taken by all men over 18 years. *Acts and Ordinances*, II, pp. 325, 391, 503, 830. When Owen took the Declaration is not known.

[3] For the letters see Nicholas Pocock, "Illustrations of the State of the Church during the Rebellion", in *Theologian and Ecclesiastic*, Vols VI-VX, especially Vol VII. Pocock took much of his material from Br Museum Harleian MSS 6942.

[4] *The Diary of Ralph Josselin*, p. 84.

[5] In contrast the average parish minister received between £75 and £100.

[6] Asty, p. x. The letter is not extant. In Christ Church a Senior Student was the equivalent of a Fellow.

uprooting the influence of antichrist from the nation in order that the Gospel of Jesus Christ could be freely preached and the Church purified. Indeed, the battles fought and the victories won, were clearly prophesied in Revelation 17–19 as part of God's programme for the last days. The latter-day glory of the Church would soon dawn. Before that great time arrived, however, it was the duty of the saints to make the best of the available means and opportunities. So whilst he had no wish to abolish the long established system of parish churches he did want to ensure that the organisation of the churches was such that it was not controlled by either a prelatical or presbyterian tyranny. He wanted to see a flexible system that allowed ministers who taught orthodox doctrine a measure of freedom. He saw his primary task at Oxford as that of providing the right atmosphere, means, teachers and opportunities for the Gospel to be expounded, defended and instilled into the hearts and minds of the young scholars, and through them to the nation.

Despite the historical associations of Oxford with prelacy it was Owen's high regard for traditional learning, conservative approach to ancient institutions that God had not condemned, and sense of divine providence which led him to accept the appointment. That his acceptance of the Deanery was to some extent a compromise of his Congregational principles he would probably have denied. In defence of his action, had he thought it necessary to give it, he would probably have argued that the saints had a responsibility to reform existing educational institutions in order to make them suitable places for training young men in the cultivation of the mind and spirit. During his days with the army he must have heard the radical views of some soldiers that the Universities were centres of heathen and papist learning; to stifle these, as well as to ensure that Oxford be a centre of solid Calvinist learning, he determined to do his part with God as his helper.

CHAPTER III

# DEAN AND VICE-CHANCELLOR

"About two years ago," wrote John Owen in early 1653, "the Parliament of the Commonwealth promoted me, while I was diligently employed in preaching the Gospel by their authority... though with reluctance on my part, to an office in the very celebrated University of Oxford." This promotion came, he confessed, despite the fact that he "dreaded almost every academic position" and felt "unequal to the task." In particular he regarded public lecturing in theology as the most demanding aspect of the work, for it required in his opinion the whole time of the most grave and experienced of divines—something which he did not claim to be.[1] The fact was that being Dean of Christ Church involved much more than academic work and his administrative duties were greatly increased when he became Vice-Chancellor. These duties were increased yet more when he also became a member of a small commission to which the Chancellor, Oliver Cromwell, delegated his powers in 1652.[2] Indeed, Owen only accepted the office of Vice-Chancellor because Cromwell insisted that he should. "I have been called upon," he told Convocation after his appointment, "by the partiality and too good opinion of him whose commands we must not dispute, and with whom the most earnest requests to be excused were urged in vain."[3]

Whatever inhibitions Owen had concerning his academic or administrative responsibilities, he was probably somewhat comforted by the knowledge that the University had been restored to the beginnings of what could prove to be, if well managed and with God's favour, a flourishing condition. When General Fairfax had called for the surrender of Oxford in May 1646, he had told the royalists in the city that "he very much desired the preservation of this place, so famous for learning, from ruin."[4] Happily, Oxford surrendered without incident and the city did not suffer harm. Two months later Parliament set up a committee

---

[1] The information and quotations come from the preface to *Diatriba de Divina Justitia* (1653) in *Works*, X, pp. 492–3, with the English title *A Dissertation on Divine Justice*.
[2] The letters from Cromwell authorising this authority shared by Owen, John Wilkins, Jonathan Goddard, Thomas Goodwin and Peter French, are in *Correspondence*, No.3, pp. 52–4. For Wilkins see B. J. Shapiro, *John Wilkins*, Berkeley, 1969, and for Peter French *Alumni Oxonienses*, ed. J. Foster.
[3] *Oxford Orations*, p. 5.
[4] Mallet, *History of the University of Oxford*, II, p. 369, quoting a news-journal.

for the regulation of the University, which had virtually ceased to exist as a centre of learning. Then in September six Presbyterian ministers, including Edward Reynolds, were sent to preach good Reformed doctrine in the churches and chapels to prepare Oxford for reform. The task of the preachers was made difficult by the jeering of undisciplined students and by the dissemination of somewhat unorthodox divinity by such army preachers as William Erbery and Colonel John Hewson.[1] The existence of both these problems did not augur well for the future as Owen himself was to find out. Parliament, however, continued its plans for further reformation by appointing twenty-four Visitors on the 1st May 1647. Their task was to enquire into all disorders, to ascertain which members of the University had failed to take the Covenant, and to list those men who had actually opposed the parliamentary forces in the recent war.[2] Each College had possessed by Statute its own Visitor, usually the King or a Bishop, and there was deep-seated opposition to the existence of one general Board. The fact also that the new Board represented the Presbyterian interest did not endear it to those who still lived in the Colleges and Halls, and who remembered with nostalgia former days.

During 1648–9, whilst Owen was still a minister in Essex, the removal of a large number of royalist Heads of Colleges, Professors, Fellows and tutors was accomplished. Only at Oriel, Lincoln, and Queen's was there no change of Head. At Christ Church Dean Samuel Fell was removed after much resistance and with him went all the Canons except John Wall.[3] The professorships in the University were filled by its own graduates and by men from Cambridge and Dublin. Henry Wilkinson, who had been an Essex minister, became Principal of Magdalen Hall and Professor of Moral Philosophy whilst Francis Cheynell, who had been ejected from Oxford in 1638 for his opposition to Laudianism, became President of St John's and Lady Margaret Professor of Divinity. From Cambridge came Seth Ward and John Wallis to be the Professors of Astronomy and Geometry and Lewis Du Moulin, who was also a graduate of Paris, to become the Camden Professor of Ancient History. And from Dublin came Joshua Hoyle to the important post of Regius Professor of Divinity. Edward Pococke, the learned Orientalist, kept his professorship of Arabic and Hebrew to which Laud had appointed him.[4] About one quarter of the 200 vacant fellowships went to Cambridge graduates.

[1] For Hewson see *D.N.B.* He was appointed one of the judges of Charles I and later a member of Cromwell's House of Lords. Erbery engaged in debate with the learned Francis Cheynell and Oxford opinion judged that Erbery had the better of the Presbyterian. For Erbery see B. R. White, "William Erbery (1604–54) and the Baptists," *Baptist Quarterly*, XXIII, No. 3, 1969.
[2] For the ordinance see *Acts and Ordinances*, I, pp. 925ff.
[3] H. L. Thompson, *Christ Church*, 1900, pp. 54ff.
[4] For Wilkinson and Cheynell see *C.R.* and for Ward, Wallis, Moulin, Hoyle and Pococke see *D.N.B.*

Anthony Wood, not an unbiassed observer, wrote of poor curates and schoolmasters from country areas, and of rude men, careless of formalities, discipline and dress, being intruded into the Colleges.¹

When Thomas Fairfax and Oliver Cromwell, fresh from their victory over the Levellers, arrived in Oxford in May 1649 to be entertained in the Warden's lodgings at All Souls, they found that the University was being reorganised and that lectures, tutorials and disputations were being resumed.² Congregation and Convocation were also meeting regularly.³ The curriculum in Arts, Law and Medicine remained the same as in former times but Theology had assumed a different emphasis. The sovereign grace of God in predestination and His irresistible grace in regeneration were again being discussed and taught. In the parish churches and College chapels, which were now purified of their high-Church adornments, the Directory had replaced the Book of Common Prayer as the basis for public worship. Arminian innovations and ceremonialism had been abandoned. Some attempts, which proved to be unsuccessful, were being made to remodel the Statutes of individual Colleges and to collect rent arrears from tenants of lands and properties owned by the Colleges and the University. Efforts were also being exerted by the Visitors and Heads of Houses to control discipline and insist on the use of Greek or Latin in both academic work and ordinary conversation. Coffee-houses were beginning to supply an alternative to taverns as places of recreation and discussion. So when Owen arrived in 1651 he faced a situation which was, though much improved since 1649, still far from satisfactory from his point of view. While the Colleges had for the most part settled down and accepted the new order, in some quarters an angry and sullen spirit was still evident. Compared with the high standard of student behaviour which Owen expected, most of the Oxford scholars were, as he himself put it, a "mere rabble and the subject of talk by the rabble." Astrologers and sectaries even speculated as to how long the University would last.⁴ Notwithstanding this, Owen was quietly confident that Oxford, and her sister institution at Cambridge, were to be, by God's grace and protection, great centres of Christian learning and evangelism.

¹ Wood, *History of University of Oxford*, II, p. 604.
² For the visit of the generals see Mallet, *op. cit.*, II, p. 385.
³ The House of Congregation was subordinate to the House of Convocation. The membership of Congregation included the Chancellor, Vice-Chancellor, Proctors and all the Regent Masters. Its main duties were connected with the granting of degrees and the incorporation of students from other Universities. See *Oxford University Statutes*, trans. G. R. M. Ward, 1845, I, pp. 81ff.
⁴ In 1657 Owen told Convocation that "our critical situation and our common interests were discussed out of journals and newspapers by every Tom, Dick and Harry. Nobody was so abjectly stupid as not to have either fear or hope on account of the situation. Such, indeed, was the will of the Sovereign Disposer of events—so that whatever is mortal would be held in lesser esteem among mortals." *Oxford Orations*, p. 41. Here we see again his habit of seeing everything in terms not of social or economic problems but of the will of God.

To simplify this account of Owen's career at Oxford, we shall not describe it chronologically, as this would make for very complicated reading. Instead we shall look first at his work as Dean and secondly at his work as Vice-Chancellor. Little reference will be made to his activities outside Oxford since his involvement in national affairs will be the subject of the next two chapters.

DEAN OF CHRIST CHURCH

From the foundation of Christ Church by Henry VIII to the year 1651 there had been sixteen Deans.[1] The first of these, Richard Cox, was known as an ardent reformer and opponent of popery; during his period of office Peter Martyr, the celebrated continental reformer, occupied a Canonry at Christ Church and was also Regius Professor of Divinity. Ten years later a Puritan occupied the Deanery. He was Thomas Sampson, who had been in exile during the reign of Queen Mary, and who eventually lost his place under Elizabeth for his nonconformity. Brian Duppa and Samuel Fell, the last two Deans before Reynolds, were of a different theological tradition for they were supporters of the religious policies of Archbishop Laud. Reynolds himself, Owen's immediate predecessor, was an able Calvinist divine who was greatly respected by his Presbyterian brethren and who had played a prominent part in the theological discussions of the Westminster Assembly. He was not, however, a doctrinaire Presbyterian of the Scottish type and would have been quite happy with a modified and reformed episcopacy as the basis of the National Church. In December 1648 he took most of the Prebends with him to London to protest against the plan to sell the lands of the Dean and Chapter.[2] Though they arrived at Westminster when Colonel Pride was "purging" Parliament, their cause triumphed because the Independents who controlled the Commons knew that Christ Church was a special case, being both a College and a Cathedral, and had therefore to be treated differently from the Cathedrals which were only the seats of bishops.[3] A year later the Chapter was in further difficulties with the same Parliament, which required all the Heads, Fellows and graduates of the University to take the Engagement. Under the leadership of Reynolds, the Oxford Convocation asked that those who had reservations in their conscience about the Engagement be allowed instead to give a promise to live peacefully, but Parliament would not agree to this compromise. The result was that Reynolds himself with two of the Canons, John Mills and Edward Pococke, and Francis Cheynell were ejected. Cheynell was replaced as Lady Margaret Professor by Henry Wilkinson, a Canon

[1] Thompson, op. cit., pp. 1-68.   [2] Wood, History of University of Oxford, II, p. 613.
[3] Henry VIII united the episcopal see of Oxford with the collegiate corporation of Christ Church in 1546. Previously the see was linked to the Abbey at Oseney. Thompson, op. cit., p. 11.

of Christ Church, whilst Owen replaced Reynolds; Peter French, brother-in-law of Oliver Cromwell, and Ambrose Upton, a Devonshire man, were made Canons, to fill the two vacancies caused by the ejection of Mills and Pococke.[1]

The eight Canons, who by tradition occupied the eight stalls in the former Cathedral during divine worship as well as the lodgings assigned to each stall, included Presbyterians, Independents and a moderate Anglican. The latter, John Wall, was appointed in 1633 and by careful compromise and moderation held his place until his death in 1666. Had he but written his autobiography before his death we would have had a most important source for comparing life in three or four fascinating decades in Christ Church. It seems, however, that all he published were a few sermons under the title, *Christian Reconcilement* (1658). The three Presbyterians were Henry Cornish, Henry Langley and Henry Wilkinson. All three were Oxford graduates who had been sent to the University in 1646 as preachers and who had been rewarded for their services by being appointed as Prebends. They had lived through and participated in the expulsions and reformation that occurred between 1646 and 1651. Wilkinson had been deeply involved in these changes as they affected the internal workings of the University since he was a member of the Board of Visitors. Langley, being also the Master of Pembroke, had experienced the changes as they affected a small College. Cornish, likewise, had been involved in reformation and change from the beginning. All three men became Nonconformists in 1662. Of the four Independents—Christopher Rogers, Ralph Button, Ambrose Upton, and Peter French—Rogers had the longest association with the University having been Principal of New Inn Hall since 1626. Button, the Public Orator, was a Fellow of Merton whilst Upton was a Fellow of All Souls. French was a Cambridge graduate whose appointment was probably due, at least in part, to the influence of Oliver Cromwell. Together with these eight men, and especially with Wilkinson, the sub-Dean in 1651-2, Owen had to guide until 1660 when he was removed the fortunes of an institution which had been both a Cathedral and College but was now only the latter. Their collective duties included the provision of services of worship in the former Cathedral, the choice of Students including the elections of boys from Westminster School, the appointment of chaplains, the provision of tutorial facilities, the administration of discipline, the oversight of property, the collection of rents and tithes, the gift of livings and the care of almsmen in Christ Church hospital.[2] Owen probably chose the actual tutors himself.

[1] This Henry Wilkinson, known as "Long Harry," is not the same man who was Professor of Moral Philosophy. Both are in *C.R.* For Upton see *Alumni Oxonienses*.
[2] From its foundation Christ Church was required to support 24 almsmen. Cf. *Correspondence*, No. 8, p. 58 for a letter from the Committee of Public Revenue to Christ Church asking for a place to be given to a Mr Cornish.

Unfortunately, very little material is available from which to construct and evaluate Owen's work as Dean. The manuscript Chapter Book is extant but it is chiefly, though not entirely, taken up with details of decisions concerning lands and property. Also a few pages of the manuscript Disbursements Book remain.[1] Owen himself wrote very little in his books about his experience in the College and his extant correspondence relating to Christ Church comprises no more than eight letters. Nor does it seem that any of the Canons left descriptions of their experiences. There are, however, a few references in letters and diaries of the period which help to supply minor pieces of information.

There is little doubt, as we noted above, that Owen regarded his preaching in and around Oxford and his lecturing and debating in the University as the most important and demanding aspect of his work. He seems to have taken administrative work in his stride and not let it worry him. Most probably he preached regularly in Christ Church on the Lord's Day and he may also have participated in the weekly lecture of the Canons there. On alternate Sundays between 1652 and 1657, he preached with Thomas Goodwin at St Mary's, the University Church. Explaining Owen's ability and popularity as a preacher, Anthony Wood declared that "his personage was proper and comely and he had a very graceful behaviour in the pulpit, an eloquent elocution, a winning and insinuating deportment and could, by the persuasion of his oratory . . . move and win the affections of his admiring auditory almost as he pleased."[2]

The type of material on which his sermons were composed may be seen from a perusal of *On the Mortification of Sin* (1656) and *Of the Nature and Power of Temptation* (1658), both of which were published in Oxford.[3] and which were, in origin, sermons preached to the University. In the preface to *On the Mortification of Sin* he made his aims in preaching and publishing clear. "I hope," he wrote, "I may own in sincerity that my heart's desire unto God, and the chief design of my life in the station wherein the good providence of God hath placed me, are, that mortification and universal holiness may be promoted in my own and in the hearts and ways of others, to the glory of God, that so the Gospel of our Lord and Saviour Jesus Christ may be adorned in all things." The sermons were based on Romans 8:13 ("If ye through the Spirit do mortify the deeds of the body, ye shall live"), and explained the principles of mortification according to the teaching of the Apostle Paul. The book of sermons on temptation originated in his observation that many people were being tempted to believe erroneous and strange things concerning God's providence in English affairs. In the introduction

---

[1] I am grateful to the Dean and Chapter for permission to see these books.
[2] Wood, *Athenae Oxonienses*, IV, col. 102.
[3] The two treatises are in *Works*, VI.

Owen expressed his concern that the mid-1650s were filled "with fearful examples of backsliding such as former ages never knew." Anyone who did not realise that there was "an hour of temptation" come upon the world to "try them that dwell upon the earth" was either under the power of some lust or stark blind. So, from Matthew 26:41 ("Watch and pray that ye enter not into temptation"), he examined the nature of temptation, how it prevails in human experience, and the ways laid down in Scripture to prevent its success. Being series of sermons both books are not balanced treatments of their themes: Owen was far too busy to rewrite and replan their contents. However, they do reveal that Owen was becoming an exponent of the puritan spirit—if by that term is meant the cultivation of personal godliness as exemplified in the sermons of such men as William Perkins and Thomas Taylor.[1] For the *Works* of the latter Owen wrote, or at least signed, a preface.[2]

From two other books we gain some insight into his academic, Latin disputations and lectures. In *Diatriba De Divina Justitia* (1653), from which we have already quoted, he expanded the position that he had defended in a public disputation. It concerned the intellectual question as to whether it was necessary for God to punish sin, and was a theological problem which had much concerned some Calvinist divines. Owen held that God, by virtue of His holy and righteous nature, could not forgive guilty sinners without an atonement being made for their sins. Other divines argued that God, being God, could forgive, if He so wished, without the atonement of Christ. In *Theologoumena Pantodapa* (1661),[3] a Latin treatise with a Greek title, he outlined the nature, rise and progress of "true" theology from the time of Adam to the fully developed and revealed theology of the New Testament. He argued that the true statement of Biblical theology was to be found in Calvinist orthodoxy. This was a theme he must often have lectured upon. This work, which was highly valued in Dissenting Academies in the eighteenth century contains a Latin poem by T.(homas) G.(oodwin).[4] Unfortunately the *Theologoumena* has never appeared in a complete translation and by now has been superseded by other books on the history of the development of Christian theology.

The Dean's belief in the importance of preaching and expounding Biblical theology is seen in three of the earliest orders of the Chapter after he moved into Christ Church. On the 15th May 1651 it was ordered that College chaplains who were Masters of Arts and others of suitable

---

[1] For Perkins see *William Perkins*, ed. Ian Breward, Abingdon, 1970, and for Taylor see D.N.B. For the "puritan spirit" see Haller, *The Rise of Puritanism*, chap's iii and iv.
[2] The *Works* were published in 1653 and, along with Owen, Caryl and Goodwin also signed the preface.
[3] *Works*, XVII, pp. 1ff.
[4] Cf. *Works*, I, p. x, for the comments of Goold and references to writers and teachers who appreciated this Latin treatise.

ability should preach in neighbouring vacant pulpits on Sundays. One young man affected by this ruling was Philip Henry, who later became a distinguished Nonconformist minister and father of the famous Bible Commentator, Matthew Henry. In his Diary for the 9th January 1653, Philip wrote: "I preacht my first sermon at South Hincsey in Oxfordshire, the text, John 8:34."[1] On the 2nd June 1651 it was ordered by the Chapter that glass pictures representing God or angels should be taken out of the windows of the former Cathedral and the glass used to repair broken windows in other parts of the foundation. To have allowed such pictures to remain would have appeared to Owen and his brethren as an open violation of the commandment to make no graven images. In June 1651 it was also required that all scholars give a report to their tutors of the sermons they heard each Sabbath. This helped to ensure that they listened carefully to what they heard and missed no opportunity of receiving the salvation of God.

Since Owen was as much committed to the ideal of the Congregational way as to the necessity of preaching the Gospel, it is somewhat surprising to find a curious lack of information about his own church membership whilst he lived in Oxford. Some years later one of his critics alleged that he had tried to form a gathered church in Christ Church.[2] In 1657, John Beverley, the Congregational pastor at Rothwell in Northamptonshire, virtually accused the Dean of forgetting the churches of visible saints, suggesting that Owen was so busy with University matters and government business that he had no time left to help the Congregational churches.[3] The fact that Beverley treated Owen as a fellow Congregationalist as well as the fact that Owen was a prominent member of the Savoy Assembly in 1658 prove that he was in good standing in the churches and thus a member of a gathered church. But the problem is: of which church was he a member and in which church did he hold office from 1651 to 1659? If there was a gathered church in Christ Church then the problem is solved but unfortunately there is no evidence to prove that one ever existed. In Magdalen College, where Thomas Goodwin was President, there was a church of visible saints but in the list of members provided by Goodwin's son, Owen is not mentioned—which suggests that he was not a member.[4] The only other possibility seems to be that he gathered a church in the house which he bought at Stadhampton, the village of his youth. From 1660 to 1662 he held services of worship there and it could be that these were the continuation of

[1] *Diaries and Letters of Philip Henry*, ed. M. H. Lee, 1882, p. 14. As the Chapter Book is not consistently paginated no folio references are supplied. South Hinksey is now in Berkshire.
[2] George Vernon, *A Letter to a Friend*, 1670, p. 15.
[3] For this letter see *Correspondence*, No. 47, p. 96.
[4] *The Works of Thomas Goodwin*, ed. J. C. Miller, Edinburgh, 1861, II, p. xxxiv. Included in the membership were Thankful Owen, Francis Howell, Theophilus Gale, Stephen Charnock, Samuel Blower, and Edward Terry, all of whom are in C.R.

earlier services of a gathered church. Of the three possibilities the existence of a church in Christ Church seems the most probable.

A Congregational Dean in what was a former seat of a prelate was vulnerable to criticism from both the right and the left. If Beverley, a moderate Independent, was angered by Owen's seeming lack of concern for the churches, the sectarians and radicals were even more incensed by the attachment of Owen and his colleagues to the old order and its institutions. They made a concerted attack upon the Universities both in 1653 and again in 1659; the former attack was deeply felt by Owen and we shall make reference to it later in this chapter. Criticism from the right came from at least two former members of Christ Church and concerned Owen's views on episcopacy and the use of the Lord's Prayer.

The religious services in Christ Church were carefully watched by former members of the House and from one of them came a report that Owen had put on his hat at the close of a service as a mark of disapprobation when a preacher ended the service by asking the congregation to recite the Lord's Prayer. When he heard this gossip, Owen vehemently denied it and claimed that he had no opposition to the Lord's Prayer. To emphasise his belief that the Prayer was truly divine he had printed in both French and English a denial that he was opposed to the Lord's Prayer.[1] In fact what he was opposed to was worship based on a written liturgy for he believed that it "quenched the Spirit of God," and he looked upon the Lord's Prayer as the most perfect prayer ever prayed. But the gossip could not be silenced and from two Anglicans came written criticism.[2] And ten years later the charge was repeated once more by an Anglican rector.[3] In reply Owen affirmed that he had always believed the Lord's Prayer to be part of canonical Scripture and that it was composed by the Lord Jesus. However, it was not necessary to repeat it in every service of worship. Rather it was a model to be imitated.

With Henry Hammond, the former Canon and University Orator, and the current leader of the high-Churchmen, Owen was involved in private meetings, correspondence and printed controversy concerning two matters. They were first, whether or not the so-called letters of Ignatius of Antioch were genuine, and, secondly, to what extent if any, Hugo Grotius, the learned Dutch writer, was guilty of teaching Socinian theology in his Biblical commentaries.[4] The contents of the letters of

---

[1] Owen referred to this printed statement in *Reflections on a Slanderous Libel*, in *Works*, XVI, p. 278. I have not been able to trace a copy of it.
[2] Meric Casaubon published *A Vindication of the Lord's Prayer*, and Thomas Long published *An Exercitation concerning . . . the Lord's Prayer*. For Casaubon and Long see *D.N.B*.
[3] George Vernon, rector of Bourton-on-the-Water, in *A Letter to a Friend*, 1670.
[4] J. W. Packer, *The Transformation of Anglicanism, 1643–1660, with special reference to Henry Hammond*, Manchester, 1969, pp. 45, 96–7, 103, 201–2. As far as I am aware none

Ignatius were considered crucial at this time for the determining of the origin and early development of diocesan episcopacy, and it was to be expected that Hammond, a committed episcopalian, should entertain different views about them and their value to those of Owen. Indeed, it must have been a humiliating experience for Hammond to see a learned opponent of diocesan episcopacy occupying the lodgings of an office which should, in his opinion, have provided an advocate of diocesan episcopacy. Modern scholarship has declared in favour of Hammond's views on the genuineness of the epistles but is still divided about the nature of the early development of the episcopate. On a further point, the late addition of the vowel points in the Hebrew Bible, it has also vindicated the views of Hammond and of his friend, Brian Walton, who became Bishop of Chester in 1660.[1] Owen engaged in controversy with Walton concerning the printing of variant readings of the various manuscripts of the Hebrew Scriptures in the *Biblia Polyglotta* of which Walton was the editor. Owen believed that these would provide papists with further ammunition to defend the Latin Vulgate, which they held to be the only valid and reliable text of the Old Testament. In the course of the controversy Owen set forth his view, which was shared by many of his learned contemporaries, that the vowel points in the Hebrew text were as ancient as the letters themselves.[2] It is significant that Owen prefaced his attack upon Walton's views with a letter addressed to the Canons and senior Students in Divinity of Christ Church. He wished to commend to them the diligent study of Holy Scripture. Satan, he told them, was daily seeking "to assault the sacred truth of the Word of God in its authority, purity, integrity or perfection." Satan's attack came from all sides and so students of theology had to be prepared.

Before printing this written exhortation to his colleagues, Owen had been pressing the same duty upon them for seven years. Indeed, it may be said that he had tried to establish the whole life of the College upon the Word of God. But of necessity, since he was a man of the seventeenth century, much of what he thought was agreeable to the Scriptures was in fact a reflection of the Protestant, Puritan culture of his day. Whilst his great emphasis on the need for preaching and the efficacy of the Word is in the spirit of the New Testament, his administration of a class system in the College was much the same as that of former days and was based upon contemporary views of society.[3] The following

of Owen's letters to Hammond is extant. See also Owen's prefaces to *The Doctrine of the Saints Perseverance* (1654) in *Works*, XI, *Vindiciae Evangelicae* (1655) in *Works*, XII, and *A Review* . . . (1656) in *Works*, XII.

[1] For Walton see *D.N.B.* For his relationship with Hammond see Packer, *op. cit.*, p. 99.
[2] In *A Vindication of the Hebrew and Greek Texts* in *Works* XVI. For the significance of this debate see F. F. Bruce, *Tradition Old and New*, Exeter, 1970, pp. 154-162.
[3] At least one member of the nobility was at Christ Church. He was Henry Herbert, son of Lord Herbert of Cherbury. *Correspondence*, No. 11, p. 61, Lord Herbert to John Owen.

order concerning food in College reflects this class system and also shows that the students needed much discipline:

> For the repressing of the immoderate expenses of youth in the College, no gentleman-commoner shall battel in the buttery above five shillings weekly; no under-commoner above four shillings weekly; and the butler is hereby required to give notice to the Dean or Sub-Dean at the end of the week of such as shall exceed this allowance.

Twelve days earlier a Master of Arts was admonished because he had been seen at a "tippling house on the Lord's Day." John Busby, who came to Christ Church from Westminster School in 1647, was expelled in 1653 for a speech he made at a funeral, which contained "matter of profanation and abuse of Scripture." Happily the emphasis on discipline, the maintenance of the social order and the preservation of ancient academic customs were balanced by Owen's exercise of compassion. He was "hospitable in his own house," wrote Asty, "generous in his favours, charitable to the poor, especially poor scholars, some of whom he took into his own family and maintained them at his own charge."[1] In particular there was one poor scholar whose mastery of Latin so impressed the Dean that he took him into his own house to teach his own children. In addition, he was so impressed with the hospitality shown by other Colleges that in his oration at the Act in 1657 he made special mention of the kindness shown to young men from foreign churches who were studying at Oxford.[2]

It seems, however, that Owen's personal influence was somewhat diminished by his frequent absence from the College when national and University affairs caused him to make journeys to London. Though he obviously chose tutors who shared his religious views, they could never have the influence over the younger scholars and older graduates which was open to him if he was in residence.[3] From its foundation Christ Church had been required to have one hundred Studentships for young men resident on the premises.[4] These were usually taken up by undergraduates at the time of matriculation and retained for

---

[1] Asty, p. xii. Wood, *Fasti Oxonienses*, ed. P. Bliss, pp. 190-1 speaks of Hungarians receiving free meals in Christ Church.

[2] He referred to "many outstanding youths, the hope and seed of many churches" which the generosity of the University "had sustained and nourished ... for more than five years." *Oxford Orations*, p. 36.

[3] It is not easy to determine who were the tutors since there are no records which specifically name them. Only the name of Thomas Cole, John Locke's tutor, is sure. (For Cole see C.R.) However, the names of the following young men appear in the Chapter Book as those who supervised disputations and studies and they were also probably tutors. Samuel Bishop, Charles Blackwell, Anthony Brett, Henry Bold, John Dod, William Hawkins, Thomas Johnson, Charles Pickering, Anthony Ratcliffe, John Singleton, Henry Thurm Edward Veal and Thomas Vincent. Veal, Vincent and Singleton became Nonconformists and are in C.R. For the rest see *Alumni Oxonienses*.

[4] Thompson, *op. cit.*, p. 12.

anything from four to thirteen years. The holders were called "Students of Christ Church." Senior Students were the equivalent of Fellows in other Colleges. With the Studentship went a small allowance of up to ten pounds each year. There is every reason to believe that in the 1650s the Studentships were all taken and that when vacancies occurred the Dean and Chapter immediately elected suitable young men to the places. Certainly Studentships were found each year for at least three scholars from Westminster School (otherwise called St Peter's College, Westminster).¹ Since 1561, when Queen Elizabeth assigned certain of its Studentships, as well as certain places at Trinity College, Cambridge, to boys educated at her royal foundation of St Peter's, Christ Church had received some of her most able scholars from the school. Each year the Dean of Christ Church and the Master of Trinity, appearing in person or by deputy, visited St Peter's College for several days in order to meet the candidates and to hear selected boys recite declamations on appointed theses before the final choice was made. How many times Owen visited the school in person is not known but he does not seem to have been impressed with it and is reported to have said that it would never be well with the nation until the school was suppressed. Had this been so Christ Church would have lacked one of its most honoured evangelical students who went from Westminster to Oxford some seventy-five years later—Charles Wesley, the hymn-writer. Perhaps Owen felt that the Master of the School, Richard Busby, was too much of a royalist and too little committed to practical godliness, with the result that the scholars were being educated by a man whose principles were in reality contrary to those of the leaders of the University of Oxford. It was probably with this in mind that Owen urged Busby in 1656 to take as his second Master, Edward Bagshaw, a Student of Christ Church and a man of strong puritan convictions.² Unfortunately Busby and Bagshaw did not get on well together and so the latter was forced to leave Westminster and return to Oxford.

Few of the scholars who came from Westminster proved to be of the type that had sufficient puritan conviction or inclination to become Nonconformists after 1662. Indeed, only one, Samuel Angier, actually became a nonconformist minister.³ The most well-known scholars of

¹ John Sargeaunt, *Annals of Westminster School*, 1898, pp. 21ff., and John Welch, *The List of the Queen's Scholars of St Peter's College' Westminster*, 1852. The pages of the Disbursements Book of Christ Church for 1659 reveal that 100 young men were in receipt of quarterly payments which varied from 1s. 0d to £2. 10s. 0d. The Chaplains of the House were listed as Students so it is difficult to ascertain exactly who they were but the following were recognised as Chaplains in 1660 (Cf. "The Restoration Visitation of Oxford", ed. F. J. Varley, in *Camden Miscellany*, XVIII, 1948): Benjamin Berry, John Hibbert, John Ward, Andrew Bruce and Richard Washbourne. Berry became a Nonconformist and Bruce a Professor at St Andrews. The rest became Anglican clergy.

² Sargeaunt, *op. cit.*, pp. 79ff. For Bagshaw see C.R.

³ For Angier see C.R. In 1660 he lived with Owen for a few months. Other young men in Christ Church at this time who became nonconformist ministers were Edward Bagshaw,

this period who came from Westminster to Oxford were all Conformists in and after 1662. William Godolphin, elected in 1651, was knighted in 1668 and then became Ambassador to Spain. Robert South, also elected in 1651, became Public Orator of the University in 1660 and a noted opponent of Protestant Nonconformists. In 1657 South insisted on using the Prayer Book in Christ Church and greatly annoyed Owen who sought to oppose his graduation as Master of Arts. Perhaps the most famous Student of all, who came from Westminster in 1652, was John Locke, the distinguished philosopher. Owen placed Locke in the care of Thomas Cole and from him Locke may have gained the rudiments of his doctrine of religious toleration and his belief in the independency of churches. In general the young Locke found his undergraduate course rather boring. He felt that disputations were not the best way of arriving at truth. However, he enjoyed the friendship of the other young men. The accounts he kept during his first winter reveal some of the expenses of a Student.[1] On his arrival he had to buy the furniture and fittings from the young man whose rooms he was taking over. Other expenses included fees to his tutor and to the butler. And for one shilling he received "an antidote against infection from the small-pox." The allowance he received as a Student could not have covered more than one-fifth of his total expenses.

Apart from the scholars who held Studentships, Christ Church also had young men attached to the House who lived in premises adjoining the College. So the total membership of the House must have been in excess of one hundred and twenty people. About twenty or thirty new scholars were admitted each year. An average of fifteen gained the B.A. and another ten the M.A. each year.[2] Amongst those who graduated were several who had interesting backgrounds or careers. Cyril Wyche, for example, who graduated in 1652 was named after the Patriarch of Constantinople where he had been born. After graduation he became interested in experimental science and was one of the earliest Fellows of the Royal Society. Nathaniel Hodges received the M.A. in 1654 and the M.D. in 1659. His claim to fame rests on his work in London during the great plague when he gave himself unreservedly to the service of

Benjamin Burgess, Thomas Cole, William Crompton, Thomas Curl, Richard Dyer, Samuel French, Philip Henry, Obadiah Hughes, James Janeway, John Jennings, John Kempster, William Maddocks, John Manduit, Thomas Newnham, Price Owen, John Sayer, William Segary, John Singleton, John Thompson, Edward Veal, Nathaniel Vincent, Thomas Vincent and Edward West. All are in C.R.

[1] For Godolphin and South see *D.N.B.* For Locke's views on toleration see H. R. Fox Bourne, *The Life of John Locke*, 1876, I, pp. 72–9 and for a brief description of Locke's life at Oxford see Maurice Cranston, *John Locke, a biography*, 1957. The MSS in which are Locke's accounts for the year 1653/4 are Bodleian Library MSS. Locke, F. 11.

[2] The average annual number of graduations for the whole University was about 130 for B.A. and 70 for M.A. I base these numbers on the lists of graduates in the "Register of Congregation, 1647–1658," in the University Archives.

those who suffered. Jonathan Edwards entered the College in 1655. In 1662 he became a Fellow of Jesus College and twenty-four years later its Principal. He is chiefly remembered as a controversialist and he took part in both the Socinian and Antinomian controverises of the 1690s. Henry Stubbe gained his M.A. in 1657 but became a critic of the organisation and curriculum of the University so that he was removed from his Studentship in 1660. After the Restoration he went to live in Jamaica but ill-health drove him back to Britain where he practised as a physician.[1] Also among the young men at Christ Church were two of the Dean's relatives. One was his nephew, John Singleton, and the other was Roger Puleston, the son of his cousin, Elizabeth Puleston of Flintshire.[2]

Owen's letter to Lady Puleston dated the 26th January 1658 and her reply contain the only two extant references to Mrs Mary Owen in this period.[3] She and her children lived with their servants in the Dean's lodgings. Her life cannot have been completely happy since in 1655 two of her children died in the plague which affected Oxford in that year.[4] The other children probably had an exciting life with plenty of servants and scholars to play with them. One thing they would not have seen, however, was the presence of builders in the College grounds. Unlike Brian Duppa, Owen does not seem to have felt the need or possessed the money to embark on a new building programme: he judged that there were more important matters with which he had to deal. So there was as yet no Peckwater Quadrangle or Library. Neither was Wren's Tom Tower put over the gate-house. Only the Cathedral, the Hall, the small Quadrangle and three sides of the great Quadrangle were then as they are today.

VICE-CHANCELLOR

It was on the 26th September 1652 that Daniel Greenwood, who was then Vice-Chancellor, handed a letter from Lord General Cromwell to the senior Proctor, Francis Howell, so that he could read it aloud to Convocation.[5] By this letter John Owen was recommended to those present as the new Vice-Chancellor for the year 1652-3. Convocation solemnly assented to the nomination and Greenwood left the seat of honour and handed over the ensigns of his authority, the statute-book,

[1] For Wyche, Hodges, Edwards and Stubbe see *D.N.B.*
[2] For Singleton see *C.R.*, and for the father of Roger Puleston, Judge John Puleston, see *D.N.B.*
[3] *Correspondence*, No's 55 and 56, pp. 103-4.
[4] *The Report of the Manuscripts of the Earl of Egmont*, 1905, I, Pt. II, p. 576. The death of the boys is mentioned in a contemporary letter.
[5] For the letter see "Register of Convocation, 1647-1658," p. 170. It is printed by Abbott in *Writings and Speeches*, II, p. 577. The office of Vice-Chancellor lasted one year but there was the possibility of being invited for further periods of one year. Owen was re-elected in 1653, 1654, 1655 and 1656.

the keys and the seal of office, to the Proctors. Owen was then asked to accept the office of Vice-Chancellor and to pledge to perform faithfully its duties. After sitting down in the Vice-Chancellor's chair and receiving the ensigns of office, he proceeded, according to ancient custom, to deliver a brief Latin Oration.[1]

He began by expressing his inadequacy:

> I am well aware, gentlemen of the University, of the grief you must feel that, after so many venerable names, reverend persons, providers and depositaries of the Arts and Sciences, the fates of the University should have finally placed him as leader of the company, who should almost come last of all. Neither, indeed, is this state of our affairs . . . very agreeable to myself, which compels me, having returned after a long absence to the *alma mater* I have greatly missed, to engage, as a sort of prelude, in the performance of a laborious and difficult office.

The office was a difficult one in the best of times but the situation at Oxford in 1652 made it the more difficult. Sectarian bitterness between Independents, Presbyterians, and less orthodox groups as well as the shocking behaviour of some scholars were to blame for this.

> In what difficult times, what manners, what diversities of opinion—dissension and calumny raging everywhere because of party spirit; what bitter passions and provocations and emotions beset with what arrogance and envy our academic authority has occurred I both know and lament. Nor is it only the character of the age that perplexes us, but another calamity to our literary establishment, which is daily becoming more conspicuous. Indeed, with no attention paid to the sacred authority of the laws, the reverence due to superiors, or the watchful envy of evil-wishers; and treating almost with disdain the tears and sobs of our ailing *alma mater;* with eternal damage to the good name of the whole of the gowned community, and not without danger to the whole academy, detestable audacity and a licentiousness almost Epicurean, a very large section of the students are now—alas—wandering beyond all bounds of modesty and piety.

In his own strength Owen could not remedy such a situation; all he could do was to work diligently and cast himself on the mercy of the Lord, trusting in the divine promises. His aims were clear:

> We ought to attempt in our own sphere greater things, corresponding in some measure to the notable attempts of all kinds, the like of which former ages had never produced. Or is it the wish of the Universities alone to remain inglorious when the fame of the English has been extended through all the world? Europe stands agape at the acts of Parliament, the laurels of our soldiers and the enhanced glory, both civil and military, which the Parliamentarians and com-

---

[1] The ceremony of installation was governed by statute. See *Oxford University Statutes*, I, p. 180. For the Oration see *Oxford Orations*, pp. 5ff.

manding generals . . . have achieved. Let it not be, gentlemen, that our special trust, the honour of religion and literature, should alone be debased as though we were completely unequal to the demands of the age.

One thing was certain. If determination and commitment had anything to do with it, Owen himself intended to be equal to the demands of this revolutionary age.

In an institution which was just recovering from the severe problems caused by civil war and which was under a new type of leadership, the duties of, and pressures upon, the new Vice-Chancellor were manifold. He was a leading member of the Board of Visitors, he had to ensure that sermons, lectures, disputations, and academic exercises were duly carried out, that offenders were punished, that heretical sermons and books were suppressed, that the goods and possessions of the University were preserved, that the Oxford market was kept well supplied and clean, that the Vice-Chancellor's Court was properly run, and that the Halls and Inns were carefully supervised. Furthermore, he had to attend the meetings of the Delegates of Convocation, preside at meetings of Congregation and Convocation, and participate in the *Vesperia* and *Comitia* at the close of the academic year. With all these duties in mind we shall look first of all at his contribution to the work of the Visitors. Following this we shall examine his reaction to the attack on the Universities in 1653, his attempts to reform aspects of University life and administration and his general view of discipline.

The first appearance of Owen's name in the Register of the Board of Visitors is in the entry dated the 1st April 1652.[1] It occurs again on the 13th April after which the Register is silent for fourteen months. The silence was due to the dissolution of the Committee for the Universities and the subsequent doubt whether the Visitors could act without it. During this period some senior members of the University, including Owen, agitated for a new, smaller, resident Board to complete the work of reformation.[2] Their request was eventually granted and a temporary Board of ten members was appointed. They sat for the first time on June 20 1653 and continued to meet regularly until September 1 1654, when a revised and permanent Board replaced them.[3] Owen was certainly the dominant personality on this temporary Board. It met twice a week during terms at the Dean's lodgings "at one of the clocke in the afternoone" until "six at the furthest." Much of the work

[1] *Register of the Visitors of the University of Oxford, 1647–1658*, ed. Montagu Burrows, 1881, p. 353. The manuscript Register is in the Bodleian Library.
[2] Wood, *History of the University*, II, p. 650.
[3] *Register of the Visitors*, pp. 356ff. The members of the Board were John Owen, Thomas Goodwin, Peter French, Jonathan Goddard, John Conant (Rector of Exeter), Edmund Staunton (President of Corpus Christi), Thankful Owen (President of St John's), Samuel Basnett (Fellow of All Souls) and Francis Howell (Fellow of Exeter).

was concerned with the administrative and disciplinary problems within the Colleges and Halls. One man who gave the Board a great deal of trouble was Dr Daniel Vivian, a Fellow of New College. When he was away in Ireland on government service he believed that he was unjustly deprived of his College dues. On his return he petitioned the Visitors who at first sympathised with him but later, on the production of more evidence, found him guilty of "many misdemenours and miscarriages" of justice and ordered his expulsion.[1]

The emphases of the first Board were maintained. Reckless behaviour or profane language was punished. On the 22nd August 1653, for example, two young men from New College were disciplined "for abusing a maid in the fields."[2] Scholars were required to use either Latin or Greek in academic work and in public conversation in Halls. Though social distinctions were recognised, gentlemen-commoners and the sons of noblemen were required to do the same academic exercises as their socially inferior contemporaries.[3] A public register of all tutors was made and it was ordered that tutors be godly men, fit and able to spend some time each evening between the hours of seven and ten in prayer with their charges. One important order, as far as the independency of the Colleges was concerned, was the procedure in the appointment of Fellows and Chaplains. Candidates had first to convince the Visitors of their "godliness, studiousness and good proficiency in learning" before they were allowed to stand for election.[4] Another important order of 14 November related to preaching:[5]

> Upon consideration that the one maine end of the University is to traine up men as well in Divine as Humane Learning that they may be able (when the providence of God shall call them) to publish the Gospell of Christ to the conversion and building up of soules to eternal life, and that exercise in the things of God doth much increase knowledge and savour therein: the Visitors think it meete that there should be frequent preaching in every Collegde in this University, as far as the number of persons qualified for that service will allow.

Since there was no effective control available at this point in time for the central direction of the National Church (the presbyterian legislation being a dead letter), Owen and his colleagues obviously saw the Universities as the places which must produce the evangelical and ministerial leaders of the community. This order also had added urgency since it was made at a time when, as we shall discuss below, the traditional

---

[1] *Register of the Visitors*, pp. 363–385.
[2] *Ibid*, p. 361.
[3] *Ibid*, p. 366.
[4] *Ibid*, p. 369.
[5] *Ibid*, p. 372.

role of Oxford and Cambridge as the places were ministers and gentlemen were trained was under attack in London in the Barebone's Parliament.[1]

Being Vice-Chancellor Owen was also a member of the new Board that began work in January 1655.[2] Burrows assumes that it was under the dominant influence of Thomas Goodwin, whom he mistakenly thinks was theologically opposed to Owen since he confuses him with John Goodwin, the noted Republican and Arminian.[3] Burrows bases his view on two basic grounds. First, the claim of Anthony Wood who stated that Goodwin placed on the Board "several of his own confidants... and none of Owen's, making him sit thereby as a cipher;" as a result Owen left them "and would not at all act among them but by way of revenge sided with the University."[4] Secondly, the fact that Owen's signature is absent from the minutes of the Board for the first three years. But, though Owen's signature is not found in the minutes between 1655 and 1657 the meetings were often held in his lodgings at Christ Church, which strongly suggests he was present. Furthermore, Wood himself specifically states that Owen was at a meeting in February 1655.[5] What seems to have happened was this. Goodwin and Owen differed as to whether the temporary Board should continue after the calling of the Protector's first Parliament in September 1654. Goodwin felt that a new Board should be created by the government and then its existence and membership be confirmed by the Parliament, but Owen favoured the continuance of the small (temporary) Board coupled with a reverting to a modified form of the former practice whereby each individual College had its own Visitor. However, it was Goodwin who had the ear of the Protector in this matter and so it was he who suggested the membership of the new, permanent, central Board of Visitors. This in turn led to Wood's comment about "confidants" of Goodwin. This explanation fits the facts and allows for a little bitterness between Goodwin and Owen, who normally were the very best of friends.

The other half of Wood's comments, relating to Owen siding with the University, had its origin in what happened after January 1655.[6] Before the actual Ordinance for the Visitation was put into operation, that is before the Visitors first met, there were moves both inside and

[1] See below pp. 70ff.
[2] *Register of the Visitors*, p. 400. The members of the Board who were also members of the University were: Christopher Rogers, Henry Wilkinson, Peter French and John Owen from Christ Church; Thomas Goodwin and James Baron from Magdalen; Robert Harris from Trinity; Jonathan Goddard from Merton; John Conant from Exeter; Philip Stephens from Hart Hall and Francis Howell from Exeter. The non-resident members, who seem to have played no effectual part in the work of the Board were mostly London politicians—Bulstrode Whitelockes for example.
[3] For John Goodwin see *D.N.B.*
[4] Wood, *History of the University*, II, p. 662.
[5] *Ibid*, p. 665.
[6] *Ibid*, pp. 666ff.

outside Convocation, instigated by Owen, to send a petition to the Lord Protector asking him to annul or change the Ordinance. A large group, who included at least four Heads of Houses, favoured the reinstitution of some form of College Visitors and the right of Convocation to nominate members of any future central Board of Visitors. A meeting was arranged between the new Board and representatives of Convocation on the 9th February 1655 but this came to nothing. So Peter French and Jonathan Goddard, both closely associated with the Protector and his family, and both in London at this time were asked to try to have the Ordinance annulled but their efforts were unsuccessful. Perhaps because of this failure Owen did not attend some of the early meetings of the Board. Nearly a year earlier, Convocation had expressed its confidence in his leadership by electing him as its burgess to sit in the Protector's first Parliament. One of his aims in allowing himself to be nominated and elected was obviously to represent the interests of Convocation with regard to the Visitation; but he failed to do this, being deemed to be ineligible for membership of the Commons since he had been ordained by a Bishop. The University protested on Owen's behalf but failed to have its burgess take his seat.[1]

Owen's disagreement with Goodwin cannot have been too intense since both men continued to preach at St Mary's. Further, Cromwell still had sufficient confidence in Owen to reappoint him as his Vice-Chancellor in 1655 and 1656.[2] Also the five members of the new Board who had not been on the previous temporary Board were not opponents of Owen. Rogers and Wilkinson were Canons of Christ Church and Stephens worked closely with Owen in 1655 when preparations were made to defend the University from a possible royalist attack.[3] And the emphases of the new Board were essentially the same as those of the two earlier Boards. Measures were taken to remedy the neglect of public worship, to ensure that prayers were said regularly and to provide for the regular catechising of scholars. Owen's last recorded appearance at a meeting of the Visitors was on the 11th January 1658 and the Board itself ceased to meet after the 8th April of that same year.[4]

The Registers of the Visitors and of Convocation bear little obvious trace of the fact that during 1653 the Universities of Oxford and

---

[1] Cf. M. B. Rex, *University Representation in England, 1604–1690*, 1954, p. 188, and see "Register of Convocation, 1647–1658," p. 254 for the letter of protest from Oxford to Westminster. Owen was removed on the basis of the Clerical Disabilities Act of 1642—*The Constitutional Documents of the Puritan Revolution*, ed. S. R. Gardiner, p. 254.

[2] For Cromwell's two letters to Owen stating this see *Correspondence*, No's 35 and 45, pp. 84 and 94.

[3] The fear of an attack followed the rising in Wiltshire for which see A. H. Woolrych, *Penruddock's Rising*, 1955. In a letter to Secretary Thurloe Owen described his preparations: Cf. *Correspondence*, No. 32, pp. 82–3. See also Wood, *op. cit.*, II, p. 668 for the role of Captain Stephens.

[4] *Register of the Visitors*, pp. 438–9.

Cambridge believed themselves to be under a real threat of being closed down or totally remodelled. Nevertheless, a perusal of the titles of books published in 1653-4, of the contents of the annual orations of the Oxford and Cambridge Vice-Chancellors, of the pages of the weekly news-journal *Mercurius Politicus*, and of the proceedings of the Barebone's Parliament, clearly demonstrates that there was a general panic at this time.[1] The views of the educational reformers—be they of the moderate variety like Samuel Hartlib and John Durie, or of the radical variety like certain Fifth Monarchists and Quakers—received wide recognition, or, at least, reached a wide public.[2] Criticisms of the Universities (or for that matter of the Inns of Court) were not new. The English Separatists, for example, led by such men as Henry Barrow and Robert Browne had severely criticised the content of University education and stated that it was basically unsuitable for the preparation of godly preachers.[3]

But the calling of the Long Parliament, followed by civil war, the abolition of prelacy and the execution of the King, provided the atmosphere in which would-be reformers could publish their revolutionary views for the complete reconstruction of the Church and social institutions. Many of them were inspired by the belief that the end of all things was at hand and that new institutions were necessary which would survive into the coming millennium. One of the earliest attacks in the two revolutionary decades against the claim of the Universities to be the proper training ground for ministers of religion came from the "mechanick" preacher, Samuel How, in his widely read and several times reprinted book, *The Sufficiency of the Spirit's teaching without humane learning* (1640).[4] A typical sentence reads: "If a man have the Spirit of God, though he be a Pedler, Tinker, Chimney-sweeper, or Cobler, he may by the help of God's Spirit give a more public interpretation than they (i.e., men trained in the Universities)." This emphasis was taken up and developed by radicals of all types. Often it was allied with the protests of the socially-underprivileged groups in society. The Levellers and Diggers, for example, criticised Oxford and Cambridge

---

[1] See F. Madan, *Oxford Books*, Oxford, 1931, Vol. III and *Catalogue of the Pamphlets, Books, Newspapers collected by George Thomason, 1640-1661*, 1908, Vol. II for details of books. Owen's orations are in *Oxford Orations;* for Cambridge orations see John Lightfoot, *Works*, ed. J. R. Pitman, 1824, V, pp. 391-2, and John Arrowsmith, *Tactica Sacra*, 1657. Lightfoot was Vice-Chancellor in 1655; Arrowsmith was Master of Trinity. For details of the Barebone's Parliament see Tai Liu, "Saints in Power," Ph.D. thesis, Indiana University, 1969.

[2] See further Charles Webster, *Samuel Hartlib and the Advancement of Learning*, Cambridge, 1970, and R. L. Greaves, *The Puritan Revolution and Educational Thought*, New Brunswick, 1969, and Hugh Kearney, *Scholars and Gentlemen*, 1970, pp. 110ff.

[3] Kearney, *op. cit.*, pp. 71ff.

[4] For How see Haller, *Rise of Puritanism*, pp. 267-8. The 1655 edition had a commendatory preface by the Baptist, William Kiffin.

in 1649 not only because of their scholastic curriculum and reliance on Greek and Latin but also because they restricted the professions to a limited social class who could afford to attend their Colleges and then if necessary go on to the Inns of Court.[1] So when the decision was taken by Cromwell to call a Parliament of nominated saints radical opinion saw its opportunity. Both before the Barebone's Assembly met and during its short life, the Universities, Church, tithe-system, legal and medical professions came under attack from the left wing of the puritan movement. Petitions, sermons and books called for radical changes in the basis of the social structure of the institutions and learned professions of the nation.

At both Oxford and Cambridge the Colleges were compared, not as most of their incumbents would have preferred, with the "schools of the prophets" of ancient Israel, but rather with the idolatrous high places dedicated to Baal in ancient Canaan. Whilst a few daring spirits in Oxford called for the closing of the famous Bodleian Library,[2] Cambridge saw a bitter exchange of views between, on the one side, Joseph Sedgwick of Christ's and Sidrach Simpson of Pembroke, and, on the other, William Dell of Caius.[3] In a sermon at Great St Mary's on the 1st May 1653 Sedgwick protested against the "spirit of enthusiasm and pretended inspiration that disturbs and strikes at the Universities." His protest, which was extended when the sermon was printed, was in part aimed at Dell who, though Head of a College, had printed an attack upon the traditional curriculum at Cambridge in his *Stumbling Stone* (1653). Sedgwick felt it necessary to defend the following propositions all of which were under debate in Oxford and Cambridge that year: "A National Church is not antichristian; that a congregation of external believers and professors is an apostolic church; that set times and places are designable under the Gospel; that the ministry of the Gospel requires ecclesiastical ordination; that all believers are not ministers; that the teaching of the Spirit is not enablement enough to the ministry; that philosophy, arts and sciences accomplish a minister; that tongues are necessary to a full understanding of Scripture; that University habits and degrees are lawful and speak nothing of antichristianism; and that the institution of the University for the supply of the ministry is according to Christian prudence and the duty of the Christian State."[4] With most of these propositions Owen agreed.

Two months after the delivery of Sedgwick's sermon, Simpson also used the opportunity offered him in the preaching of the Commencement

---

[1] Kearney, *op. cit.*, pp. 111–2.
[2] This is what Owen reported in *Oxford Orations*, p. 11.
[3] For a description of their contest see J. B. Mullinger, *The University of Cambridge*, Cambridge, 1911, III, pp. 448ff. A recent study of Dell is E. C. Walker, *William Dell, Master Puritan*, Cambridge, 1970.
[4] Sedgwick, *A Sermon preached at S. Maries*, 1655, pp. 25–6.

sermon, that is in July 1653, to defend the traditional role of the Universities. They were, he maintained, as the outwork to the citadel of religion and as the outer court to the Temple of the Gospel. Dell, who heard the sermon, was incensed by it and printed a reply. "Human learning," he wrote,[1] "mingled with divinity, or the Gospel of Christ understood according to Aristotle, hath begun, continued and perfected the mystery of iniquity in the outward Church." Following his attack on the scholastic curriculum he condensed into six pages his own suggestions for "the right reformation of learning."[2] He wanted schools to be founded in all cities, towns and large villages offering a wide range of subjects related to the needs of an area; he deprecated the monopoly of higher education by the two ancient Universities. From another former army chaplain, who had studied as a youth at Cambridge, came a further attack upon traditional education. He was John Webster and he dedicated his *Academiarum Examen* to Major-General Lambert, a fellow Yorkshireman. In his opinion Oxford and Cambridge placed too much emphasis on the use of Latin and on the writings of Aristotle. He wanted to see greater emphasis placed on the contribution of mathematics and the practical disciplines associated with it, on a practical medical education which included such activities as dissection, and on a study of recent philosophy, the writings of Descartes for example.

Webster proved an easy prey for the dialectical skill of two former Cambridge men who were now prominent at Oxford. The *Vindiciae Academiarum*, written by John Wilkins and Seth Ward of Wadham College, sought to show that Webster was ill-informed as to what went on at Oxford. The two men, however, carefully avoided the basic issue of changing the curriculum. To the scientific society, which met at Wadham and which developed into the Royal Society, science was a subject to be studied outside the normal curriculum by mature students.[3] This is confirmed by the note-book belonging to a certain Nicholas Floyd, an undergraduate at Wadham, which clearly shows that he and his colleagues pursued the old-style scholastic curriculum as in former times and that this was unaffected by what was done in the scientific society. Similar notebooks of scholars at Christ Church and Exeter reveal the same emphasis in those Colleges.[4] Professor Kearney attributes the continuance of this old tradition at Oxford primarily to the influence of Thomas Barlow, Owen's former tutor. Barlow, Bodley's Librarian and Provost of Queen's from 1657, wrote a guide for young scholars

[1] Quoted by Mullinger, *op. cit.*, p. 454, from Dell's *Tryal of Spirits*.
[2] Dell, *The Right Reformation of Learning*, 1654. Cf. Walker, *op. cit.*, p. 161.
[3] For the Oxford society see Marjery Purver, *The Royal Society* 1967, and Shapiro, *John Wilkins*, chap. 5. On pp. 122ff, Purver confuses John Owen with Thankful Owen; it was the latter who helped in the work of cataloging books on science.
[4] Three notebooks are in the Bodleian: MSS Rawlinson D. 233, 254, and 258. One is in the Br. Museum: Sloane MS 1472.

which seems to have been widely used and whose basic premise was that the liberal arts are the handmaids of divinity.[1]

Simpson, Sedgwick, Wilkins and Ward, together with others who defended traditional learning, had the full support of Owen. Though the Vice-Chancellor did not himself write a defence of Oxford education, he saw to it that the University congratulated the City of London when the latter petitioned the Barebone's Parliament on the 2nd September 1653 that the precious truths of the Gospel should be preserved, that faithful ministers should be encouraged and that the two Universities be zealously preserved and maintained.[2] Also he expressed his relief in July 1654 at the Act that the University was "not so far breathing its last as to have need to draw up its last will and testament." He was glad to report to the crowds who had come to Oxford that "Almighty God still had men who were actively engaged vigorously to preserve His worship and the University still had men similarly engaged to watch over its preservation."[3] Even in 1657, in his parting oration to the University, he still vividly remembered the attacks on learning made in 1653 and God's gracious deliverance of the University from ruin.

> No man among us, I believe, is ignorant of the position of the gownsmen and that state of our affairs at the beginning of my term of office and since then. For the first two years we were a mere rabble and a subject of talk to the rabble. Our critical situation and our common interests were discussed out of journals and newspapers by every Tom, Dick and Harry. Nobody was so abjectly stupid as not to have either fear or hope on account of our situation. Such, indeed, was the will of the Sovereign Disposer of events—so that whatever is mortal would be held in lesser esteem among mortals. Further, it was not perhaps equitable that, whilst decay was invading empires and the highest ornaments of the world, the University alone should keep its blossom unimpaired. Meanwhile, very few ventured to the best of their powers to defend our cause, which ought to have been held sacred but was exposed to the greatest hazards. Indeed, such was the pitch of madness that to have stood up for the gownsmen was designated as a violation of religion and piety. On the other hand, everything that is rejected by respectable men and which is truly criminal was most plentifully charged on you every day by the malicious . . . After it had become only too obvious to what an extreme, the audacity, rage and ignorance of some, from whom better things might have been expected, would have gone, the Governor of all things so quickly defeated all their councils and all their attempts that with difficulty were those able to provide for their own interests who, three days before, were most eagerly intent on swallowing up ours.[4]

[1] Kearney, *op. cit.*, pp. 124–5.
[2] *Correspondence*, No. 10, p. 59, Oxford Convocation to the Lord Mayor and Aldermen of London.
[3] *Oxford Orations*, p. 11. John Evelyn was present at this Act from 6–10 July and left a very brief description. See *The Diary of John Evelyn*, ed. E. S. De Beer, 1959, p. 339.
[4] *Oxford Orations*, p. 41.

## DEAN AND VICE-CHANCELLOR

The last sentence obviously refers to what happened in the Barebone's Parliament in its final week, when, after a report from the Committee on Tithes had been rejected by a very small majority, its brief existence came to an end.[1]

Part of the attack of the radicals on the Universities was directed at the actual granting of degrees in divinity and the wearing of academic costume, which was, in origin, derived from medieval monastic dress. Within the Reformed Churches of Europe there had been differing views as to whether or not Protestant Academies should grant the degree of Doctor of Divinity. In Scotland, for example, no degree of D.D. was awarded from the Reformation until the reign of James VI, and from 1638 to 1661.[2] As if to emphasise that it wished to remain as conservative as possible, the Oxford Convocation decided, just a few days after the end of the experiment of the rule of the saints, to bestow the D.D. degree on Thomas Goodwin, Peter French, and John Owen. The latter's diploma, dated the 22nd December 1653, described his theological and philosophical powers in glowing terms.[3] But, as he later explained, it was only gratitude and "respect unto them" who had conferred it upon him which made him "once own it:" for "freed from that obligation" he would never have used the title. And as for the title *Reverend* "I have very little valued it," he wrote, "ever since I considered the saying of Luther—'nunquam periclatur religio nisi inter Reverendissimos'."[4] He preferred to be called "John Owen" as the Quakers addressed him. So in this matter at least he did have some basic agreement with the critics of the Establishment.

He did also with regard to academic dress. According to Anthony Wood's colourful description, Owen "scorned all formality and undervalued his office by going in quirpo like a young scholar, with powdered hair, snakebone bandstrings, lawn bands, a large set of ribbons pointed, and Spanish leather boots with large lawn tops, and his hat mostly cocked."[5] In other words, Owen regarded the usual square cap and hood (which are still part of academic dress) as "Romish" and therefore in order not to appear to be in any way associating with popery he dressed in a cocked hat, a velvet coat and jack-boots with cambric tops. During 1656 he made determined efforts in meetings of Convocation and its delegates to persuade the University to make the wearing of

---

[1] S. R. Gardiner, *History of Commonwealth and Protectorate*, II, p. 327.
[2] Cf. G. D. Henderson, *Religious Life in Seventeenth-Century Scotland*, Cambridge, 1937, p. 41. For the radicals and academic dress see Greaves, *op. cit.*, pp. 135–6.
[3] For the Latin wording of the Diploma see "Register of Convocation, 1647–1658," p. 229.
[4] For these statements of Owen see *Works*, XIII, p. 302. Cf. Nuttall, *Visible Saints*, p. 90. Luther's statement literally means: "religion is never put in danger except amongst the most reverend."
[5] Wood, *Athenae Oxonienses*, IV, col. 98.

"habits" optional.¹ A somewhat exaggerated report of his activities reached his old friend, Ralph Josselin, who wrote in his Diary on the 8th July 1656: "Heard how Dr Owen endeavoured to lay down all the badges of scholars distinction in the Universities; hoods, caps, gowns, degrees . . . : he is become a great scorne, the Lord keep him from temptations."² Convocation rejected Owen's proposal on the 10th April. This was a memorable day at Oxford for, as Anthony Wood put it: "I think we may well say that there was more of real public reformation voted at one Convocation than had been before by the Visitors since their first meeting."³ Whilst Convocation agreed to the introduction of new exercises in divinity and to the removal of certain promissory oaths,⁴ Owen's further, important, proposal that the Act, which closed the academic year, be abolished was rejected. He believed that it made no valid contribution either to the academic progress of scholars or to the general propagation of the Gospel. It simply allowed the young men and the crowds who came to Oxford for the occasion to behave in an unseemly manner. Though Convocation was willing to agree to the introduction of certain reforms in the activities, Owen was not really interested; for him it was all or nothing. Righteously indignant at the failure of the Senate of the University to do what he believed was the will of God, Owen called the Visitors together and asked them to use their powers to impose on the Convocation an order to abolish the Act. Whilst Goodwin, Thankful Owen, Francis Howell and James Baron from the Board agreed with him, the other members doubted whether the Visitors had such powers over Convocation. So Owen decided to take the matter to London. He also wanted to remodel the constitution of Convocation. He believed that his proposals to abolish the Act and to make "habits" optional had been rejected on account of the large number of young Masters of Arts who had equal voting rights with the older, more experienced men. Yet all his efforts came to nothing—except that perhaps moderate opinion in Oxford and in London was antagonised and made more conservative.

---

¹ Wood, *History of University*, II, pp. 668ff. The Laudian Statutes amde academic dress obligatory. In 1658 John Conant made further efforts to make it optional. See Walter Pope, *The Life of Seth, Lord Bishop of Salisbury*, ed. J. M. Bamborough, Oxford, 1961, pp. 26ff. Pope was a Proctor in 1658.
² *The Diary of Ralph Josselin*, p. 116.
³ Wood, *History of University*, II, p. 671.
⁴ At matriculation all boys aged 16 years had, according to the Laudian Statutes, to subscribe to the 39 Articles and take their corporal oath to acknowledge the supremacy of the King, to be faithful to the University, and to observe its Statutes, privileges and customs. On becoming Regent Masters, the young Masters of Arts had to take further oaths of loyalty to the House of Congregation etc. Admission to offices of the University (Proctor, Orator, Registrar etc.) meant more oaths. As both Presbyterians and Independents regarded the taking of an oath as the making of a binding promise they wanted oaths kept to a minimum. For oaths see *Westminster Confession of Faith*, chap. xxii, and *Savoy Declaration of Faith*, chap. xxiii.

## DEAN AND VICE-CHANCELLOR

Owen's desire to reform the closing ceremonies of the year proceeded from his understanding of the nature of education and the need for discipline and godliness. As a young student, and now as Vice-Chancellor, Owen knew how manners and morals deteriorated in the festive atmosphere. On one occasion, probably in 1657, Owen intervened in the proceedings to arrest a student who was acting and speaking irresponsibly in his capacity as the *terrae-filius*, the elected wag of the students. "When one from Trinity College was *terrae-filius*," wrote Asty, "before he began the Doctor stood up and in Latin told him he should have liberty to say what he pleased, provided that he would avoid profaneness and obscenity, and not go into any personal reflections. The *terrae-filius* began, and in a little time transgressed in all the foregoing particulars; upon which the Doctor did several times desire him to forbear those things which reflected so much dishonour on the University; but, notwithstanding, he went on in the same manner: at length, the Doctor seeing him obstinate sent in his beadles to pull him down; upon which the scholars interposed and would not suffer them to come near him: then the Doctor resolved to pull him down himself; his friends dissuaded him for fear the scholars should do him mischief; but he replied, 'I will not see authority trampled on'; and hereupon he pulled him down and sent him to Bocardo (the Oxford prison), the scholars standing at a distance amazed to see his courage and resolution."[1] At the close of the Act for 1657 he felt moved to speak of the revelry and gluttony of the weekend. In this extract he speaks in the third person:

> Someone ... not so long ago, disgusted with these ineptitudes, has dared in his ignorance to overturn this order of things amongst us, which he has always found prohibited, always condemned and always retained. He wanted, indeed, that jokes pleasantries and lies should be banished from the *Comitia* of the University, celebrated by the crowded gathering of earnest men from all parts: that we should have a richer crop of exercises and disputations in all branches of learning; a dearth of insults, malice and most inept jokes; and that there should be no remembrance in posterity of inert and gluttonous men, who know nothing except to live in disgrace and die of laughter every day, who flock to our ceremonies in great crowds.[2]

It must have been one of Owen's greatest disappointments at Oxford that he failed to reform the *Comitia*.

As Vice-Chancellor Owen was the man primarily responsible for discipline within the University. We have noticed above that as Dean and Visitor he did not shirk from this duty. Likewise, with his deputy, Edmund Staunton, the President of Corpus Christi, he sought to use his powers to keep the scholars in good behaviour. On the 28th February

---
[1] Asty, p. xi. For an example of a typical *terrae-filius* speech see that of Robert South given in this period and printed in his *Opera Posthuma Latina* (1717).
[2] *Oxford Orations*, p. 32.

1654, for example, Staunton issued an order to all scholars.[1] There had been some disorders in Oxford caused by the "rude carriage" of certain young men. If this occurred again they would be expelled. Meanwhile tutors were required to have "a more vigilant eye" over their respective scholars. Owen also issued a Latin proclamation on the 29th January 1656 which warned that dissident influences had wormed their way into the University in order to foment trouble. Students were to refrain from all forms of fighting either with fists or stones and were to conduct themselves in a sober manner.[2] If they did not, they would be sent home.

Eighteen months earlier two young ladies had been banished from Oxford.[3] In June 1654 Oxford was visited by a group of Northern Quakers, whose missionary zeal was pushing them into Southern England. Two brave but eccentric girls, Elizabeth Fletcher and Elizabeth Homes, sought to preach to the students and reveal to them the unchristian nature of University learning and their need for the inner light of the Holy Spirit. The rough treatment they received from the excited undergraduates so moved Miss Fletcher that she felt God was calling her to be a living testimony for Him. Accordingly, in the style of an Old Testament prophet, she took off her clothing and walked semi-naked through the streets, proclaiming the terrible day of the Lord. For the young men this was at best a great joke and they drove her into the grounds of St John's College where they pumped water over her and her friend. On the following Sunday, seemingly unaffected by their rough ordeal, the young ladies visited an Oxford church and in Quaker fashion interrupted the service in order to utter a warning from heaven. They were arrested and put in prison. Next day, since the city authorities were hesitant to punish them, the Vice-Chancellor was called. He accused them of speaking blasphemy and abusing the Spirit of God. He ordered that they be whipped and driven out of Oxford. They were punished not for being Quakers but because their behaviour incited civil disorder, being aimed at the downfall of the University.[4]

In contrast to his treatment of the Quakers, Owen "suffered to meet quietly three hundred Episcopalians every Lord's Day, over against his own door (in the house of Dr Willis) where they celebrated divine service according to the Liturgy of the Church of England; and though he was often urged to it, yet would he never give them the least distur-

---

[1] The original is in the Oxford Archives. *A Bibliography of Printed Works relating to the University of Oxford*, ed. E. H. Cordeaux and D. H. Merry, Oxford, 1968, item 1267.
[2] Ibid, item 1268.
[3] Cf. *Here followeth a true Relation of some of the Sufferings inflicted upon the Servants of the Lord who are called Quakers* (1654), and *A True Testimony of Oxford-Professors and University-Men who for zeal persecute the Servants of the living God* (1654). The former was anonymous; the latter was by a Richard Hubberthorne.
[4] Owen attacked Quaker doctrine in *Exercitationes adversus Fanaticos* (1658) in *Works*, XVI. The use of Latin was deliberate; it emphasised his defence of traditional learning against a group who would have abolished it.

bance."[1] Possibly they recited the services from memory and were thus technically not breaking the law. Possibly also Owen did not feel powerful enough to risk antagonising such men as Willis, who was greatly respected as a scientist. Or maybe, since this group did not threaten the peace of Oxford, and were not actively propagating Anglicanism, he decided it was best to leave them alone. Certainly it was not necessarily, as Asty seems to suggest, an exercise in religious toleration.

Owen's term as Vice-Chancellor came to an end in October 1657. Oliver Cromwell had resigned as Chancellor on the 3rd July 1657 and Convocation had invited his son, Richard, to succeed him.[2] The latter was installed in a ceremony at Westminster on the 29th July.[3] After this Owen persuaded the new Chancellor that another person should now assume the office of Vice-Chancellor.[4] Richard agreed and John Conant, the Rector of Exeter College, was appointed. At a ceremony in Convocation on the 9th October Owen handed over the ensigns of office to Conant and delivered his final oration as Vice-Chancellor.[5] He rejoiced that the University was safe and once more a great centre of learning. "Behold your ship, the University, tossed by mountainous billows, is now safe and sound," he boldly affirmed, "even beyond the expectations of almost all hope—stronger than she normally is when fitted with all her trimmings, very soon to be entrusted to the hands of a skilled captain while fortune smiles and the sea is calm." To God alone the praise was due for the settled state of things and for the great improvement in the University.

> Professors' salaries lost for many years have been maintained; the rights and privileges of the University have been defended against all the efforts of its enemies; the treasury is tenfold increased; many of every rank in the University have been promoted to various honours and benefices; new exercises have been introduced and established; old ones have been duly performed: reformation of manners has been diligently studied despite the grumbling of profligate brawlers; labours have been numberless; besides submitting to enormous expense, often when brought to the brink of death on your account, I have hated these limbs and this feeble body which was ready to desert my mind; the reproaches of the vulgar have been disregarded; the envy of others has

---

[1] Asty, p. xi. Included in this group were John Dolben, who became a Canon in 1660, John Fell, who became Dean of Christ Church in 1660 and Richard Allestree, who became Regius Professor in 1663.

[2] For Cromwell's letter of resignation addressed to Owen see *Correspondence*, No. 45, p. 98.

[3] The ceremony is described in *Mercurius Politicus*, No. 373, and the description is reprinted in Zachary Grey, *An Impartial Examination*, 1739, p. 200.

[4] Cf. *Oxford Orations*, p. 40 where Owen states that he "sought to persuade very important men to allow" him to resign.

[5] *Oxford Orations*, p. 47.

been overcome: in these circumstances I wish you all prosperity and bid you farewell.

The new Captain, John Conant, was taking over the ship in a calm sea, but, concluded Owen, there was still need for full co-operation from the members of Convocation.

Though Owen remained as Dean of Christ Church for two more years, he seems to have resided very little in Oxford during 1658 and 1659. He was not, for example, in Convocation on the 12th April 1659 when the important petition against the foundation of the University of Durham was drafted and approved in order to be sent to Richard Cromwell.[1] Therefore it will be convenient now to make a brief assessment of Owen's work at Oxford. As has been emphasised, he saw his task, and that of all the Heads of Colleges, as an extremely important aspect of the work of the kingdom of God in England. He told his colleagues in 1654: "The whole of your employment, I confess—both in the general intendment of it for promoting and diffusing of light, knowledge and truth in every kind whatever, and in the more special design thereof, for the defence, furtherance, and propagation of the ancient, inviolable, unchangeable truth of the Gospel of God—is, in the days wherein we live exposed to a contention with as much opposition, contempt, scorn, hatred and reproach, as ever any such undertaking was, in any place in the world wherein men pretended to love light more than darkness."[2] Their aim and his was the propagation of the Calvinistic view of God, the universe and salvation and in this they were probably very successful. Theology was central and of this Owen was proud. In 1654 he told the crowds at the Act that "theology, the queen and mistress of the other branches of learning" was again highly honoured at Oxford. Not "that confused theology drawn from the ditches of the scholastics, nor the theology that is merely common and teachable material handed down in a variety of manuals . . . but theology that is free, pure, and undefiled drawn in from the fountain of fountains with the Holy Spirit and the power of the Almighty aiding—and indeed completing—the whole task."[3] Efforts were made in teaching, debating and disciplinary action to achieve the great end of the propagation of the Gospel, and Owen's special emphasis was to insist that the whole academic curriculum be submerged in preaching and catechising and prayer. He wanted the graduates of Oxford not only to be proficient in the Arts and Sciences but also to aspire after godliness. Nor were academic standards allowed to suffer because of the stress on practical godliness. Lord Clarendon admitted this when he wrote that Oxford "yielded a

[1] "Register of Convocation, 1647–1658," pp. 340ff.
[2] *Works*, XI, p. 8. Dedicatory letter to Heads of Houses, prefacing *The Doctrine of the Saints' Perseverance*.
[3] *Oxford Orations*, p. 15.

harvest of extraordinary good and sound knowledge in all parts of learning."[1]

Not a few students, who later became Protestant Nonconformists, believed that God had specially blessed Oxford during the 1650s. Philip Henry, for example, "would often mention with thankfulness to God, what great helps and advantages he had then in the University, not only for learning, but for religion and piety. Serious godliness was in reputation, and besides the public opportunities they had, there were many of the scholars that used to meet together for prayer, and Christian conference to the great confirmation of one another's hearts in the fear and love of God and the preparing of them for the service of the Church in their generation."[2] George Trosse, who became a nonconformist minister in Exeter, greatly enjoyed his life at Oxford. "I thank God from the bottom of my heart," he wrote,[3] "that I went to Oxford when there were so many sermons preached and so many excellent and practical divines to preach them ... Then, Religion was in its glory in the University and was a qualification for respect and advancement."

Yet, whatever their achievements, Owen and many of his colleagues were really misfits at Oxford. The University had been a centre of Anglicanism and royalism since the days of Henry VIII and would continue to be so after 1660. The Laudian statutes seemed hardly to blend with the anti-prelatical emphasis of the Independents and Presbyterians. The rule of the two Cromwells and their Vice-Chancellors was but a brief interlude in Oxford's continuing history and tradition. Indeed, Owen's activities reveal a basic tension between a conservative academic and social outlook and a fairly radical religious viewpoint. On the one hand he favoured the retention of the scholastic curriculum, the use of Latin and the preservation of higher education as the rightful domain of the sons of clergy, gentlemen and noblemen, whilst, on the other hand, he attempted to change the ancient customs of Oxford with regard to the membership and rights of Convocation, academic dress and the annual Act. Neither he nor his Independent colleagues satisfactorily resolved this tension. In their own way their critics on the right (e.g. Henry Hammond) and on the left (e.g. John Webster) were more logical.

---

[1] Clarendon, *The History of the Rebellion*, Oxford, 1849, IV, p. 284. Matriculations were high: cf. *Register of Visitors*, p. cxxx.
[2] Matthew Henry, *An Account of the Life and Death of Philip Henry*, 1698, p. 19.
[3] J. Hallet, *The Life of . . . Geo. Trosse*, 1714, p. 81.

CHAPTER IV

## ECCLESIASTICAL STATESMAN

As a friend of Oliver Cromwell a former preacher to the Council of State, and a prominent theologian and academic, John Owen was often called upon to take an active part in the affairs of the Commonwealth and Protectorate. On many occasions he travelled by coach from Oxford to London to preach to Parliament, to sit on committees, to meet Cromwell or to deal with matters relating to the University. Despite his poor health, he made these journeys gladly since for him the progress of the Commonwealth was a significant matter; he saw its moral and spiritual prosperity as intimately connected with the progress of the kingdom of God amongst the people of Europe and the world. As at Oxford his primary aim in all his varied activities in London was to prepare for the propagation of the Gospel of Jesus Christ, which he firmly believed, included at least the following ingredients: faithful and regular preaching of the Bible in parish churches; the freedom under the law of gathered churches of visible saints; the duty of government to protect and encourage the profession of the Christian Faith; the training of young men in the Faith in order to fit them for the lives of either Christian gentlemen or godly preachers; the support of persecuted Protestants in Europe; the encouragement of the settlers in New England and the provision of means to aid the conversion of the Jews to Christianity.

To achieve all or any of these aims Owen was willing to co-operate with or seek to influence whatever government was in power. It seems that he held no particular, dogmatic, political theory. He was opposed to rule by kings at this particular juncture in British history but only because God had revealed Himself as opposed to the House of Stuart. As he made clear over and over again, what he wanted to see was a Council of State and a Parliament in which were men whose hearts worshipped Christ and whose wills sought to do His bidding. This meant that he was happy to be associated with the Rump of the Long Parliament, the Barebone's Assembly, and most of all with the Lord General, and later Lord Protector, Cromwell. The relationship and understanding between Cromwell and Owen, first initiated at the home of General Fairfax in 1649, and deepened by their life together with the army in 1650-51, was now able (at least until 1657) to be utilised for what both men believed was the good of the nation. From their united efforts, for example, together with the advice and help of others, came the famous Settlement of Religion of 1654 with its "triers" and "ejectors." Whilst they were not to agree on all matters there was a spiritual bond between them and this cemented their friendship until, as we shall see, the question of kingship sadly separated them.

As both men, and Owen in particular, set their understanding of the necessity for the preaching of the Gospel in the light and context of what they understood to be God's purposes for His Church as revealed in Holy Scripture, it is perhaps necessary first of all to examine Owen's views of God's plan before looking at his practical efforts to realise a small part of it on British soil. The best short summary of Owen's views of the future of the Church on earth is found in the *Savoy Declaration of Faith* (1658), which he helped to write.

> As the Lord in His care and love towards His Church, hath in His infinite, wise providence exercised it with great variety in all ages, for the good of them that love Him, and His own glory; so according to His promises, we expect that in the latter days, Antichrist being destroyed, the Jews called and the adversaries of His Son broken, the churches of Christ being enlarged and edified through a free and plentiful communication of light and grace, shall enjoy in this world a more quiet, peaceable and glorious condition than they have enjoyed.[1]

We have already met this eschatological optimism in sermons preached to soldiers and politicians in 1648 and 1649 and it reoccurs very noticeably in the sermons Owen preached to the Rump of the Long Parliament in 1651 and 1652.

On the 24th October 1651, a day of thanksgiving for Cromwell's victory over the Scots whom he had finally fought at Worcester after their invasion of England, Owen described the Lord General's "crowning mercy" as one of the most outstanding manifestations of the power of Christ in the Christian era.[2] He urged his hearers to believe that there were "three principal seasons of the Lord's eminent appearances to carry on the kingdom of Christ and the Gospel." Each one had "dreadful providential alterations" attached to it. The first was the preaching of the Gospel to the Jews which was followed by the destruction by the Romans of the city of Jerusalem in A.D. 70. The second was the preaching of the Gospel to the Gentiles of the Roman Empire which was followed by the destruction of the city of Rome by the barbarians of the North. But the third is the greatest of all—"the coming of the Lord to recover

---

[1] This quotation is from chap. xxvi. The origin of the *Declaration* is examined in chap. V below. See P. Toon, "A Message of Hope for Parliament," *Evangelical Quarterly*, XLIV, April 3 1970 for Owen's eschatology.

[2] The sermon was entitled *The Advantage of the Kingdom of Christ* and is in *Works*, VIII, pp. 3ff.

His people from antichristian idolatry and oppression"—prophesied in Revelation 17:14 and 19:11-21. As Owen put it:

> This is the head whereunto the present actings of Providence in this nation are to be referred; they all tend to the accomplishment of God's main design therein. He that thinks Babylon is confined to Rome and its open idolatry, knows nothing of Babylon or of the new Jerusalem. The depth of subtle mystery doth not lie in gross visible folly. It hath been insinuating itself into all the nations sixteen hundred years, and to most of them is now become as marrow in their bones. Before it be wholly shaken out, these heavens (i.e. the political glory of nations) must be dissolved and the earth (i.e. the people on the earth) shaken . . . This, I say, is the work that the Lord hath now in hand; and this is the day of thankfulness in reference to what He hath done for us in this nation.[1]

Both victory over Charles I and victory over the Scots, who had supported the young Charles, were seen as part of God's removal of those barriers in Britain which prevented the dawn of the latter-day glory of the Church.

The Scots had prepared "a Procrustes bed, a heavy yoke" for the English Church and people. This iron burden of presbyterian discipline which they intended for the parishes of England was "fleshly, carnal and cruel;" it was uncompromising and opposed to the "meek and gentle" rule of Christ. To make matters worse the Scots had wanted to set up a "son of Tabeal"[2] as King of England; or, put another way, they wished to re-enthrone tyranny. Happily, God had crushed these moves against His true spiritual kingdom and His victory was plain for all to see. And in His appointed time, God would "bring forth the kingdom of the Lord Christ unto more glory and power than in former days." There would be peace on the earth, harmony in the Church, purity of Gospel worship and ordinances, multitudes of converts and the subjection of all nations to the cause of Christ.[3]

A year later, on the 13th October 1652, at the time of the naval war with the Dutch, he again emphasised that "God will surely shake the heavens and the earth . . . until all the Babylonish rubbish, all their original engagements to the man of sin be taken away."[4] Then the "civil powers of the world, after fearful shakings and desolations, shall be disposed of into a useful subserviency to the interest, power and kingdom

---

[1] *Works*, VIII, p. 322.
[2] Tabeal is mentioned in Isaiah 7:6. He was probably an Aramean of the Damascus Court, whom the Syrians intended to place on the throne of Judah. Owen refers to Prince Charles.
[3] A similar conception of the future of Christianity is seen in the dedicatory letter signed by Owen and other Independents in the book *Strengthe out of Weakness* (1652) edited by Henry Whitfield, and describing missionary work in New England.
[4] The sermon is in *Works*, VIII, pp. 365ff. Owen believed that since the Netherlands "whose being was founded" upon the kingdom of Christ, had joined "with the great antichristian interest of Spain" it would inevitably come to ruin. *Works*, VIII, p. 382.

of Jesus Christ." In this fulfilment the Jews will play an initial and major part: "the beginning of it must be with the Jews; they are to be 'caput imperii'." Or, put another way: "all the promises of the glorious kingdom of Christ are to be accomplished in the gathering of the Gentiles, with the glory of the Jews. 'The Redeemer comes to Zion and to them that turn from transgression (that great transgression of unbelief) in Jacob.' (Isaiah 59:20.)" All this will be accomplished by the pouring out of the Spirit of God.

> Great wars, desolations, alterations, shall precede it; but it is not the sons of men that, by outward force, shall build the new Jerusalem; that comes down from heaven adorned as a bride for Christ, fitted and prepared by Himself. Certainly the strivings of men about this business shall have no influence into it. It shall be by the glorious manifestation of His own power and that by His Spirit subduing the souls of men unto it.

This, however, did not mean that Christian men were to do nothing and merely wait for God to act. Owen's belief was that divine sovereignty of action is always placed in Scripture alongside human responsibility to do the will of God. The former is most evident when the latter is being done, and all is, ultimately, by the grace of God.

This sermon included a statement of the duties of human rulers with regard to the propagation of the Gospel since Owen and others were emphatically urging upon the Rump at this time the need for a Settlement of Religion for the nation. Naturally Owen saw this need in the light of God's current redemptive activity in England. The initial stages of this pressure for a Settlement may be traced to February 1652 when Owen was in London to preach at the memorial service for his friend, Henry Ireton, whom he had come to know at the siege of Colchester and who had been Lord Deputy of Ireland since 1650.[1] Owen took this opportunity to confer with other like-minded ministers concerning the provision of a preaching ministry for all parts of the nation as well as what action ought to be taken about the recent publication of the Socinian *Catechesis Ecclesiarum Poloniae* (commonly called *The Racovian Catechism*[2]). This catechism denied the orthodox doctrine of the Holy Trinity; its innovations were heresies. So, on 10 February, a group of ministers, led by Owen and including Philip Nye, Sidrach Simpson and John Durie, appeared at the bar of the Commons to condemn the Socinian teaching and to plead for the prohibition of sales of the catechism. The House immediately appointed a committee of forty

---

[1] The sermon is in *Works*, VIII, pp. 341ff. It was essentially a funeral sermon and has no religio-political ideas in it.
[2] *The Racovian Catechism* was published in Polish at Rakow in 1605 with later versions in German (1608) and Latin (1609). For its use in England see H. J. McLachlan, *Socinianism in Seventeenth-Century England*, 1951.

to discuss the matter with the ministers.[1] The result of this quick action was an order that the whole edition of the book be recalled and burnt.

Also on the 10th February the ministers had made specific requests and proposals to ensure that godly preachers were able to occupy the parish pulpits of the nation. To discuss the questions raised by this second request the House appointed a committee of fourteen who were to receive proposals for the propagation of the Gospel both from these ministers as well as from any other groups who wished to submit their ideas. On the 18th February nine of the original ten ministers together with six more met the committee to submit definite, written proposals, which were printed soon afterwards as *The Humble Proposals of Mr Owen, Mr Tho. Goodwin, Mr Nye, Mr Sympson and other ministers.*[2] The proposals involved, on the one hand, the fullest utilisation of educated, godly men in the task of preaching, and, on the other, the removal from the parishes of ignorant, scandalous, and non-resident clergy. A group of godly and respected men, both lay and clerical, were to travel through the country to examine parish ministers and to eject those who were not fulfilling a preaching ministry. As they went through each county this commission was to recommend to Parliament the names of laymen and ministers there who would then act in that area as examiners (triers) of men who wished to become parish ministers. Conventicles were to be tolerated as long as they were carefully controlled and registered by the Committee for the Universities, and by the local magistracy. Everybody was to be required to go to their local parish church on the Lord's Day and Parliament was requested "to take some speedy and effectual course for the utter suppressing of that abominable cheat of judicial astrology." This form of astrology explained events not with reference to God and His righteousness but to the movement of celestial bodies. Then, as now, it was extremely popular.[3] The idea was to preserve the parishes of the National Church at a time when its legal, Presbyterian character was possible of no fulfilment. Classes only existed in a few parts of the country and no national synod had yet met. The proposals were also designed to achieve the maximum co-operation

[1] The ten ministers were: John Owen, Philip Nye, Sidrach Simpson, William Strong, John Durie, William Bridge, William Greenhill, Adoniram Byfield, George Griffith, and Thomas Harrison. All were known Independent except Durie, the ecumenist, and Byfield, who had been a scribe to the Westminster Assembly.

[2] George Griffith was the one who was not present and the six were: George Marshall, Augustine Plumsted, Matthew Barker, Richard Lee, Ralph Button and Jenkin Lloyd. The printed proposals had a further twelve names attached, including Thomas Goodwin. Cf. F. J. Powicke, "The Independents of 1652," in *Transactions* of the Cong. Hist. Society, IX, 1, April 1924, pp. 22–8, where the *Humble Proposals*, with comments, are printed in full.

[3] Owen and his colleagues may have been affected by the "Black Monday" scare. For some time before Monday, the 29th March 1652, when a solar eclipse was due, astrologists were prophesying that terrible events would take place. So much so that many people left London in order to avoid the forecasted doom! In the event nothing happened! For details of this and of Calvinistic attitudes to astrology see Keith Thomas, *Religion and the Decline of Magic*, 1970, pp. 299–300 and 367.

between Presbyterians, Congregationalists and Baptists in preparation for the time when, in the coming millennium, denominational differences would be irrelevant. However, the proposals were basically conservative and cautious in that conventicles were to be carefully controlled, tithes retained, and graduates of the Universities used to staff the parishes. There was little in them to cheer the hearts of the sectarians and radicals.

The invitation by the committee of fourteen to others to offer proposals did not go unheeded. Two Baptist groups submitted their ideas but they were not printed.[1] Captain Robert Norwood, a recalcitrant member of the church of which Sidrach Simpson was pastor, submitted his proposals and then printed them as *Proposals for the Propagation of the Gospel*. From William Butler, soon to be made a Major-General, came proposals which were printed as *The Fourth Paper*.[2] Butler's paper was in part an attack upon the proposals of Owen and his colleagues. He complained that if their ideas were adopted there would be no place for religious toleration for either Christian radicals or for Jews, whom he wished to see readmitted to Britain. He also wanted to see the disestablishment of the Church and the abolition of tithes. From a totally different viewpoint came criticism also. Richard Baxter felt that proposals merely from one party, the Independents, was not in the national interest; further, if the proposals of Owen were accepted they would not solve two major problems facing the parish ministry, the questions of church discipline and worship.[3]

Owen and his brethren did not know of Baxter's views, and if they had they would not have worried them. However, because of the four sets of proposals from the sectarians, which if implemented would have aided and abetted error, heresy, and schism, they made it known that they wished to add certain doctrinal articles to their own proposals to ensure that the theology preached in the parish churches and registered conventicles was orthodox and such as would be pleasing to the Almighty. It was probably these doctrinal articles (and not the original proposals as such) that John Milton, knowing that Cromwell disagreed with their addition, criticised in his sonnet, "To the Lord General Cromwell, May 1652, on the proposals of certain ministers at the Committee for the Propagation of the Gospel."[4] In fact the doctrinal

[1] G. F. Nuttall, "Presbyterians and Independents," *Journal* of the Presbyterian Hist. Society, X, May 1952, p. 5. for reference to these proposals.
[2] In the preface to this R.(oger) W.(illiams) stated that Cromwell said that "he had rather Mahometanism were permitted amongst us than that one of God's children be persecuted."
[3] Baxter was writing to Durie: see Dr Williams's Library MSS. 59.6.90. The letter was written on May 7.
[4] Milton the Latin Secretary to the Council of State wrote that:
. . . "new foes arise
Threatening to bind our soules with secular chaines:
Helpe us to save free Conscience from the paw
Of hireling wolves whose Gospell is their maw."
See *The Poetical Works of John Milton*, ed. Helen Darbishire, Oxford, 1955, II, p. 153.

articles were first published in December 1652 attached to a second edition of the *Humble Proposals* and under a modified title, *Proposals for the furtherance and propagation of the Gospel in this nation*, with the date 1653 attached.[1] They affirmed the supreme authority of Holy Scripture, the Nicene doctrine of the Trinity, the centrality of Christ's atonement, resurrection and ascension, the Chalcedonian Christology, the necessity of regeneration and saving faith in sinful mortals who would obtain eternal salvation, and the worship of God according to His revealed will. If this statement effectively removed Socinians and Unitarians from a legal part in the religious life of England, it also prohibited both Roman Catholic and Anglican worship which was based on either an erroneous or a dead liturgy.[2] The question as to whether or not it allowed Arminians is more difficult since, though the doctrines of predestination and limited atonement are not specified, they are implied.

Before the *Proposals* appeared, Owen had preached to Parliament on the 13th October. We noted above the eschatological references contained in his sermon, but it was much more than an exposition of the doctrine of the last things. It was also a strong statement of the duty of rulers and magistrates with regard to the Christian Faith. Owen complimented the members by recounting how God had used them in the past. "From the beginning of the contests in this nation," he said, "when God had caused your spirits to resolve that the liberties, privileges and rights of this nation, wherewith you were entrusted, should not, by His assistance, be wrested out of your hands by violence, oppression and injustice; this He also put upon your hearts, to vindicate and assert the Gospel of Jesus Christ, His ways, and His ordinances against all opposition, though you were but enquiring the way to Zion, with your faces thitherward." Now in the autumn of 1652 when there was a general confusion caused by the expression of radical religious views, Owen was afraid that members would be influenced by them or by the proposals of such men as Major Butler. So he asked the Commons:

> What now, by the lusts of men, is the state of things? Say some, There is no gospel at all; say others, If there be, you have nothing to do with it;—some say, Lo, here is Christ; others, Lo, there:— some make religion a colour for one thing; some for another:— say some, The magistrate must not support the Gospel; say some, Your rule is only for men as men, you have nothing to do with the interest of Christ and the church; say others, You have nothing

---

[1] S. R. Gardiner, *History of the Commonwealth* . . . , II, pp. 98ff. and Shaw, *History of the English Church* . . . , II, pp. 82ff. seem not to have realised that this was the second edition. For the original proposals they go only to the *Journals* of the Commons. Masson, *Life of Milton*, 1877, IV, pp. 392ff. seems only to have known the first edition.

[2] This is the implication of Art. XV: "God is to be worshipped according to His own will and whosoever shall forsake and despise all the duties of His worship cannot be saved."

to do to rule men but upon the account of being saints. If you will have the gospel say some, down with the ministers of it, chemarims, locusts.[1]

In the face of such varied views, the members must not be confused but remember what were their duties as rulers. To make these clear Owen expressed them in five propositions. These summarised views he had previously expressed.

1. The Gospel of Jesus Christ has a right to be preached and propagated in every nation and to every creature under heaven.
2. Wherever the Gospel is by any nation owned, received, embraced, it is the blessing, benefit, prosperity and advantage of that nation.
3. The rejection of the Gospel by any people or nation to whom it is tendered is always attended with the certain and inevitable destruction of that people or nation; which, sooner or later, shall, without any help or deliverance, be brought upon them by the revenging hand of Christ.
4. It is the duty of magistrates to seek the good, peace and prosperity of the people committed to their charge, and to prevent, obviate, remove, take away everything that will bring confusion, destruction, desolation upon them; as Mordecai procured good things for his people and prosperity for his kindred. Esther 10:3.
5. Although the institutions and examples of the Old Testament, of the duty of magistrates in the things about the worship of God, are not in their whole latitude and extent to be drawn into rules that should be obligatory to all magistrates now, under the administration of the Gospel . . . yet, doubtless, there is something moral in those institutions, which, being unclothed of their Judaical form, is still binding to all in the like kind, as to some analogy and proportion.[2]

Of necessity Owen and others of this period had to refer to the Old Testament for the basis of their view of the Christian magistrate since there was little, if anything at all, explicitly stated in the New Testament about the duties of rulers with regard to the Gospel. In the first century the Church was too small to have been faced with this problem. Obviously he wanted Parliament to act quickly with reference to the proposals which he and his brethren had laid before the committee eight months earlier.

Owen's sermon had no immediate effect but on the 11th February 1653 the Committee at last reported to the House. During February and March the *Humble Proposals* were debated *seriatim* and were well on the way to being accepted when Cromwell and his officers dissolved the Rump on the 20th April. Unfortunately we have no information concerning Owen's reaction to Cromwell's intervention at Westminster. Neither do we have any record of what were his thoughts concerning

[1] *Works*, VIII, p. 381.
[2] *Works*, VIII, p. 390.

the calling of the Nominated Assembly of Saints.[1] It is very probable that he shared Cromwell's optimism for a Parliament of elect saints since on more than one occasion he expressed the view that a nation stood a better chance of receiving God's favours if that nation had committed Christians as its rulers.[2] And when the Barebone's Assembly (as the Parliament of saints was called) met, Owen preached before it. This was on the 25th August 1653, a day of thanksgiving for the victory over the Dutch fleet on the 31st July.[3] Had this sermon been printed we would perhaps have had a clear indication of Owen's hopes for this Assembly but as it was not we can only guess at them. One fact is certain: if he had entertained hopes that the Barebone's Assembly would be the great preparer of the way for God to bring in the latter-day glory of the Church on earth, these hopes were soon shattered. Indeed, it is quite possible that, as a result of what happened during the last part of the life of this short Parliament, with its repercussions at Oxford and Cambridge, Owen became less convinced of the nearness of the end of the age. We may recall that the rise to power of the Independents from 1646 to 1649 had had a similar effect upon the eschatological views of the Presbyterians: their optimism had been severely dampened.[4] Owen's optimism was cooled by what were for him the dangerous opinions, wild ideas and impractical schemes of some of the supposed saints. His conservative temperament reacted against their desire to change the face of England by abolishing tithes, reforming the law, and remodelling the Universities. Christopher Hill writes that "it is impossible to exaggerate the psychological importance of the failure of the Barebone's Parliament for Oliver Cromwell."[5] Exactly the same may be said of John Owen.

The longer the Barebone's Assembly sat, the more Cromwell was troubled and bewildered by the course which events were taking; he had hoped, as had Owen, for a sensible, broadly-based settlement of religion and all he got was frustration. So in late October he called a conference of leading Congregational, Presbyterian and Baptist ministers in order "to persuade them that hold Christ the Head, and so the same in fundamentals, to agree in love, that there be no such divisions among people professing godliness, nor railing and reviling each other for differences in only some forms."[6] Among those present were Philip Nye, Stephen Marshall, Henry Jessey and John Owen. No doubt the frustration of Cromwell and Owen was increased when a vote of 58 to 41 on the 7th

[1] See above, p. 69.
[2] Cf., for example, *Works*, VIII, pp. 444-5.
[3] *C.J.*, VII, pp. 297 and 308.
[4] Cf. Wilson, *Pulpit in Parliament*, pp. 230ff.
[5] Hill, *God's Englishman*, p. 143.
[6] Quoted by Abbott in *Writings and Speeches of Cromwell*, III, p. 119, from a contemporary news-journal.

November within the Assembly abolished tithes. The Committee to consider the propriety of incumbents in tithes then had to find alternative means of maintenance for the ministers. Moderates and radicals were about equally represented on this Committee but somehow the former gained the ascendancy and proposals for the propagation of the Gospel were brought into the House for debate on 2 December. They were similar to those in the *Humble Proposals* and included both the sending out of eighteen named commissioners, of whom Owen was to be one, to travel throughout the land to set up local committees of "ejectors," and the compromise suggestion that alternative ways of raising church finance be used in areas where there was deepseated opposition to tithes. As other business intervened it was not until the 6th that this scheme was considered. Then for five whole sittings the discussion continued until Saturday, the 10th, when the first clause of the report which provided for the ejection of scandalous ministers was rejected by fifty-six votes to fifty-two. The moderates had suffered a real defeat. Radicals and possibly a few moderates had voted against it, the former because they were opposed to the very existence of a National Church, and the latter because they feared that the powers delegated to the commissioners might lead to tyranny and persecution. The basic reason, however, for the defeat was growing absenteeism from the House which in this instance was mostly moderates. The rejection of this report left the way open for the radicals to launch a new attack upon the public ministry. Fearing this, the moderates, thoroughly exasperated by recent events and probably at General Lambert's suggestion, voted on the 12th December to resign their authority to the Lord General Cromwell. Owen was in London at this time and viewed the end of this Assembly with great relief. In 1657, looking back to this period when the radicals were out-manouvered, he described the dissolution on the 12th December in terms of "the Governor of all things so quickly defeating all their councils and all their attempts" against His gospel.[1] God had come once more to the aid of His saints but this time His coming involved the punishment not of wicked papists or royalists but of the extreme left of the Puritan movement. The Almighty had, as it were, set in motion a conservative reaction.

With many others, Owen must have been deeply relieved that Cromwell became the Lord Protector of England, Scotland and Ireland. The new constitution, which defined the office of the Protector, was set

---

[1] *Oxford Orations*, p. 42. A. H. Woolrych, "The Calling of the Barebone's Parliament," *English Historical Review*, LXXX, 1965, p. 500 has suggested that Cromwell collaborated with Lambert, Desborough, Pickering, Whalley, Goffe and Owen to pack this Assembly with conservatives. His view is based upon an interpretation of words in *A Faithful Searching Homing Word* (1659), pp. 14-16. However, as Tai Liu points out in "The Calling of the Barebone's Parliament Reconsidered," *Journal of Ecclesiastical History*, XXII, 1971, p. 229, the reference in the tract is to what occurred after the 12th December 1653.

forth in a document known as the *Instrument of Government*.[1] At last the revolution had a written constitution. Congratulations to Cromwell flowed into Whitehall from all parts and among the messages was a Latin letter from the Convocation of Oxford.[2] "Let it be fitting that in the public rejoicing," said the letter, "the University, your fosterchild (to whom your good fortune extends first and foremost) should respectfully approach you and join the rest in congratulation." Cromwell had protected both learning and religion, the letter continued, and, as we would expect, the confident hope was expressed that he would continue to do so. The place of religion in the State was explained in the *Instrument*. Since Articles XXXV–XXXVII became the legal basis for the Cromwellian Settlement of Religion and were also the basis of the longer statement (with which Owen was to confess full agreement) in the *Humble Petition and Advice* of 1657, it is perhaps necessary to quote them in full here.

XXXV. That the Christian religion, as contained in the Scriptures be held forth and recommended as the public profession of these nations; and that, as soon as may be, a provision, less subject to scruple and contention, and more certain than the present, be made for the encouragement and maintenance of able and painful teachers, for the instructing the people, and for discovery and confutation of error, heresy, and whatever is contrary to sound doctrine; and until such provision be made, the present maintenance shall not be taken away.

XXXVI. That to the public profession held forth none shall be compelled by penalties or otherwise; but that endeavours be used to win them by sound doctrine and the example of a good conversation.

XXXVII. That such as profess faith in God by Christ Jesus (though differing in judgement from the doctrine, worship or discipline held forth) shall not be restrained from, but shall be protected in, the profession of the faith and exercise of their religion; so as they abuse not this liberty to the civil injury of others and to the actual disturbance of the public peace on their parts: provided this liberty be not extended to Popery, or Prelacy, nor to such as, under the profession of Christ, hold forth and practice licentiousness.

In general there was nothing here with which Owen would have disagreed. From his point of view the weakness was the lack of definition of the Christian religion and, as we shall see, he did seek to have this matter remedied.

Before we examine the Cromwellian ordinances for the Settlement of Religion and Owen's part in their creation, we must notice a significant and important letter which, together with Nye and Goodwin, he wrote to the Congregational churches of England and Wales.[3] One of the results

[1] For the text see *Constitutional Documents*, ed. Gardiner, pp. 406ff.
[2] *Correspondence*, No. 16, pp. 64–5.
[3] *Correspondence*, No. 18, pp. 66–8.

of the calling of the Barebone's Assembly was to intensify eschatological speculation and general instability amongst the separatists and sectarians, be they of the Baptist or Paedobaptist variety. This speculation involved the belief, held by not a few members of the former Assembly of saints, that Christ would soon return to earth to inaugurate the millennial reign of the saints (the Fifth Monarchy) and thus He and His Word (as interpreted by the saints) were the only legitimate source of authority. So, politically speaking, the Fifth Monarchists were anarchists. Worried by the political and social ramifications of this chiliasm, the Congregational leaders wrote in early 1654 to warn their brethren of the dangers inherent in the views of the Fifth Monarchists. They had no complaint with millenarianism since all three were millenarians of one kind or another; rather, it was the false deductions made from the belief in the millennium which they attacked. Whether any churches or individuals were saved from anarchical chiliasm through this circular letter we do not know; what certainly happened was that the gulf which existed between the conservative Congregationalists and the radical separatists (e.g. Vavasor Powell and John Rogers) was made wider.[1] This of course was also helped by the controversy over the place given to education in the training of ministers which we discussed in the last chapter.

The presence of a large and growing sectarian movement made it all the more necessary for the conservative Independents to move quickly to provide for a preaching ministry in the parishes of England and Wales. So Cromwell met Owen and other leading divines to discuss with them how this could be achieved. On the 22nd February 1654, for example, various "ministers and some from the Universities" were at Cromwell's lodgings.[2] As a result of the advice which the Protector received at this and at other meetings, he and his Council of State produced two Ordinances. A general Board, whose members became known as "triers," was set up on the 20th March 1654 for the approbation of public ministers.[3] Thirty-eight men, both ministers and laymen, were named as commissioners and invested with the power and responsibility of judging the qualifications of men who wished to be presented to a benefice or lectureship. The commissioners represented Congregational, Baptist and Presbyterian opinion, but men engaged in teaching at Oxford and Cambridge were a dominant influence. From Oxford came John Owen, Thomas Goodwin and Thankful Owen; from Cambridge came John Arrowsmith, Master of Trinity, Anthony Tuckney, Master of

---

[1] Cf. for example the comments of John Rogers in the "Epistolary Perambulation" to *The Time of the End* (1657) by John Canne. Addressing himself to the Independents he wrote that some "of your chiefest heads were once of the same mind with us." For Powell and Rogers see D.N.B.

[2] This is what Durie told Baxter in a letter of the 22nd Feb. Dr Williams's Library MSS. 59.5.199. Cf. also *Writings and Speeches of Cromwell*, III, p. 206., and *Diary of Archibald Johnston*, ed. Fleming, II, p. 214.

[3] For the text see *Acts and Ordinances*, II, pp. 856ff.

St John's and Thomas Horton President of Queens'. Other important ministers included Joseph Caryl, Philip Nye, Henry Jessey, and Obadiah Sedgwick.[1] The Board of whom nine members formed a quorum sat regularly at Whitehall. Each man who presented himself was required to provide three testimonials from men of known godliness and integrity, including one minister, testifying to his holy and good conversation and behaviour. Patron's rights were kept intact and so was the support of the churches by tithes, despite the promise of Article XXXV of the *Instrument*. So, as S. R. Gardiner has remarked, "the conservative instinct of the country protesting against further change than was necessary to promote efficiency was abundantly satisfied."[2]

A month after its constitution, the Board announced in an open letter to the nation that it was ready to begin work and would seek to conduct its examinations with justice and care. All men appointed to livings since the 1st April 1653 had to be examined. Ministers who recommended candidates should only commend those whom they knew well and whose spiritual state was sufficiently developed to enable them to preach with conviction and usefulness. Unfortunately, no detailed record exists of any examination of candidates in which Owen was involved. However, the names of twenty-seven men for whom he wrote testimonials are known and, as we would expect from his known concern for unity, they include both Independents and Presbyterians.[3] As to the general work of the Board, in which Philip Nye played a major part, Baxter pointed out that certain of its members were "overbusie and over-rigid . . . against all that were Arminians, and too particular in enquiring after evidences of sanctification . . . and too lax in their admission of unlearned and erroneous men that favoured antinomianism and anabaptism." But he was willing to admit that "so great was the benefit above the hurt, which they brought to the Church, that many thousands of souls blest God for the faithful ministers whom they let in, and grieved when the prelatists afterwards (between 1660 and 1662) cast them out again."[4]

On the 28th August a second Ordinance completed the administrative structure of the Settlement by providing for the supervision of ministers

[1] All these men are either in *D.N.B.* or *C.R.* or in both.
[2] Gardiner, *History of Commonwealth*, III, p. 24.
[3] The Admission Books of the Triers are in Lambeth Palace Library, MSS L996–999. Cf. Shaw, *op. cit.*, II, pp. 467ff. From these manuscripts the late Canon C. Jenkins compiled a list of all those ministers who signed testimonials for intending incumbents. The 27 men whom Owen commended are listed under Owen's name in Jenkins MS 1662. Of these the following are in *C.R.*: Samuel Malbon, John Francis, John Johnson, Stephen Ford, John Kempster, William Burnet, Abraham Dye, Thomas Waterhouse, John Meadows, Edward West and Thomas Bruce.
[4] Baxter, *Reliquiae*, I, p. 72. For criticisms of the methods of the triers see Anthony Sadler, *Inquisitio Anglicana* (1654) to which Nye replied in *Mr Sadler Re-Examined* (1654). Sadler was one of those who were not accepted. There is an urgent need for a study of the work of the triers. Little seems to have been written on them in recent years.

at the county level through the expulsion of those deemed unfit to hold parish livings.[1] Lay commissioners and their ministerial assistants were named for each county (or group of counties) and they were given the power to call for examination any minister, lecturer, or schoolmaster who was reported to be ignorant, scandalous, or negligent. Negligence meant, for example, omitting to preach on the Lord's Day; scandalous behaviour included such activities as dancing around the may-pole, taking part in stage-plays, or writing or preaching against the government. Where an ejected minister left his benefice without resistance, the commissioners were empowered to set aside for the benefit of his family a fifth of his successor's income from the parish.

John Owen and his brother William, the minister at Remenham, were nominated as ministerial assistants to the Oxfordshire "ejectors." Nominated also from the University of Oxford were Thomas Goodwin, Thankful Owen, Christopher Rogers, Ambrose Upton, Peter French, Henry Wilkinson (of Christ Church), Edmund Staunton, Robert Harris, Ralph Button, Francis Howell and Henry Cornish.[2] Again, nothing is known of Owen's participation in the work of ejection. His general attitude, however, may be illustrated by his efforts to prevent the ejection of Edward Pococke, the Laudian Professor of Arabic, from his living at Childrey. In 1655 some of the parishioners at Childrey complained about their minister to the local lay commissioners who seemed to be in favour of ejecting Pococke. So with Seth Ward, John Wilkins and John Wallis, Owen travelled to Abingdon where he laboured to convince the commissioners of the absurdity of ejecting for insufficiency one of the most learned scholars in Europe. He also wrote to Secretary Thurloe in London complaining about these "men of mean quality and condition, rash, heady and enemies of tithes."[3] Obviously Owen preferred to see learned, moderate men like Pococke in parishes rather than the unlearned, enthusiastic radicals who wished to eject him.

There are similarities between the provisions suggested in the *Humble Proposals* and the two Cromwellian Ordinances. It appears that the basic ideas of Owen and his Congregational brethren (which were themselves perhaps based on earlier experiments in London and Wales[4]) were reduced to practical shape by the Protector and his advisers. No doubt the latter took care to notice the comments of the committees of both the Rump and Barebone's Parliaments. It could well be that the roles of "triers" and "ejectors" were reversed because of comments

[1] For the text see *Acts and Ordinances*, II, pp. 968ff.
[2] As far as I know no material is extant to show how these men worked with their lay colleagues.
[3] *Correspondence*, No. 32, pp. 82–3, Owen to Thurloe. See also L. Twells, *Life of Edward Pococke*, 1816, pp. 156–175.
[4] See p. 22, n. 1 above for London and Thomas Richards, *A History of the Puritan Movement in Wales*, 1920, pp. 81ff.

made in these committees. Whereas Owen's proposal had been for a national Board to do the ejecting and local Boards the accepting, the Cromwellian Settlement, as we have seen, set up a Board in London to examine candidates and local Boards to eject unsatisfactory clergy. Perhaps Gardiner claimed too much for Owen when he stated that the "Cromwellian Church" was "conceived in the mind of Owen and reduced to practical shape by Oliver."[1] We have no proof, for example, that Owen was the one who conceived the idea of the propagation of the gospel as set out in the *Humble Proposals;* all we know is that he led those who presented the proposals to Parliament, and that he did much to keep successive governments and Parliaments thinking in terms of propagating the gospel. However, Gardiner was right to say that "with the exception of the condemnation of the use of the Book of Common Prayer the scheme was in the highest degree broad and generous." And he correctly pointed out that many of those who sought to promote the use of the Prayer Book were a political as well as an ecclesiastical party and therefore the prohibition was not without solid reasons.

Gathered churches were allowed to meet as and where they pleased as long as they did not cause any public inconvenience. They were not required to be licensed as the *Humble Proposals* suggested. Many men of the Congregational way held parish livings, preached in the "public-place" (as the parish church was often called by those for whom the word "church" signified "people" not buildings) and were pastors of Congregational churches. For this activity they were accused of being schismatics. Indeed, such was the strength of this accusation in 1656, that early in 1657 (as we noticed in the last chapter) John Beverley, the incumbent of Rothwell in Northamptonshire, wrote to Owen in agonising terms asking him to arise and to defend his brethren from what they believed were unjust charges of schism.[2] That Owen was also very conscious of what Beverley was experiencing is seen not only from the frequent references to the "party-spirit" in his Oxford oration for 1656, but also from the pleas he made for unity amongst Protestants in the two sermons he preached before Oliver's second Parliament in September and October 1656.[3] Partly in response to Beverley's cries for help, he did write three books principally aimed against Daniel Cawdry, presbyterian minister at Great Billing, also in Northamptonshire.[4] All three books, though firm in their principles, display what was for those times a generous spirit and lack of acrimony. In this Owen practised what he preached.

Though he wanted the National Settlement of Religion to include

[1] Gardiner, *op. cit.*, III, p. 24.
[2] *Correspondence*, No. 47, pp. 96-8.
[3] The sermons are in *Works*, VIII, pp. 398ff.
[4] These were: *Of Schism* (1657), *A Review of the True Nature of Schism* (1657) and *A Defence of Mr John Cotton* (1658), in *Works*, XIII.

all godly, learned, orthodox preachers, and though he believed that sound religion would be propagated by their influence in the parishes, Owen still felt that such a Settlement needed a less ambiguous theological basis than that offered by the *Instrument of Government*. This is made clear by the doctrinal statement which Owen and his brethren had added to the *Humble Proposals*, and by the draft of a Confession of Faith which, with Thomas Goodwin, he was preparing at Oxford in April 1654.[1] So, despite the fact that he was prevented by the Clerical Disabilities Act from taking his place in Oliver's first Parliament, he was nevertheless glad to be invited to act as an adviser to one of its committees. This had been set up to provide an explanation of what were the "fundamentals" of the Faith and, therefore, of what types of theology and worship were legally permitted by the Instrument of Government. Other divines who were invited to offer advice included Baxter (whose Worcestershire Association of ministers was now well known as a practical experiment in unity), the Presbyterians, Manton, Cheynell and Marshall, and the Independents, Nye, Simpson, and Goodwin.[2] Baxter, renowned for his catholicity, would have defined the fundamentals in terms of the Apostles' Creed, the Lord's Prayer, and the Decalogue, but the majority preferred to set them out in a series of propositions, "the great doer" of which, according to Baxter, was Owen who was helped by "his assistants," Nye, Simpson, and Goodwin, with Cheynell acting as scribe.[3] The sixteen articles upon which they agreed were printed soon afterwards by Owen's "assistants" under the title, *The Principles of Faith presented by Mr Tho. Goodwin, Mr Nye, Mr Sydrach Sympson and other ministers*, but were never accepted by the Commons. The chief reason for this was the brevity of the Parliament. A brief study of this document reveals that the propositions are vitrually the same as the fifteen articles printed in the *Proposals* of December 1652. The only additions were an article on the resurrection of the dead and the strengthening of the article on the authority of Scripture. It does not need emphasising that Owen, the "great doer," regarded doctrinal accuracy as tremendously important and it was for this reason that he acceded to the Council of State's request of March 1654 to write against the Socinian views of John Bidle, the father of English Unitarianism, set forth in his *Twofold Catechism*.[4] The same motivation was behind his long defence of the Calvinist doctrine of the perseverance of the saints against the Arminian notions of John Goodwin in 1654, as it

---

[1] The preparation of the Confession is mentioned in *The Diary of Sir Archibald Johnston*, II, p. 246. This is the only reference which I can find to it and so what became of it I cannot tell.
[2] Cf. Masson, *Life of Milton*, V, pp. 12ff. for an account of the meetings of the divines and the committee.
[3] Baxter, *Reliquiae*, II, pp. 197ff.
[4] C.S.P.D. (1654), p. 3. Owen's book was entitled, *Vindiciae Evangelicae* (1655) and is in *Works*, XII.

was also behind his earlier defence of Calvinism against Laudian innovations in 1643 and against Baxter's compromise position on the atonement in 1650.[1] Never at any time, however, did Owen advocate the defence of orthodoxy by the use of force.

Oliver's first Parliament did not last long On the 22nd January 1655 it was dismissed and there was no further Parliament for twenty-one months. The pattern of the interim period was set by an abortive royalist rising early in March, at which time, as was noted in the last chapter, Owen hastened to prepare the defence of Oxford. In August, England and Wales were divided into ten (later eleven) military districts each under a Major-General, whose duties were both military and civil. With most of these senior officers (Desborough, Fleetwood and Berry, for example), Owen was on the best of terms and would remain so for many years. He remained also on good terms with the Protector and was chosen by him to preach at the opening of his second Parliament in 1656. Owen's sermon, published as *God's Work in Founding Zion*,[2] was in essence a call for Britain to live up to the calling of God which had been revealed in His wonderful dispensations in recent history. He judged that there was need for such a call since, as he also made clear in the sermon he preached six weeks later to the same assembly, the good old cause was being forgotten, and private, selfish interests were beginning to cloud or obliterate the cause of Christ and His kingdom.[3] England, he felt, needed a continuing reformation, and Wales still needed sound preachers of the Gospel. It is not coincidental that Owen's observation that the spiritual temperature of the House of Commons and its supporters was cooling should occur just a short time before open moves were made to persuade Oliver to accept the title of king. Enthusiasm for those spiritual ideals which Owen held sacred was certainly waning in 1656 amongst many of those who had taken part in the revolution and who now wanted to stabilise the country on familiar social and political patterns.[4] However, this is not to say that there was no governmental and national concern after 1656 over such matters as the preaching of the Gospel, the peace of the Church and religious toleration. Therefore, before we look at Owen's part in the opposition to the move to make Oliver the King of England, we shall note his involvement in these very areas, in particular at the conferences he attended concerning the settlement of religion in Scotland and the question as to whether or not Jews should be allowed to re-enter Britain from where they had been excluded since 1290.

In December 1655, the Lord Protector called a series of meetings

[1] His book against Goodwin was entitled *The Doctrine of the Saints' Perseverance* and is in *Works*, XI.
[2] *Works*, VIII, pp. 398ff.
[3] Entitled, *God's Presence with His People*, in *Works*, VIII, pp. 428ff.
[4] Ivan Roots, *The Great Rebellion*, 1966, pp. 210ff.

in London to discuss the petition of Menasseh ben Israel, the Jewish rabbi who was living in Amsterdam, which requested that Jews be allowed to settle in Britain. The petition raised serious theological and economic problems for the advisers whom Cromwell called in to study the matter. Most of the advisers, whether divines or laymen, were of the opinion that before the end of the age many Jews would be converted to the Christian Faith. Some of those present even went so far as to believe that the whole Jewish race would soon turn to Christ and then make Palestine the centre of a regenerated earth. At the same time, the merchants and the divines (who, in the main were "conservative" Englishmen) were well aware of the thrift and ability of the Jews and they feared the competition that would arise if Jews were allowed equal rights and opportunities. So they had to reconcile their desire to see the Jews given the opportunity to turn to Christ in what they believed was the most Christian nation on earth, with the challenge that the competitive ability of those Jews in finance and commerce would bring. Whilst no description exists as to what exactly was Owen's point of view, it is very probable that he favoured their entry on a strictly controlled basis. This would have meant that religion, relationships with the native English and the places of their habitation should be carefully defined and limited. The members of the conference, however, could not agree among themselves. Little was achieved except perhaps the revelation that it was easier to be Judaiophiles if the Jews remained in Holland or Spain then if there was a serious possibility of their entry into England! Conservatism triumphed in the conference but not in the mind and actions of the Protector. He was incensed at the lack of guidance he received from the divines and laymen and on his own initiative allowed a good number of Jews to settle in and around London during 1656 to 1658.[1]

The settlement of the problems of the Scottish Kirk was also complex and difficult. At various times after 1656 Owen was called to London to act as a negotiator or mediator between the two groups from Scotland who were in dispute and had been since 1650. During that year, when Owen himself was in Scotland talking to some of them, the Scottish clergy and leading laymen became divided into two parties: the Resolutioners, who were prepared to accept the aid of any man or party in their opposition to and war against the English and the Remonstrants (or Protestors), who signed a Remonstrance against all, including Charles II, who were not wholeheartedly for the Covenant. The quarrel continued after Cromwell's victories over the Scots and it kept the Kirk in constant tension. Each side wanted to control policy and place men of its choice into vacant livings. After Cromwell and his

[1] For a discussion of the conference and the events leading up to it see P. Toon, "The Question of Jewish Immigration," in *Puritans, the Millennium and the Future of Israel*.

Council had appointed fifty-seven men in August 1654 to act as "triers" in Scotland each party tried to gain control of this Board. Eventually both parties in dispute agreed to send representatives to London and to put their respective points of view to the Protector and his advisers. Owen was at Whitehall in February and April 1657 and from what James Sharp, the leader of the Resolutioners, had to say, he was a careful listener.[1] He was also much in demand: "Dr Owen is no small person here as to courtship" said Sharp on one occasion.[2] Since the early conferences did not lead to a speedy reconciliation, further meetings were arranged for July, and the Council of State appointed referees to hear the various arguments. This time Sharp definitely felt that Owen, with Joseph Caryl and George Griffith (two of the referees), was prejudiced against his party. Neither was Sharp pleased when a report, framed by Owen and Patrick Gillespie, a leader of the Protestors, with whom Owen became very friendly, was put before a meeting.[3] The report seemed to accept as just most of the demands of the Protestors. But Cromwell refused to be bound by the recommendation of Owen and his Independent colleagues. Two or more years earlier the advice of the Dean of Christ Church would probably have been acceptable; it was not so any longer. Sharp noticed this fact and reported back to Scotland that Owen was under a cloud at Court.[4]

If this was so, it was partly because Owen and the Lord Protector had become estranged over the question as to whether the latter should become King. This estrangement must have been painful to both men. To Owen, Cromwell was the greatest Englishman of the century, a man greatly used of God in the accomplishment of His purposes, and a man who held the preservation of Biblical religion and traditional learning near to his heart. This great respect is seen in the dedicatory epistles to Cromwell in *The Branch of the Lord* (1650), *Musarum Oxoniensum* (1654), and in the Latin Orations delivered at Oxford.[5] On the other hand, the appreciation of Owen by Cromwell is seen in his choice of him as chaplain, his nomination of him for five successive years as Vice-Chancellor, and in the choice of him as a preacher and adviser.

Perhaps the fact that Cromwell and Owen would eventually come to real disagreement was implicit in the report that reached London from Oxford in January 1656 to the effect that "Dr Wilkins of Wadham is likely to prove the man of men there, having lately married the

[1] *Register of the Consultations of the Ministers of Edinburgh*, ed. W. Stephen, Edinburgh, 1921, I, pp. 365-8.
[2] Ibid, p. 368.
[3] Ibid, II, pp. 66ff. Before this happened Owen was reported to have said that "he would be content to make a journey to Orkney" if this would help to bring peace to the Kirk.
[4] Ibid, II, p. 88.
[5] In 1657 Owen described Cromwell as "the wisest and most gallant of all men whom this age, rich in heroes, has produced." *Oxford Orations*, pp. 25 and 12.

Protector's sister, Dr French's widow."[1] It was also strangely foreshadowed in the strange episode of Owen's arrest at Whitehall Gate in May 1656.[2] Nearly a year later, London gossip, anticipating that Cromwell would soon accept the offer of the crown made to him by Parliament, was suggesting that when this happened Philip Nye would become Archbishop of Canterbury and John Owen the Archbishop of York.[3] This kind of talk could not have pleased Owen and it is not surprising to learn that, as Richard Cromwell told his brother Henry on the 7th March 1657, "Dr Owen hath been very angry and went in great haste out of London."[4] At this very time the the House of Commons was actually proposing to restore the House of Lords and also to raise Oliver to the status of King.[5] So Owen had good cause to be angry. He believed that the Republic had been created under the guidance of God in order to fulfil a particular role; he had taken the Engagement to be faithful to the Commonwealth without a King or House of Lords, and he well knew that, in England at least, if past experience was a useful guide, a monarchy and prelacy went hand in hand. Even if Oliver himself opposed prelacy his successors could so easily reintroduce it and thereby destroy all that which the revolution had achieved.

It was Owen's concern for the purity of the religion professed by the nation that obliged him, even if with reluctance, to help in the moves a few weeks later which finally persuaded Oliver not to accept the offer of the crown. On the 6th May 1657 Oliver met his brother-in-law, John Desborough, in St James' Park and was told by him that, because of the kingship issue, he "gave the cause and Cromwell's family up for lost." Though he would never act against his friend and brother, he would never act for him if he became King. After further discussion, reported Edmund Ludlow:[6]

> Desborough went home and there found Colonel Pride ... and having imparted to him the design of Cromwell to accept the crown, Pride answered,

[1] *The Flemings in Oxford*, ed. J. R. Magrath, Oxford, 1904, I, p. 101.
[2] C.S.P.D. (1655–6), p. 319, and (1656–7), p. 108. For some reason he was arrested whilst on his way to a service in Whitehall.
[3] C.S.P.D. (1656–7), p. 381. At least this is what Marchamont Needham, the newswriter, told the Protector in mid-March.
[4] Br. Museum Lansdowne MSS. 821. f.324.
[5] *Writings and Speeches of Cromwell*, IV, pp. 399ff. According to the *Diary of Sir Archibald Johnston*, ed. J. D. Ogilvie, III, p. 67, Owen was asked to preach before the Commons at a fast-day on Friday, 27 February 1657, but only after two hours of debate over the matter. Obviously he was not universally popular at Westminster. Cf. *C.J.*, VII, p. 497, and *Writings and Speeches*, IV, p. 415.
[6] *Memoirs of Edmund Ludlow*, ed. C. H. Firth, 1894, II, pp. 25–6. Orme, p. 126, states that Owen merely acted as a scribe for Pride and Desborough, but he is obviously wrong. Christopher Rogers, a Canon of Christ Church, signed a petition against kingship, C.R. s.v. C. Rogers. Henry Owen, John's brother, who was a Major in the army in Ireland and a member of Oliver's second Parliament, supported the move to make Oliver the King. C. Firth and G. Davies, *The Regimental History of Cromwell's Army*, p. 595. This must have distressed Owen also.

"He shall not." "Why," said Desborough, "how wilt thou hinder it?" To which Pride replied, "Get me a petition drawn and I will prevent it." Whereupon they both went to Dr Owen and having acquainted him with what happened, they persuaded him to draw up a petition according to their desires.

The petition was presented to Oliver and it did have some part in his final decision not to accept the offer of the crown. However, it opened a gulf between the Protector and his former chaplain which was never healed. From a reference that he made in a series of sermons in 1657 on the topic of temptation it would appear that Owen believed that Cromwell and many of his associates succumbed to the temptation of Satan during this period.

> We are like a plantation of men carried into a foreign country. In a short space they degenerate from the manners of the people from whence they came and fall into that of the country whereunto they are brought; as if there was something in the soil and the air that transformed them. Give me leave a little to follow my similitude: he that should see the prevailing party of these nations, many of those in rule, power, favour, with all their adherents, and remember that they were a colony of Puritans . . . translated by a high hand to the mountains they now possess, cannot but wonder how soon they have forgot the customs, manners, ways of their own old people and are cast into the mould of them that went before them in the places whereunto they are translated.[1]

The section from which this quotation comes begins with an explanation that the gravest temptations are usually accompanied with "strong reasons and pretences." Certainly plenty of these had been offered to persuade Cromwell to become King of England.

Even if Owen was opposed to Cromwellian kingship, he was pleased with the clauses on religion of the *Humble Petition and Advice*,[2] which became the legal basis of Oliver's second period as Lord Protector. The true Protestant Religion as contained in the Old and New Testaments and no other was to be held forth and asserted for the public profession of Britain, and at a suitable time a confession of faith was to be prepared. All who were ministers within the parish system would be expected to agree with and teach this doctrine. Nevertheless, any who professed faith in "God the Father, and in Jesus Christ His eternal Son, the true God, and in the Holy Spirit, co-equal with the Father and the Son, one God blessed forever" and "acknowledged the Holy Scriptures of the Old and New Testaments to be the revealed will and

---

[1] *Works*, VI, p. 112.
[2] For the text see *Constitutional Documents*, ed. Gardiner, pp. 447ff. Owen expressed his agreement with the articles of religion in his preface to the *Defence of Mr John Cotton* (1658) in *Works*, XIII, pp. 294-5. "The Parliament of the three Nations," he wrote, "has come up to my judgement."

Word of God," but who differed on secondary matters from the public profession were to be allowed to practise their religion under the law. No dissenter from the National Church was to be injured or molested except if he abused his liberty, inflicted injury on others, or disturbed the public peace. Popery, prelacy, and all forms of blasphemy and licentiousness were, however, to be totally banned.

Several interesting but unanswerable questions arise from Owen's agreement with the articles in the *Humble Petition*. Did the Congregationalists who met at the Savoy Palace in October 1658, for example, originally intend to produce a confession of faith which could have served as the basis for the confession required by the *Humble Petition*? An affirmative answer is probably the right one but no evidence is available to prove it and, furthermore, by the time the synod met the Protector was dead. Another question is: What did Owen think about the case of James Naylor, whose re-enactment at Bristol in October 1656 of Christ's entry into Jerusalem on a donkey caused so much discussion and trouble in the Commons and in Whitehall? During the debates at Westminster Sir John Reynolds suggested that Naylor would profit from having a conference with "Dr Owen, Mr Caryl and Mr Nye."[1] Whether or not Naylor did talk to Owen is not known but, knowing how the Vice-Chancellor treated the Quaker girls at Oxford in 1654, we may suppose that his attitude to Naylor would have been similar. That is, Naylor should be punished for his blasphemy, not for holding erroneous views.

One of the last appearances of Owen in London to take an active part in the affairs of Cromwell's administration was, it seems, to attend a meeting in November 1657 of the Committee on the Protestants of Piedmont.[2] Ever since news of the plight of these people had reached London in April 1655, men like Cromwell and Owen had been deeply touched by it. Milton spoke for them and for many others when he wrote:[3]

> Avenge O Lord thy slaughter'd Saints, whose bones
> Lie scatter'd on the Alpine mountains cold,
> Ev'n them who keep thy truth so pure of old
> When all our Fathers worship't Stocks and Stones
> Forget not: in thy book record their groanes
> Who were thy Sheep and in their antient Fold
> Slayn by the bloody *Pietmontese* that roll'd
> Mother and infant down the Rocks.

---

[1] *Diary of Thomas Burton*, ed. J. T. Rutt, 1823, I, pp. 79–80. There is a helpful chapter on the significance of the Naylor episode in Roots, *op. cit.*, pp. 203ff. A committee of ministers was actually appointed to meet Naylor but it did not include Owen. Cf. *Writings and Speeches of Cromwell*, IV, p. 359.

[2] *C.S.P.D.* (1657–8), p. 149. Cf. Paul, *The Lord Protector*, pp. 336–9, and Masson, *op. cit.*, V, pp. 40ff and 342.

[3] Entitled *On the Late Massacher in Piemont* in *Poetical Works*, II, p. 154.

A collection of money was taken for them in Oxford and at many other places and Owen spoke movingly of their plight in his Oration at the Act in 1655.[1] It was fitting that one of Owen's last activities for Oliver's administration should have been to work out ways of helping suffering Protestants, for this was a matter that touched both their hearts deeply.[2] During the winter and spring of 1658, Oliver's health deteriorated, and eventually, on the anniversaries of his great victories at Dunbar and Worcester, he died. And his former chaplain was not there to minister to him at his bedside. "I saw him not in his sickness nor some long time before," wrote Owen twelve years later.[3] It seems, however, that he took part in the State Funeral some weeks later.[4] In and through death they were finally reconciled.

---

[1] *Life and Times of Anthony Wood*, I, p. 198 and *Oxford Orations*, p. 29.
[2] Cf. *Correspondence*, No. 19, pp. 68–70. From Owen and others to the Evangelical Churches of Europe commending John Durie in his search for Protestant Unity. Durie also carried letters from Cromwell. In their search for Protestant Unity Owen and Cromwell were also at one.
[3] *Reflections on a Slanderous Libel* (1670) in *Works*, XVI, p. 274.
[4] *Public Intelligencer*, Nov. 22–29, 1658, and *Diary of Thomas Burton*, II, p. 529.

CHAPTER V

# CHANGING RESPONSIBILITIES

JUST BEFORE HIS DEATH ON THE 3RD SEPTEMBER 1658, OLIVER CROMWELL had nominated his son, Richard, as his successor in the Protectorate. To the dismay of royalists, the transition from Oliver to Richard took place without any major incidents. At Oxford a few energetic undergraduates pelted the Sheriff and also Owen's friend, Colonel Unton Croke, as the former proclaimed the new Protector; but the University and town accepted the news quietly.[1] So also did the Dean of Christ Church, who, according to Bishop Gilbert Burnet, was at Whitehall a week after Oliver's death taking part with Thomas Goodwin, Joseph Caryl and others in a day of fasting and prayer in which God was supposedly blamed for causing further troubles for England.[2]

Later that same month public interest was aroused in London as representatives of Congregational churches throughout England and Wales began to arrive for a synod scheduled to begin on the 29th September at the Savoy Palace. Those Londoners who claimed some ability to read the signs of the times could not have believed that the purpose of the synod was merely to discuss the finer points of theology. The state of the nation necessitated that the discussion be related to the political and religious situation in England and Wales. Church assemblies were rare occurrences. More than a decade earlier the famous Westminster Assembly of divines had met, but strictly speaking it was neither a Church Assembly nor even a Presbyterian Assembly. It was a meeting of divines who had been chosen by Parliament, and who submitted their work to Parliament.

It seems that the proposals for this Congregational gathering were made at Oxford in July after the annual Act. George Griffith, minister of the church meeting at the Charterhouse, was appointed correspondent and from him invitations went out to the churches. Some refused to send messengers fearing the synod had unacceptable, political implications, but in the end about two hundred men, mostly "lay" elders, representing over one hundred churches attended, Griffith was appointed clerk and a committee of six—Thomas Goodwin, Philip Nye, William Bridge, William Greenhill, Joseph Caryl (all of whom had been members

[1] Wood, *Life and Times*, I, p. 259.
[2] Burnet, *History of my own Time*, ed. O. Airy, Oxford, 1897, I, p. 147. I share Orme's suspicion (p. 190) that Burnet's account of these devotions is highly coloured and not reliable.

of the Westminster Assembly) and John Owen—was appointed to prepare the draft of a declaration of faith and church order. Six of these seven men were "triers" in the Cromwellian settlement of religion and the seventh, Bridge, was a ministerial assistant to the Norfolk "ejectors." Thus as a group they were deeply committed to the propagation of the Gospel through the parish system and this is clearly reflected in Article XIV of the statement they produced on the institution of churches.[1]

Days of fasting, prayer and hearing of the Word of God were held between sessions and on Sundays. By the 12th October the final draft was approved and John Owen, probably assisted by Philip Nye who had acted as chairman, was asked to write the preface.[2] Two days later a deputation from the conference waited on his highness, the Lord Protector, and presented him with a copy of *The Declaration of Faith and Order*. From the speech which Thomas Goodwin made on this occasion it appears that the basic purpose behind the conference and this document was—from the Congregational standpoint—"to clear ourselves of that scandal which not only some persons at home but of foreign parts have affixed on us, viz. That Independentism is the sink of all heresies and schisms."[3] The theological doctrines of the *Declaration of Faith* are those of orthodox Calvinism and in general agreement (though with perhaps a stronger emphasis on federal theology) with those set forth in the *Confession of Faith* produced by the Westminster Assembly. But whilst the former Confession was seen as a "testimony of faith" by its framers the latter was seen as "a test of faith." There were, however, important changes or additions with respect to the sections on the civil magistrate, the church and the Gospel.[4] It is in the *Declaration of*

---

[1] This article related to those "who are ingaged in the work of Publique Preaching, and enjoy the Publique Maintenance" and states that they need administer the Lord's Supper only to the members of the gathered church.

[2] There is some question as to the authorship of the preface but it is generally attributed to Owen. Sharp spoke of a "sweet preface penned as is thought by Owen," *Register of the Consultations of the Ministers of Edinburgh*, ed. William Stephen, II, p. 154.

[3] There is an abridgement of Goodwin's speech in *Mercurius Politicus* No. 438, and this is quoted by A. G. Matthews in *The Savoy Declaration of Faith and Order*, 1959, p. 12.

[4] Chap. xxix, sec. iii. reflects the Independent view of the magistrate:
Although the Magistrate is bound to encourage, promote and protect the professors and profession of the Gospel, and to manage and order civil administrations in a due subserviency to the interest of Christ in the world, and to that end to take care that men of corrupt minds and conversations do not licentiously publish and divulge Blasphemy and Errors in their own nature, subverting the faith, and inevitably destroying the souls of them that receive them; Yet in such differences about the Doctrines of the Gospel, or ways of the worship of God, as may befall men exercising a good conscience, manifesting it in their conversation, and holding the foundation, not disturbing others in their ways or worship that differ from them; there is no warrant for the Magistrate under the Gospel to abridge them of their liberty.
(In contrast the *Westminster Confession*, Chap. XX gave greater powers in ecclesiastical, doctrinal and moral affairs to the Magistrate.)
Chap. xxvi. sec. ii and v reflects the Independent view of the "visible Catholic Church of Christ" and its latter-day glory. In the first section it is emphasised that there are no

*the Institution of Churches* (part two of the document) that the principles of the Congregational way are expounded and acclaimed as "the Order which Christ himself hath appointed to be observed." We must briefly summarise these.

By the will of God the Father, all authority in the Church belongs to Jesus Christ. It is He who through the ministry of preaching and by the Holy Spirit, calls people out of the world into communion with Himself. Those whom He thus calls He commands to walk together in gathered churches for the purpose of mutual edification and for public worship. To each particular church, composed of regenerate saints who obey God's will, Christ gives all the necessary power and authority for the administration of worship and discipline. In a church there are four types of church officer: pastor, teacher, ruling elder and deacon. The ordination or setting apart of any church officer is administered by the local church usually in the presence of "messengers" from other churches. Only the pastor and teacher may administer the seals of the covenant of grace (Baptism and the Lord's Supper), but, in some cases, "gifted brethren" who do not hold office may preach. A pastor or a teacher may hold a parish living within the State Church and receive the "Publique Maintenance" and at the same time be an officer within a gathered church. By the powers given by Christ the individual church has full internal authority to govern its affairs and excommunicate guilty members, but synods of representatives from churches are helpful and may give advice to the churches.

A. G. Matthews suggests that anyone seeking a concrete example of the type of Congregationalism for which the *Declaration* was the *apologia* cannot do better than consult the records of the church at Yarmouth during the pastorate of Bridge, who was also the town preacher.[1] The experience of this large and influential church was probably drawn upon in the wording of the articles on church order. Yet the origins of this type of Congregationalism are to be traced to John Cotton and his book *The Keyes of The Kingdom of Heaven* (1644) which, as we saw in chapter one, was introduced to the British public by Nye and Goodwin and was instrumental in leading Owen to appreciate the Congregational way. Nevertheless, the *Savoy Declaration* shows no signs of dependence on the *Cambridge Platform* (1648), the most important monument of early New England Congregationalism. The reasons for this are obvious.

church officers who have authority to exercise their ministry to the whole number of professing Christians in the world. This reflects Congregational thinking and is opposed to Presbyterian and Anglican theology which teach that a man is ordained to the Catholic Church not to a congregation.

The whole of chapter xx is an addition and emphasises that salvation is received through the hearing of the word of God. The works of creation or providence, or the light of nature, cannot "make discovery of Christ." Obviously this section had been inspired by the growth of natural religion since 1648.

[1] *Savoy Declaration*, ed. Matthews, p. 25.

The situation in Massachusetts was vastly different from that in Britain and the *Declaration* was written partly with the non-Congregational public in mind while the *Platform* was composed as a concise text-book to regulate the churches of the new colonies.

The preface to the *Declaration* provides very interesting reading. After a justification of the need for confessions of faith in the Church of God, and of religious toleration for those of orthodox theology, whatever their churchmanship, there are sections which describe in what particulars the *Declaration* differs from the *Westminster Confession*, and upon what legal basis current English Protestant Christianity was based. A. G. Matthews declares that "anyone reading Owen's preface might interpret its concluding pages as a thinly veiled plea for the restoration of the remanant of the Long Parliament, the Rump." Furthermore, he asserts that Owen was "not putting into print an invention of his own, but repeating a fiction from the doctrinaire stock-in-trade of his party (the Republican party) which he had swallowed with the credulity of a recent convert."[1] This is an extraordinary statement but Matthews justifies it on three basic grounds. First, a small but significant republican group existed in London (Ludlow, Vane, etc.) and Owen knew its members. Secondly, the Accommodation Order, passed by the Commons in 1644, was printed in thick black italics in the preface and described as "the foundation of that freedom and liberty" enjoyed in 1658 by the Congregational churches.[2] Finally, there is no mention of the Cromwellian Ordinances of 1654 for the settlement of religion in which so many of the men who were at the synod were intimately involved. These are passed over as if they never existed.

Against Matthews it must be emphasised that no evidence (if the Preface is not taken into account) exists to prove that at this time Owen was a doctrinaire republican who wanted to overthrow the Protectorate. The main purpose of the final section of the preface is to argue that orthodox Christians, whether of Congregationalist or Presbyterian opinion, should have the right to practise their different types of church government and that this right was guaranteed by the Long Parliament in 1644. Indeed, Owen argued, the so-called Presbyterian settlement of 1645-6 was not considered to be a full Presbyterian settlement by dedicated Presbyterians. The London presbyterian classis made this clear in its book *Jus Divinum Regiminis Ecclesiastici* (1646), which declared their views on church government and showed just how much the

---

[1] Ibid, pp. 42-43. For the political thought of the Republicans see Perez Zagorin, *A History of Political Thought in the English Revolution*, 1954.

[2] This Order required that a Committee of Lords and Commons seek to unite the Presbyterian and Independent groups in the Westminster Assembly and if this was impossible to endeavour to find a way to provide toleration for those of tender conscience who could not submit to a Presbyterian Settlement. Jordan, *The Development of Religious Toleration. 1640-1660*, pp. 53ff, and *Savoy Declaration*, ed. Matthews, p. 43.

national legislation fell short in implementing them. In like manner, the Congregational churches were now publishing to the world their views on church government, which they practised. If asked where the Cromwellian Settlement fitted into all this, Owen would probably have replied that it was simply a State system of providing for a godly and learned ministry in the parishes of England and Wales and thereby filling a gap created by the failure to implement the legislation of the Long Parliament. He may even have believed that the ordinances of the Protector and his Council were invalid now that he was dead unless they were renewed by the new government and confirmed in Parliament. So, it seems that the Congregational brethren, realising that their period of ascendancy in the counsels of the nation was virtually at an end and that Richard favoured Presbyterianism, decided that their best plan was to plead for a basic religious toleration and for unity amongst those conservative Protestants who were opposed to prelacy and the Book of Common Prayer. They were being wise and tactful in appealing to the order of a Parliament which was held in such honour by both Independents and Presbyterians. This explanation does not solve all the problems raised by the preface, especially the large claim made for the Accommodation Order, but it does cast serious doubts on Matthews' assertion that Owen was a doctrinaire republican. Furthermore, as we shall see later in this chapter, Owen's activities during 1659, though difficult to unravel and interpret, do not provide evidence for doctrinaire republicanism.

Soon after the Congregational synod ended Richard and his Council made the decision to call a Parliament.[1] Oliver's Lords were to be summoned to the other house and the Commons to be elected "according to the ancient rights of the nation" in the days of Charles I, except for the disqualification of overt papists and royalists. This return to the old ways was possible because the *Humble Petition and Advice* had been silent on electoral provisions. Though the elections brought back into Parliament some swordsmen and some commonwealthsmen the majority were moderates or neuters who could be swayed one way or the other on most topics but who were in general agreement that the independence and power of the army had to be reduced. As part of the official opening ceremony on the 27th January, 1659, Thomas Goodwin was chosen to preach to Richard, his Council, and the Lords and Commons in Westminster Abbey. He spoke from Psalm 35:10, "Mercy and Truth are met together; righteousness shall look down from heaven."[2] Later that day the Commons chose their Speaker and other officials and then decided to set apart the 4th February as a day of humiliation. Four

[1] For the complicated history of this period see Godfrey Davies, *The Restoration of Charles II*, San Marino, 1955.
[1] Ibid, p. 49. The sermon was never printed.

ministers were chosen to assist but the order in which they were to be named provoked a discussion. Eventually they were named as Edward Reynolds, Thomas Manton, John Owen and Edmund Calamy.[1] Had it not been for the forceful speaking of General John Lambert then Owen would probably have been named last of the four. Yet the fact that Owen was to be named last suggests that he was regarded by most M.P.s as being in close contact with the army leaders and therefore not to be trusted to the extent that the three Presbyterian ministers could be trusted.

Whilst Owen was certainly a close friend of the grandees of the army, his sermon on the 4th February shows no signs of being a defence of the power of the army in national affairs.[2] It was a call (and a fairly unpopular one if the reaction against it mentioned by Owen in the dedicatory epistle is to be taken at its face value) to promote the kingdom of God in England and not add to the bitterness caused by sectarian and denominational rivalry. From his text, Isaiah 4:5, he deduced two basic propositions which were then applied to the situation in the country. They were: "the presence of Christ with any people is the glory of any people" and "the presence of God in special providence over a people attends the presence of Christ in grace with a people." In his view Christ was present with a people in two ways. First, in the preaching of the Gospel and the administration of its ordinances, and secondly, through His Spirit dwelling in the hearts of true believers. So looking back on British history since 1642, it could be said that all spiritual reformation which had been achieved in the revolution was by "the Spirit of the Lord of Hosts." "It was not by prudence of councils, or strength of armies above that of our enemies that we prevailed," stated Owen, "but by faith and prayer: and if any one be otherwise minded I leave him for his resolution to the judgement of the great day, when all transactions shall be called over again." The great danger in 1659 was that many people were falling to temptation and were doubting the glorious work of God in England in the last two decades. And as the true greatness of Britain was intimately connected with the progress of the cause of Christ, it was most necessary that men realise that the strategy of Satan was to cause the doubts, quarrels and divisions within the ranks of professing Christians. In knowledge of this, the preacher's advice to his hearers was that they each seek to let Christ rule in their own hearts, that they oppose the "overflowing flood of profaneness" that was spreading through the land, and that they "value, encourage

---

[1] *C.J.* VII. 595-6.
[2] It was published as *The Glory and Interests of Nations* and is in *Works* VIII, pp. 453ff. Davies, *op. cit.*, pp. 453ff. describes this sermon as though it were preached in May 1659 to the restored Rump. Only one of the other three sermons was printed and even that was in an abbreviated form. It was by Reynolds and is in *The Substance of Two Sermons* (1659). His theme was "unity of Judgement and love of the brethren."

and close with them in and with whom is the presence of Christ." The question naturally followed as to who were the people in whom was Christ's Spirit. Owen answered this by saying that they were people who not only spoke in religious language but who were obviously righteous in their living. Righteousness was not to be judged by men's views on either civil or church matters but by the quality of their lives. Those who were committed to a particular form of church polity or a particular philosophy of the civil state could not have been greatly encouraged by Owen for his intention was to persuade men to seek after those essential spiritual principles which united men who were of different judgements on secondary matters. His view that the unity of the true saints and their encouragement was of far greater importance than the promotion of any theory of the government of Church or State was, needless to say, not a popular one. At this time it seemed that each religious and political group was intent on promoting its own ends without regard to the good of the nation and its people.

Unfortunately, unity of the saints seemed less probable as the months of 1659 went by. During February a whole crop of pamphlets appeared, written by sectarian preachers and republicans, which called for a return to the "good old cause" as they understood it.[1] By early March many soldiers were showing signs of losing patience with the Parliament since nothing was being done to settle their arrears of pay. As the junior officers resumed their regular meetings, which they had last held in 1657, it became obvious that the army was faction-ridden. Colonels Ingoldsby, Goffe and Whalley, with many officers in Ireland and Scotland, supported the Protector. Others, the Commonwealthsmen, including Colonels Ashfield, Lilburne and Fitch, with many inferior officers, objected to the kingly nature of the régime established under the Humble Petition and Advice and wanted a return to some form of republicanism. A third grouping, the Wallingford House Party—so called after the residence of General Fleetwood—which included most of the senior officers, stood for the maintenance of the power of the grandees both in the army and civil matters.[2] It was Owen's wish to remain on the best of terms with each group and seek to heal the differences. He abhorred the existence of faction and party-spirit as much in the army as in Parliament or at Oxford.

Possibly it was with a view to healing the divisions in the army that Owen gathered a Congregational church of officers and their families in London. On the 15th March it was reported by Arthur Annesley to Henry Cromwell that "Dr Owens hath gathered a church in the

---

[1] For an account of this preoccupation with the "good old cause" see A. H. Woolrych, "The Good Old Cause and the Fall of the Protectorate," *Cambridge Historical Journal*, XIII, 2. pp. 133–161.
[2] Davies, *op. cit.*, p. 74.

Independent way and that Lord Fleetwood, Lord Desborough, Lord Sidenham, Berry, Goffe and divers others were admitted members." And significantly, he added that this church "hath divers constructions put upon it and is not that I heare well liked at Wallingford House."[1] A week earlier James Sharp had told a Scottish correspondent that "Owen hath lately erected a congregation about Whitehall of which Fleetwood, Desburrie, Lambert, Berrie, Whaley are members, upon a state project."[2] These two references supply us with all the known members of the church. Baxter stated that it met in Wallingford House but this is unlikely at this stage.[3] The known membership does indicate that representatives from at least two of three factions in the army were on friendly terms with Owen and with each other; and it may be that amongst the membership which is not known to us there were Commonwealthsmen. In view of the political situation in London Owen was probably tactless to engage in the role of pastor of such a church since its very existence, as the above two quotations make clear, was open to misunderstanding. His aims were honourable but he would perhaps have been better employed in Christ Church, where he was still Dean, and where he was leaving the main work of the College to the Sub-Dean and Chapter. He judged, however, that the cause of Christ was best served by his presence in London where he could plead for unity amongst the saints.[4]

Towards the end of March the Wallingford House party made overtures to the civilian Republicans in the House of Commons and a meeting was arranged with Edmund Ludlow. At this meeting Ludlow asked the officers to join with the Commonwealthsmen in the army and the Republicans in the Commons to restore the government "which had cost the nation so much blood to establish"—the Rump of the Long Parliament.[5] The senior officers, however, had no desire to ruin their friends who supported the Protector, and nothing definite was agreed; but, as subsequent events showed, they underestimated the strength of the Commonwealthsmen in the army. The next move of the grandees was to call a General Council of officers. This met in a dark mood on the 2nd April and composed a strongly-worded statement, *The Humble Representation and Petition*. They contended that the good old cause was frequently derided in public, that many Cavaliers were entering Britain, that the army was in great extremity for lack of pay and that they, the

[1] Br. Mus. Lansdowne MSS. 823. f.251.
[2] *Register of the Consultations*, II, p. 154.
[3] Baxter, *Reliquiae Baxterianae*, I. p. 101.
[4] It is interesting to note that during Owen's prolonged absence from Oxford there was further disagreement over the nature and type of University Visitors. According to Wood, *Life and Times*, I, p. 268, Conant wrote to Owen telling him that "he must haste to Oxon for godliness lay a-gasping." Unfortunately we have no account of Owen's reaction to this request.
[5] Ludlow, *Memoirs*, ed. C. H. Firth, II, pp. 61ff.

officers, intended to help the Protector and Parliament "in plucking the wicked out of their places."

The sober Whitelocke judged that the petition was "the beginning of Richard's fall" and Annesley compared it to "lightning before thunder, both to the Protector and to the House."[1] Richard received this potentially explosive document on the 6th April and two days later sent a copy of it, with his own letter attached, to both Houses of Parliament, but, as was expected, it was not received with enthusiasm. The dilatoriness of Parliament served to increase the frustration of the army which decided to set aside the 13th April as a day of fasting and prayer. With Hugh Peter, Owen took part in the devotions but afterwards Peter complained that he did not know what was the true purpose of the gathering.[2] He felt that many officers saw it as a means of paving the way for a momentous decision—the overthrow of Richard—just as a prayer-meeting at Windsor in 1648 had prepared the ground for the decision to put Charles I on trial. Owen, it seems, made no such protest, for his close relationship with the officers served to provide him with information about their intentions. His agreement to participate would have been made because he wished to seek to heal differences and promote unity despite his knowledge of the intentions of some of the 500 officers.

A few days later Richard ordered Desborough to disband the General Council of officers. The latter, however, refused, claiming the Council's right to meet whenever it pleased until its just demands were met, and suggesting that in the view of the Council the Parliament should be dissolved. On the 19th and the 20th April there was a deceptive calm before the decisive events of Thursday the 21st. On that day Richard sent a messenger to Fleetwood requesting that he come to Whitehall. The general, knowing the intention was to arrest him, refused. So Richard decided to call a general rendez-vous of the army at Whitehall in opposition to Fleetwood's order that it meet at St James. Though Oliver could have done this and met an obedient army, his son did not have the necessary prestige and so most of the army assembled at St James. Richard had failed and later that same evening he was visited by the grandees led by Desborough. With suitable threats they persuaded him to sign a commission for the dissolution of Parliament on the next day. This visit to Richard followed some hours of intense discussion at Wallingford House at which Owen was present. Thomas Manton had also been invited but, arriving late, he heard what he believed to be the loud voice of Owen from within the room saying "he must down and he shall down." Taking this as a possible reference to the overthrow of the Protector he decided to go home and have no part in the proceedings.[3]

[1] Cited by Davies, op. cit., pp. 77–8.
[2] Davies, op. cit., p. 79 n. 42.
[3] Daniel Neal, History of the Puritans, 1738, IV, p. 209 and Orme, p. 213.

The dissolution of Richard's Parliament marked the practical collapse of the Protectorate. One contemporary witness noted, with some sarcasm, that "Wallingford House is the scene for action. There . . . the greatest officers seeke God for counsel and act their own way."[1] Owen took part in their devotions as well as in those of the junior officers at St James.[2] From the *Diary* of Sir Archibald Johnston of Wariston we are able to gain some indication of Owen's thoughts and activities between the 30th April and the 3rd May, the period which led to the decision to recall the Rump of the Long Parliament. On the 30th April Sir Archibald wrote:

> Foranoon I mett with Doctor Owen, Col. Sydnham, Mr King, Griffeth and at last with my Lord Fleetwood, and told them largely my reasons aginst calling the Long Parliament. I heard they had agreed to byde one be another and manteane civil and spiritual libertyes already obteaned, and submit to what government God shal inclyne them to. I heard the Protector was not very sensible of his condition tho Doctor Owen spak thryse to him.[3]

This clearly indicates that no decision had yet been taken by Fleetwood and his fellow grandees to call a Parliament despite the many petitions they had received for the recall of the Rump. Also, it seems, Owen was acting as an intermediary between the Protector and the senior officers. By the 3rd May, after more thought and prayer a major decision seemed in sight.

> I mett, after a report of the resolving on a long Parliament with Dr Owen who told me he had better hoopes of things going in a better waye nor before to eschow the calling of the Long Parliament unles they were secured anent the gourvernment, what they thought fittest, to keepe the Protectors title and dignitye, to haive an good Counsel and the uther House or Senate fixed and the new representative qualifyed. I heard the officers was at fasting and praying this daye, thereafter that some of them was meeting at Sir Hary Vaynes with him, Hazelrig, Salloway, Ludlow and with them Jones, Sydnham, Lambert and Berry.[4]

The notion of a titular Protectorate, a godly Council of State, a Senate and a new Parliament was not Owen's idea. The grandees wanted to retain a nominal Protectorate, appoint a Council of State they could trust, and have a second chamber acting as the guardian of certain fundamental laws as well as of their own continued existence. Only few senior officers wanted to recall the Rump although as Sir Archibald mentioned they were having discussions with the Republican leaders.

[1] *Nicholas Papers*, ed. G. F. Farmer, 1886-1920, IV, p. 122.
[2] Woolrych, *op. cit.*, p. 155.
[3] *Diary of Archibald Johnston*, III, p. 106,
[4] Ibid, III, pp. 107-8.

CHANGING RESPONSIBILITIES                        113

These talks were not conclusive and it was left to Owen to intervene. He decided that the recall of the Rump was the only feasible solution to the complex situation and so he acquired from Ludlow a list of about one hundred and sixty names of men who were still alive who had been members of the Rump and presented them to Fleetwood in order to convince him that they could make a viable Parliament.[1] Whether or not Owen felt that a titular Protectorate could be preserved alongside the Rump or whether or not he felt some senate could also be nominated we do not know. Relunctantly, and, it seems, with little thought of what problems a restored Rump would pose, the army leaders accepted the idea and on 6 May the order was given for the members to return to Westminster after their long absence of six years. On the 8th May, which was a Sunday, they heard a sermon from Owen, but regrettably, this was never printed. So we are deprived of an important indication of how he saw the rôle of this resurrected Parliament. By this time Richard had realised that the existence of a titular Protectorate was intolerable and on the 25th May he resigned to return to the life of a country gentleman.

It is most difficult to evaluate Owen's share in the responsibility for the necessary resignation of Richard Cromwell. Richard Baxter had no doubts as to Owen's guilt:

> Dr Owen and his assistants did the maine work: his high spirit now thought the place of Vicechancellor & Deane of Christs Church to be too low: and if the Protector will not do as he would have him, he shall be no Protector: he gathereth a church at Lieutenant Generall Fleetwoods quarters at Wallingford House, consisting of the active officers of the Army! (This Church-gathering hath bin the Church-scattering project.) His parts, & confidence, and busybodiness, & interest in those men who did give him the opportunity to do his exploits; & quite put Hugh Peters besides the chairs (who had witt enough to be against the fall of Rich. Cromwell, seeing how quickly his owne would follow). Here fasting & prayer, with Dr Owens magisteriall counsell, did soon determine the Case, with the proud & giddy headed Officers, that Richards Parliament must be dissolved, and then he quickly fell himself.[2]

In the main Baxter's facts are right (except perhaps for the placing of the church as meeting initially in Wallingford House), but his interpretation, as we would expect from one who had little sympathy with the Independents, is biased against Owen. A similar accusation was made by George Vernon in 1670.[3] He wrote that Owen became the "Instru-

---

[1] Ludlow, *Memoirs*, II, p. 74.
[2] See Geoffrey F. Nuttall, "Richard Baxter's Apology (1654); its occasion and composition," *Journal of Ecclesiastical History*, IV, 1, pp. 69ff., where this section is printed. The abridged form is in *Reliquiae*, I. p. 101. Matthew Sylvester, the editor of the *Reliquiae*, did not wish to print even the abridged form of Baxter's comments and he tried to get some explanation of them from Dr Owen's widow but she refused to co-operate.
[3] Vernon, *A Letter to a Friend*, 1670, p. 28.

ment of Ruine" to Richard "because that rickshaw of Authority and Policy espoused the Presbyterian interest." Replying to Vernon, Owen claimed that he had no more to do with the "setting up and pulling down" of the Protector than Vernon himself.[1] In saying this Owen was claiming too much. While it is true that he had had no part in making Richard the Lord Protector he certainly had some part, howbeit a small and indirect one, in the fall of Richard. Asty, however, felt that Owen could not be blamed in any way for Richard's resignation and he quoted a letter belonging to James Forbes of Gloucester to show that during the days when the grandees were deciding that Richard's Parliament should be terminated, Owen was so worried by the situation that he became sick and had to ask a friend of Forbes to preach for him in Whitehall.[2] If this is so, it is somewhat surprising that Owen did not immediately leave London and return to Christ Church where he could have served a more useful purpose. The fact that he stayed in London and involved himself in the discussions of the officers in Wallingford House as well as the fact that he preached to the Rump do involve him to some degree in culpability for what occurred. Unfortunately for him and his cause, he was involved in the complex affairs of the nation at a time when religious zeal, personal amibition and party prejudice were rampant and intertwined and so he was to some extent involved in many of the results of pride, ambition and selfishness, even though these were sins against which he had often preached. Nevertheless, his own conscience (and he was an honest man) informed him, as he told Vernon, that he was not responsible for the downfall of Richard. And, because of lack of further evidence, we must leave the matter there.

If the grandees had recalled the Rump as a smokescreen for their own rule, they soon found that life was far from comfortable for them. Fleetwood was officially Commander-in-Chief of the army but his powers were very limited. He could not, for example, personally appoint junior officers since all appointments had to have parliamentary approval. The new Council of State was also firmly civilian and closely related to Parliament. Naturally, royalist activists saw the opportunity for action and Lord Mordaunt shewed his enthusiasm for Charles II by giving himself the task of reorganising the royalist interest in England. He sought to unite the old royalists who had stood by the king in the civil wars and the new royalists who were worried by the state of the nation. In June such was gossip in London that bets were being laid that the Rump would not last more than two more weeks. Realising the gravity of the problems facing the country, Owen's church, which by this time had begun to meet in Wallingford House, sent a letter to the Congregational church at Yarmouth, which, as we noted above, was

[1] Owen, *Reflections on a Slanderous Libel*, in *Works*, XVI, p. 274.
[2] Asty, p. xix. The friend of Forbes is not named.

one of the most important churches in the country.[1] The entry for the 7th June 1659 in the Yarmouth church book reads:

> This day the Church received a letter from the Church at Wallingford House desiring advice from the Church what they apprehended was needful for the Commonwealth; the Church considering it, ordered the elders to write to them, thanking them for their love and care of them; but considering civil business, the Church, as a Church, desire not to meddle with.

Of similar import is the entry for the 10th July when another letter has been received:

> Ordered by the Church upon the receipt of a letter from the Church at Wallingford House, that Wednesday, the 13th July, should be set apart to humble our souls before the Lord, both in regard to the sins of the nation and also to seek the Lord for direction and assistance for the carrying on the Lords work in the nation.

Regrettably this second letter from Owen's church is not extant and we are thus deprived of interesting insights both into the names of the signatories and also into the contents of the letter. One thing at least is certain—Owen and the church elders (Desborough, Fleetwood, Berry?) felt that the advice of William Bridge and his church was extremely valuable. This, in turn, suggests that the grandees were totally confused as to what they could or should do for the preservation of the good old cause. Unlike such men as Ludlow and Vane and some of their junior officers they were not committed to doctrinaire republicanism; rather, they wanted to preserve their own place in the nation and also guarantee certain basic civil and religious liberties. But how to do this was a problem.

The passage of events, however, took the control of the future out of the hands of most of those who formed the church in Wallingford House. Although the royalists hoped that local rebellions would break out in many places, only in Cheshire did anything happen which looked like a serious threat to the authority of the Rump. There Sir George Booth raised about four thousand men and occupied Chester on the 2nd August with the enthusiastic support of the local Presbyterian clergy. News of this uprising reached Westminster on the 3rd which was a fast-day. Owen, Caryl and Lockyer were assisting in the devotions. Immediately John Lambert was appointed as commander-in-chief of the parliamentary army and sent North to deal with the rebellion.[2]

[1] A copy of the Yarmouth church book is among the MSS of the Library of New College, London, and I am grateful to Dr G. F. Nuttall for allowing me to consult it. The two following entries are quoted by John Stoughton, *History of Religion in England*, 1881, III., p. 28. Cf. John Browne, *History of Congregationalism . . . in Norfolk and Suffolk*, 1877, pp. 225-8.
[2] Davies, *op. cit.*, pp. 140ff.

On the 19th he scattered Booth's army at Winnington Bridge near Nantwich. Earlier in the month, when the very worst was feared, the Congregational churches had offered to raise three regiments for the use of Parliament and John Owen had hurried back to Oxford in order to raise a troop of cavalry for the defence of the University, just as he had done four years earlier when similar uprisings were expected.[1] Meanwhile the victorious army, justly claiming that the defeat of the great royalist conspiracy was largely its own work, began to show its discontent and to press for its arrears of pay and for reforms. As a result of this agitation the Rump revoked the commission of some officers and ordered the arrest of Lambert. His answer to all this was to surround the House and refuse to allow the Speaker and members to enter. Once more the Rump had been closed by the military!

The news that the army had expelled the Rump reached General Monck in Scotland on the 18th October. He had prepared for the national emergency and immediately declared that he would restore civil government. His decision meant that the armies of the Commonwealth were divided amongst themselves. After purging his forces of about one hundred and fifty officers, Monck wrote to Fleetwood, Lambert, and the Speaker of the House of Commons, to make clear to them his disapproval of what had happened and his intention to uphold Parliament. This intention was also affirmed in the *Declaration of the Officers of the Army in Scotland to the Churches in the Three Nations*, copies of which were available in London before the end of October. Representatives of the London Congregational churches studied this document and were not wholly satisfied as to Monck's promises. So they decided to send immediately to Scotland two ministers, Joseph Caryl and Matthew Barker, and two ruling elders, Edward Whalley and William Goffe, both of whom had supported the Protector in the recent troubles and were thus likely to be acceptable to Monck. They also wrote a letter to the General to be taken by the deputation; amongst those who signed it were John Owen, Philip Nye, William Greenhill, and Henry Scobell, the former clerk to the Privy Council and Council of State.[2]

The deputation was received at Holyrood by Monck, two colonels, two chaplains and the Scottish Judge Advocate, Barrow. Caryl delivered a speech the substance of which had been agreed in London. He claimed that the interruption of Parliament could not be justified but even so General Monck had no right to intervene in the matter. His work was to keep Scotland quiet. If the armies of the Commonwealth continued to quarrel only the Royalists and Prelatists, the "common enemy," would gain any benefit, whilst the saints of God would suffer. Replying,

---

[1] B. Whitelocke, *Memorials of the English Affairs*, Oxford, 1853, IV., p. 357, and C.S.P.D. (1659–60), p. 110.
[2] *Correspondence*, No. 58 pp. 105–6. The London Churches to Monck.

Monck affirmed that it was Lambert who had caused all the trouble and that Parliament must be restored. When the deputation left for London it carried Monck's reply to the letter from the London churches. In it he promised that their "interest, liberty and encouragement" would be dear to him.[1]

When Owen heard that the commissioners of the Scottish and English armies had signed an agreement in London on the 15th November, he decided to send a personal letter to the General, who he realised held the balance of power in Britain. "There are," he wrote,[2] "two evils that we have cause to fear: the one is the prevailing of the Common Enemy over us; the other the prevalency of fanatical, self-seeking persons amongst us." It is difficult to decide whom he had in mind as "fanatical:" perhaps it was Lambert or perhaps the Republican leaders, Ludlow, Vane and others. To avert the dangers from all sides the armies must unite. One obstacle to their unity seemed to be a difference of opinion concerning the Rump; Monck wanted it restored whilst Fleetwood, Lambert, Desborough and others did not. So Owen expressed his own viewpoint:

> Most of the persons of that number are my old friends and acquaintance. I may say freely that I ventured somewhat for their sitting. I know nothing at all of their dissolution, being for about five weeks before absent from this place; nor shall I take off from their esteem by a review of their actings during their session. Yet this I shall say, that it were better that both they, and I ,and hundreds of better men than myself were in the ends of the earth, than that this cause should be ruined by the armies' contest about them. For my own part I am satisfied with these two things: first, that without their restoration a free State or Commonwealth may be settled, the Common Enemy defeated, the ministry preserved, reformation carried on and all the ends of our engagements satisfied, if your Lordship and those with you concur in the work; and secondly that their reinvestiture cannot be effected without the blood of them whose ruin I am persuaded you seek not . . .

This extract makes clear that Owen's republican sentiments were not sufficiently strong to press for the restoration of the Rump. He feared that it could not return without the ruin of Lambert and others. Yet just what kind of government he had in mind instead of the Rump is not clear. His friend, Lord Fleetwood, who was still nominally the Commander-in-Chief of all the forces, and the Council of officers, talked of electing a new Parliament which would meet on the 24th January 1660, but this came to nothing. By this time all that Owen wanted was a government which would give Congregational churches the freedom to worship God according to their views of the divine will

[1] *Correspondence*, No. 60, p. 109. Monck to Owen and others.
[2] *Correspondence*, No. 59, pp. 106–8. Owen to Monck.

and would also guarantee basic civil liberties. So in closing his letter to Monck he assured his Lordship that he was "a true lover of his country's liberties, an enemy of all usurpations upon it and one resolved to live and die with the sober, godly interest."

In reply to Owen, Monck emphasised that he dared not sit still and see the laws and liberties of the people go to ruin. His concience obliged him to free his country from the intolerable slavery of government by the sword and to restore the sovereignty of Parliament.[1] As these letters were passing between London and Scotland, the London Congregational churches were busy corresponding with other churches. Owen's church at Wallingford House, for example, wrote several letters to churches in East Anglia and as a result a meeting of messengers from East Anglian Congregational churches was arranged to be held at Norwich on the 30th November. This meeting then elected representatives, including Bridge of Yarmouth, to attend a further meeting in London in December.[2] Meanwhile, it was becoming clear that the Council of Officers who met at Wallingford House no longer had much control over the situation in England. Men from Lambert's army, which had gone North to prevent the Scottish army entering England, were beginning to desert. Soldiers sent by Fleetwood to subdue the rebellious Portsmouth garrison went over to Monck's cause. So we are not surprised to learn that Owen was at Wallingford House on the 21st December sympathising with the grandees as they bemoaned the state of the nation and the loss of their power.[3] Though letters continued to pass between Scotland and London they were of no avail; Monck had made up his mind and soon he would act decisively.

At the December meeting of Congregational messengers from East Anglia and London, several important resolutions were passed. When Bridge reported back to his own church it was decided to enter four of them into the church book.[4] They were:

1. We judge a Parliament to be expedient for the preservation of the peace of these nations; and withal we do desire that all due care be taken that the Parliament be such as may preserve the interest of Christ and his people in these nations.
2. As touching the magistrate's power in matters of faith and worship we have declared our judgments in our late confession; and though we greatly prize our Christian liberties, yet we profess our utter dislike and abhorrence of a universal toleration, as being contrary to the mind of God in His Word.
3. We judge that the taking away of tithes for the maintenance of ministers

---

[1] *Correspondence*, No. 61, pp. 110–112. Monck to Owen.
[2] Browne, *op. cit.*, p. 225.
[3] Davies, *op. cit.*, pp. 186–7.
[4] Quoted by Stoughton, *op. cit.*, III, pp. 28–9. Cf. G. F. Nuttall, *Visible Saints*, p. 141.

until as full a maintenance be equally secured and as legally settled, tends very much to the destruction of the ministry and the preaching of the Gospel in these nations.
4. It is our desire that countenance be not given unto, nor trust reposed in the hands of Quakers, they being persons of such principles as are destructive to the Gospel and inconsistent with the peace of civil societies.

Again we see the desire for a Parliament but no suggestion as to how it should be elected. Perhaps such churches as that at Yarmouth who did not wish to become involved in politics insisted that the above statement was all that churches could legitimately say. The other three articles reveal the Congregational brethren as conservatives, desiring to maintain the parish system, the tithe system and a restricted religious liberty. During 1659 many radicals, and most of all the Quakers, had pressed for complete religious toleration as well as for the closing or remodelling of the Universities. Owen himself had felt obliged both to write against the Quakers in 1658 and to publish in 1659 a brief tract entitled [*Unto the two questions sent me last night, I pray accept of the ensuing answer, under the title of,*] *Two Questions concerning the Power of the Supreme Magistrate about Religion and the Worship of God, with one about Tithes, proposed and resolved.*[1] Owen affirmed that the supreme magistrate in a Christian nation should exert his legislative and executive power to support and preserve the profession of the Christian faith and the worship of God as well as to forbid and restrain such principles and practices which are directly contrary to that faith and worship. Yet he denied that the supreme magistrate had the power to make Christians subscribe to a confession of faith or to worship God according to a fixed pattern. Finally, he supported the system of tithes as the only feasible way at that time to maintain the Christian ministry. There was nothing new here but the situation in which he found himself with Quakers pressing for the abolition of tithes and Presbyterians pressing for the introduction of a Presbyterian National Church made him feel it necessary to reiterate his views.

As Monck and his army drew near London it was reported that Owen and Nye were talking optimistically of collecting £100,000 for the use of the other armies provided they would undertake to protect the liberty of the Congregational churches.[2] But, even if this money could be raised, it was too late. On the 3rd February Monck entered London and by the 21st February the excluded members of the Long Parliament were recalled to Westminster after an absence of nearly twelve years

[1] In *Works*, XIII, p. 508. The *Exercitationes adversus Fanaticos* (1658), is in *Works*, XVI. At least two tracts from Quaker circles against Owen were published in 1659–60: they were: *Winding Sheet for Englands Ministry*, which was anonymous, and *The Rustics Alarm* by Samuel Fisher. Cf. also *Correspondence*, No. 64, p. 116, for a printed criticism of Owen from Quaker circles.
[2] D. Neal, *History of the Puritans*, (ed. E. Parsons) 1811, II, p. 462.

to join those forty members who had begun to resit on the 26th December 1659. The Presbyterians were once more in the ascendant and, not unexpectedly, by a vote on the 13th March, Owen was deprived of the Deanery of Christ Church and Edward Reynolds was restored.[1]

Quickly and quietly Owen disappeared from the centre of public life and University administration and took his family to the house he had purchased in Stadhampton. He awaited future developments and prayed that God would still use him in the propagation of the Gospel. For the last fourteen years he had publicly concerned himself with the preaching of the Protestant Faith, the preparation of young men to serve their country and church, and the establishment of a controlled religious toleration for orthodox Christian groups. He had viewed political actions and military victories in the light of their effect upon the progress of the Gospel and of their relationship to what be believed were prophetic portions of Holy Scripture which related to the future of Europe and the Middle East. This had given both his hearers and himself strength of mind and of conviction. Also he had provided guidance for successive Parliaments, Protectors and army leaders on national priorities. This guidance was often based upon his interpretation of the Old Testament in which he found a divinely revealed pattern in the life of the people of Israel. They were at the height of their fortunes when their leaders were godly, or as Micah expressed it, when they "loved mercy and walked humbly with their God." This pattern Owen applied to England, which, with many of his contemporaries, he believed to be "an elect nation." So a constant call in all his sermons to Parliament was for the cultivation of godliness. Though plagued by ill-health and domestic grief, his aims had been unchanging and his efforts unceasing. Always before him had been the vision of a purified, loving and gracious Church set in the midst of a godly nation. Now other men, with different views of the order of the Church, were beginning to preach to Parliament and guide the counsels of the nation.

Providence, it seemed, had failed to bring to a glorious conclusion the expectations it had aroused in his own heart and in the hearts of many saints during the years immediately following the sitting of the Long Parliament and victory in the civil wars. Was God, therefore, abandoning His saints? Was he refusing to support the glorious reformation He had inaugurated by His Spirit? These and similar questions must have plagued the mind of Owen during 1659 and 1660. But, being a man who believed that the Bible was God's written Word, he looked for the answer to his questions within its pages, especially in the historical and prophetical books of the Old Testament, which told of God's dealings with the elect nations of Israel and Judah. He well knew that the history of these nations provided pertinent examples of

[1] C.J., VII, pp. 860 and 871-2.

how a period of great national blessing was followed by a speedy degeneration of national life and religion. This happened, for example, in the reigns of Hezekiah and Manasseh in the eighth century B.C. The blessings of the first reign quickly changed into the evils of the second reign. Thus Owen was able to interpret the collapse of the good old cause and the probable return of the "common enemy" in terms of God's judgement upon the failure of His saints to make the most of their opportunities and to obey His Word. Owen had hinted at this interpretation in his sermon of the 4th February 1659 at which time, to use the words of the book of Daniel, he saw "the writing on the wall."

> Know you not that the nation begins to be overwhelmed by the pourings out of a profane, wicked, carnal spirit, full of rage, and contempt of all the work of reformation that has been attempted amongst us? Do you not know that if the former profane principle should prove predominant in this nation, that it will quickly return to its former station and condition, and that with the price of your dearest blood? And yet, is there not already such a visible prevalency of it, that in many places the very profession of religion is become a scorn; and in others, those old forms and ways taken up with greediness, which are a badge of apostasy from all engagements and actings? And are not these sad evidences of the Lord's departing from us? If I should lay before you a comparison between the degrees of the appearances of the glory of God in this nation, the steps whereby it came forth, and those whereby it seems almost to be departing, it would be a matter of admiration and lamentation. I pray God we lose not our ground faster than we won it. Were our hearts kept to our old principles on which we first engaged, it would not be so with us; but innumerable evils have laid hold upon us: and the temptations of these days have made us a woful prey.[1]

By March 1660 his worst fears were all but realised. A decayed remnant of the Long Parliament had been reinvigorated by a transfusion of Presbyterian blood, a Council of State had been appointed composed chiefly of men who favoured the restoration of the Stuart monarch, and Monck, though still elusive, looked ready to agree to bring back Charles II to England. For a generation or more, according to God's good pleasure, the "saints" were to be recipients of divine chastisement.[2] And this heavenly judgement was to be accepted, for the apostle by divine inspiration had taught that "whom the Lord loveth He chasteneth" (Hebrews 12:6). Or as Owen himself had put it in 1656: "to dispute

---

[1] *Works* VIII, p. 467, Cf also *A Vision of Unchangeable, Free Mercy* (1646) in *Works*, VIII, p. 24 where he gave a similar warning.
[2] Robert Baillie, the Scottish divine, spoke for many Presbyterians and Anglicans when he wrote on 31 Jan. 1661 that "it was the justice of God that brought . . . to disgrace the two Goodwins, blind Milton, Owen, Sterrie, Lockier and other of the maleficient crew." *Letters and Journals*, ed. D. Laing, III, p. 443.

against the condition wherein at any time we are cast by His providence is to rise up against His wisdom in disposing of things to His glory."[1] So the deposed Dean and future Nonconformist looked upon the return of Charles II and the restitution of the prelates as part of the inscrutable, beneficent and sovereign will of God. Having done what he could to prevent this movement of events, he must now accept them as from the hand of the Lord.

[1] *Works*, VIII, p. 413.

CHAPTER VI

# PROTESTANT NONCONFORMIST

IN PREVIOUS CHAPTERS IT HAS BEEN SUGGESTED THAT OWEN'S PRIMARY motivation and aim during his crowded life in the 1650s was the propagation of the Protestant gospel. After 1660 the same aim was also always before him, but necessarily, due to the changed religious scene and to his own uncompromising principles, the public opportunities with which he was presented were severely curtailed. As it became apparent that Charles II and his advisers were intent on restoring the Church of England as far as possible to what it was before 1640, and that the Cavalier Parliament, which began to sit on the 8th May 1661, intended to enforce a uniformity of worship according to the Book of Common Prayer, Owen had resolutely to face the situation and decide what God required of him.[1] In 1637 as a young Master of Arts he had virtually escaped from a similar situation in Laudian Oxford by taking a chaplaincy; but now he was a national figure, the leading Congregational divine. Thousands looked to him for an example and for guidance: the eyes of the Reformed Churches abroad were upon him. So in his home at Stadhampton he consulted with, and provided hospitality for, some of his former Oxford colleagues, who had lost or were losing their posts. Together they prayed and discussed their problems. Students also, including William Penn, the future Quaker, came to share the fellowship and conversion of these leaders of Nonconformity.[2]

The theological ethos of Owen and his brethren categorically informed them that they must obey the will of God as they understood it to be revealed in Holy Scripture. For the former Dean of Christ Church this

[1] For the whole background to this period see David Ogg, *England in the Reign of Charles II*, 1967; for details of the actual restoration of the Church see Anne Whiteman, "The Restoration of the Church of England," in *From Uniformity to Unity, 1662–1962*, ed. G. F. Nuttall and O. Chadwick, 1962.

[2] At this time Penn seems to have been favourably attracted to the doctrines of Owen. The two corresponded but not with the blessing of William's father, the admiral. See Bonamy Dobrée, *William Penn*, 1932, pp. 13–15, and M. C. Brailsford, *The Making of William Penn*, 1930, p. 104. Another young man who lodged with Owen was Samuel Angier, for whom see *C.R.* On 15 Jan. 1661 a correspondent wrote to Joseph Williamson, a former Fellow of Queen's, telling him that "last week some of the horse went over to Mr Owen's at Stadham from whence they brought 6 or 7 cases of pistols but left him behind together with Francis Johnson and Thankful Owen." *C.S.P.D.* (1660–61), p. 473. Johnson had been Master of University College and Owen the President of St John's. The raid was occasioned by fear in government circles that Owen might be implicated in Venner's Fifth Monarchist insurrection in London earlier that month. For Thomas Venner see *D.N.B.*

meant that he must live by the same principles which had guided him since 1646 but he must apply them to a different situation. Unlike some of his Presbyterian friends he could not contemplate the idea of serving as a minister in the restored Church of England as long as it had a compulsory liturgy and was ruled by prelates. This he made clear in *A Discourse concerning Liturgies and their imposition* (1662),[1] published whilst there was public discussion concerning the Act of Uniformity which received the royal assent on the 19th May 1662. Amongst other things, this Act required all ministers in the Church to be episcopally ordained, and to make a public declaration of their "unfeigned assent and consent" to the Prayer Book, before the Feast of St Bartholomew, the 24th August 1662. The Government knew that most former Puritans would not conform and so modern Nonconformity was born in England and Wales. The Cromwellian ideal of a comprehensive National Church was rejected and the seeds of later denominationalism were sown.

However, there were ways for Owen to escape the difficulties and possible persecution that would (and did) follow Black Bartholomew's Day. He could have emigrated. Certain Dutch Universities, whose professors were well acquainted with his writings, were very ready to offer him a professorship in theology; and the churches of Massachusetts would have been highly honoured to have him in their midst. Indeed, a definite invitation came to him from the First Church of Boston, which had enjoyed from 1633 to 1652 the ministry of John Cotton, the divine whose writings had been instrumental in guiding Owen into the Congregational way. For several years after 1663, when, as we shall see, he had no fixed abode in England, he was ready and willing to go to New England but circumstances of one kind or another prevented him so that finally he resolved to stay in Old England.[2]

To serve God and the saints in Britain meant at least two things. First and foremost, it meant the encouragement of the true worship of God, the practice of the Congregational way. He solemnly believed that the Word of God condemned not only the "papistical" prelates and their ecclesiastical courts but also some of the ceremonies required by the Prayer Book. In the New Testament, which contained in his opinion a blueprint for church polity and worship, he found that community worship was inspired by the Holy Spirit and took place in the fellowship of committed Christians. So to obey God after 1660

---

[1] *Works*, XV, pp. 3ff.
[2] Wood, *Athenae Oxonienses*, IV, col. 98, refers to an invitation from Holland but research in Dutch archives has not confirmed or rejected this. It seems no copy of any letter to Owen is extant. For the letter from the governor of Massachusetts dated 20 Oct. 1663 inviting Owen see *Correspondence*, No. 71, pp. 135-6. In *The Records of the First Church in Boston, 1630-1668*, ed. R. D. Pierce, Boston, 1961, p. 59 there are references to the call sent to Owen. Cf. also the references in the "Diary of John Hull," *Archaeologia Americana*, Boston, 1865, III, pp. 211 and 221. As late as 1666 Owen was expected in Boston.

he felt obliged to expound and defend the biblical doctrine of the church and of worship, to provide suitable devotional material for members of gathered churches, and to have pastoral responsibilities within such a church. This important area of ecclesiastical doctrine and practice in which Owen made a significant contribution to Protestant Nonconformity will be examined in the next chapter.

Here we must look at the second way in which he felt he must serve the people of God. It was his conviction that the supreme magistrate (the King in Parliament) should by all legal means be persuaded that his divinely appointed task of preserving and protecting the Christian religion was not achieved by enforcing uniformity of religious practice as in the legislation commonly known as the Clarendon Code.[1] Rather it was achieved by the suppression of antichristian Roman Catholicism and the provision of a basic religious liberty for all Christians who taught and believed the basic doctrines of the Apostles' and Nicene Creeds. Accordingly Owen continually pressed for such a liberty both in his writings and through his contacts with members of the gentry, nobility, government and of the Houses of Parliament with whom he had established friendships during the period of Cromwellian dominance.

Though it is patently obvious that Owen came through the upheavals accompanying the Restoration and the persecutions which followed virtually unscathed because powerful friends shielded him, the evidence of his relationship with these important men is scanty indeed. In the last chapter we noted his friendship and correspondence with General Monck; here we must notice some of the other men who helped him between 1660 and 1683. Asty merely states (with obvious pride in his hero):

> It was not possible that the real worth of so excellent a person should be concealed; and in many instances his reputation shone out with such lustre as drew the admiration and respects of several persons of honour and quality upon him, who very much delighted in his conversation; particularly the Earl of Orrery, the Earl of Anglesea, the Lord Willoughby of Parham, the Lord Wharton, the Lord Berkley, Sir John Trevor . . . and which is much more, even King Charles and the Duke of York paid a particular respect to him.

---

[1] The Clarendon Code is usually taken to describe four Acts of the Cavalier Parliament. First, the Corporation Act (1661) which required all holders of municipal office to renounce the Covenant and to take the sacrament according to the rites of the restored Church of England. Secondly, the Act of Uniformity (1662) which required episcopal ordination of all ministers and complete assent by them to the Prayer Book. Thirdly, the Conventicle Act of 1664, which made illegal all assemblies of five or more persons under colour of religion. Fourthly, the Five Mile Act (1665) which forbade all teachers and preachers who had not taken the oaths in the Act of Uniformity to come within five miles of a corporate town or the parish where they had previously taught.

The identity of the King and his brother James is well known but perhaps the identity of the others needs to be explained.[1]

Roger Boyle (1621–1679), first Earl of Orrery and third son of Richard Boyle, first Earl of Cork, was a prominent member of Cromwell's House of Lords and one of the committee appointed by Parliament to discuss the question of kingship with Oliver in 1657. After the Restoration he spent much time in Ireland as Lord President of Munster. Just when and under what circumstances Owen and Boyle met Asty unfortunately does not inform us. Rather more is known, however, about Owen's relationship with Arthur Annesley (1614–1686), the first Earl of Anglesey. He was a M.P. in the Long Parliament and President of the Council of State in 1660. In 1661 he became an Earl and enjoyed prominent positions in the government especially in the 1670s. While keeping the letter of the law by attending services in the parish church Annesley kept nonconformist chaplains in his own home. Within the Privy Council and in other spheres he defended the interests of Protestant Dissenters. From various entries in his Diary we know that on many occasions during the 1670s Dr and Mrs Owen were the dinner guests of the Earl and Countess.[2] And eventually the Countess herself became an actual member of Owen's gathered church which met in Leadenhall Street from 1673. From the Earl Owen must have received help, protection and information about national politics.

Exactly which Lord Willoughby Asty had in mind is not clear. It could have been either Francis (d.1666), the fifth Baron Willoughby of Parham or his brother, William, the sixth Baron. Both were at different times governors of the West Indian islands of Barbados, St Kitts, Nevis, Montserrat and Antigua. Just what form this friendship with Owen took is and probably will remain a mystery. With Philip Wharton (1613–1696), fourth Baron Wharton of Wooburn, Buckinghamshire, the matter is much clearer. As a young man Wharton was a Puritan and in the civil war he fought for Parliament. Of Presbyterian sympathies he welcomed the Restoration of Charles II. But in the House of Lords he was a determined opponent of the Clarendon Code, especially the Conventicle Act. Three letters from Owen to his Lordship preserved in the Bodleian Library reveal a close relationship between the two men.[3] Wharton

[1] Asty, p. xxix. That many royalists expected Owen to be punished in 1660 is obvious from the statement of A. Wood in *Athenae Oxon.*, IV, col. 100, where he writes that Owen's not being excepted from the Act of Oblivion "was much wondered at." Other Independents were executed!

[2] The MS Diary is in the British Museum, Add. MSS 18730 and 40860. See further D. R. Lacey, *Dissent and Parliamentary Politics, 1661–1689*, New Brunswick, N.J., 1969, pp. 459–463.

[3] *Correspondence*, pp. 155ff, No's 80, 81, 82. These three letters are part of about 600 letters addressed to Lord Wharton by Nonconformist ministers between 1660 and 1693. They are preserved in the Bodleian Library in Rawlinson MSS 49–53 and 104 and are currently being transcribed and edited by Peter Toon. One of the letters from John Loder (Rawl. 51:6) suggests that it was the sixth Baron Willoughby whom Owen knew, for Loder wrote: "Dr Owen commended him [Thomas Speed, a servant] to the Lord Willoughby late

used Owen to transact delicate business, the finding of a suitable daughter-in-law for example. We also know that when he was ill Owen sometimes went to Wooburn for a rest. The Earl of Anglesey noted in his Diary that he met Owen at Lord Wharton's and from Wooburn Owen wrote a memorable letter to his London church. We may justly presume that a large proportion of the conversation over the dinner-table concerned national politics and the lot of the Nonconformists.

George Berkeley (1628–1698), the first Earl of Berkeley, was educated at Christ Church, Oxford. He was a member of Oliver's Parliaments in 1654 and 1656. His basic business interest, as was that of his wife's family, was in trade with the colonies and plantations overseas. He was on the Council for Foreign Plantations, a member of the Royal Africa Company, and the governor of the Levant Company. In 1667 he became a Privy Councillor. His piety revealed in his *Historical Applications and Occasional Meditations upon Several Subjects* (1668) is similar to that espoused by Owen and possibly here was the link between them. Perhaps also it was Berkeley, with his many contacts in the shipping industry, who was ready to help transport Owen to New England in the early 1660s. Asty's last name is Sir John Trevor (1626–1672), the M.P. for Flint in 1646 and 1654 who was knighted and appointed a Secretary of State in 1660. According to his colleague, Sir Joseph Williamson, Trevor had nonconformist leanings even though part of his duties involved making enquiries into, and if necessary suppressing, conventicles.[1] A part of his nonconformist leanings was obviously his friendship with Owen which the latter must have found most helpful in various ways, the obtaining of licences to publish books for example. One further friend of Owen who enjoyed a high position in post-Restoration affairs but whose name Asty does not mention was Sir William Morice (1602–1676), a kinsman of General Monck. Morice had Presbyterian sympathies and was one of those expelled from the Long Parliament by Pride's purge. Like Monck he warmly welcomed Charles II and believed that the promise of toleration contained within the famous Declaration from Breda (April 1660) would be honoured. In May 1660 he became a Secretary of State. However he never lost touch with his friends who became Nonconformists. He even provided a yearly pension for one ejected minister named William Oliver. Owen was very grateful to him for various forms of help but especially with regard to obtaining licences to publish books. He dedicated the first volume of his Commentary on the Epistle to the Hebrews (1668) to Sir William and asserted that "it was through the countenance of your favour that this and other treatises received warrant to pass freely into the world."

Governor of Barbados, who greatly delighted in him . . ." The date of the letter 29th August 1673 suggests the sixth Baron who died on 10th April 1673.

[1] *C.S.P.D.* (1671) p. 569 and *C.S.P.D.* (1668–9) p. 294.

The first occasion after the Restoration that Owen defended in print the principles of orthodox Protestantism was in 1662. During 1661 a crafty and plausible book was published by a Franciscan named Vincent Canes, who had been educated at Douay. The book's title reveals its general aim: *Fiat Lux: or, a general conduct to the right understanding in the great combustions and broils about religion here in England, betwixt Papist and Protestant, Presbyterian and Independent, to the end that moderation and quietness may at length happily ensue after so many various tumults in the kingdom.* It gained fame partly because its message seemed to have a contemporary relevance and partly because it took as its starting point a passage in a speech made at the adjournment of Parliament in September 1660 by Edward Hyde, the Lord Chancellor. A copy of the book was sent by "a person of honour" to Owen who quickly produced *Animadversions on . . . Fiat Lux*. Owen's reply shows a measure of wit, humour and irony that the reader does not often encounter in the writings of this ponderous divine; perhaps this pleasant quality was possible because of the comparative peaceful and quiet situation in which he lived at Stadhampton. He warned that Canes' purpose was to recall the British people to the fold of the Bishop of Rome and he insisted that the doctrinal differences which separated Catholic and Protestant were still great and not to be minimised. So there are chapters on the doctrines of Scripture, the Mass, the Blessed Virgin, saints, and the Pope. The Franciscan replied in some haste to Owen but, instead of keeping to the matters under debate, Canes wandered from his subject to attack Owen for his political activities between 1649 and 1660. In December 1663 Owen defended his *Animadversions* with a *Vindication*.[1] In this he carefully kept to the subject in hand and tried to show once more the weaknesses and errors of the claims made by Roman Catholicism.

However, since Owen did not give the title of "saint" to the apostles and evangelists of the primitive Church (believing as he did that all the regenerate are saints in the New Testament sense), and since he expressed his doubt concerning the claim that the apostle Peter was ever in Rome, he encountered great difficulty in getting a licence from the Bishop of London to print his books. Happily his friend, Sir William Morice intervened and persuaded the Bishop to grant a licence.[2] Sir William also seems to have spoken favourably of Owen's books against Canes to the Lord Chancellor who decided that he must meet the former Dean of Christ Church. His Lordship sent a message to Owen via Bulstrode Whitelocke, the former President of the Council of State, and a man who had had many previous dealings with the divine. When the

[1] *Works*, XIV, pp. 174ff.
[2] Asty, p. xxiii, asserts that it was Sir Edward Nicholas who helped Owen, but, since Nicholas gave up his post as Secretary of State on 15 October 1662 (*D.N.B.* s.v. E. Nicholas) it is much more likely that the person concerned was Morice, who became a Secretary in May 1660.

Chancellor and the Nonconformist leader met, the former expressed his surprise that a man of Owen's learning and ability should have been led astray by "the novelty of Independency." If he would give up his strange ideas and conform, then perhaps a bishopric or high ecclesiastical post could be his.[1] His Lordship must not have known how deeply the Congregational way was engraven on Owen's soul or else he would not have wasted his time in meeting him. Owen, believing that everything which happened was controlled by God's providence, used the opportunity to expound his views on the Church and to ask for toleration of gathered churches which taught orthodox doctrine. He even ventured the opinion that although the Presbyterian leaders were still optimistically talking of comprehension within the State Church, what they truly wanted was freedom to worship God according to their consciences, which in turn meant that they would eventually support the idea of toleration outside the National Church. But, come what may, he himself would follow God and his conscience.

Before this memorable interview, Dr and Mrs Owen had sent their children to stay with Lady Tyrell at Hanslope in Buckinghamshire while they themselves went to the home of Mrs Abney at Theobalds in Hertfordshire.[2] Mrs Abney was a daughter of Joseph Caryl, with whom Owen had gone to Scotland in 1650. At Theobalds they were kept well informed of the effects of the Act of Uniformity, of the possibility of an Indulgence from the King, and of the fate of "near 2,000 ejected ministers."[3] One eminent visitor was Dr Thomas Manton who had been a commissioner at the ill-fated Savoy Conference of 1661 and who now was himself an ejected minister, even though he had been a leading Presbyterian minister in London since 1649. The two men were, it seems, primarily concerned with the plight of ejected ministers, many of whom were placed in severe economic distress. What they did of a practical nature to help them is not known but they certainly would have planned something. For many a week Owen did not preach any sermons but, in a letter to John Thornton, chaplain to the Duke of Bedford at Woburn Abbey, he did say that he was to accompany Mrs Abney to London and preach in her house there.[4] This being so,

[1] The anonymous author of *The Life of Owen* (1720), p. xxiii, states "I am informed by one of the Doctor's relations that King Charles II offered him a bishopric." I have found no other reference to such an offer. For the interview with Clarendon see Asty, p. xxiv, and James Ralph, *History of England*, 1744, I, p. 52.
[2] Owen asserts this in his second letter to John Thornton: *Correspondence*, No. 69, pp. 130-1. For Lady Tyrell's husband, Sir Thomas, see *D.N.B.* The house was registered for Presbyterian worship in 1672. For Sir Edward Abney, her husabnd, see *D.N.B.* s.v. Sir Thomas Abney. Another famous Nonconformist who lived at this house about forty years later was Isaac Watts, the hymnwriter.
[3] Owen used this expression in his first letter to Thornton: *Correspondence*, No. 68, pp. 129-30. Matthews calculated that a total of 1909 ministers and teachers were ejected between 1660 and 1662. *C.R.* pp. xii-xiv.
[4] *Correspondence*, No. 69, pp. 130-1.

we must presume that at Theobalds each Sabbath only family prayers were held or that another preacher was staying there who took the service of worship.

From 1662 onwards the Owen family spent little time together and seem not to have had a family home of their own. From several references to Owen in letters to Lord Wharton during 1663-4 we know that the good doctor resided mostly at Stadham in this period. However, after 1664 Mrs Owen and the children stayed more or less permanently at the home of the former Cromwellian general, Charles Fleetwood, who had recently married Mary Hartopp, the widow of Sir Edward Hartopp and daughter of Sir John Coke. Fleetwood and his children by his first two wives moved into the Hartopp home in Church Street, Stoke Newington, and eventually the two children of his first marriage, Smith and Elizabeth, married Mary Hartopp's two children, Mary and Sir John. The house, a large one, came to be known as "Fleetwood House" but it was only one of the several houses and properties owned by Sir John Hartopp, who, happily, shared his stepfather's nonconformist opinions.[1] Though Owen himself must have spent long and short periods at Stoke Newington, then a village on the outskirts of London, he moved around a great deal. In 1663 he was preaching in Moorgate near one of the traditional northern gates of the City of London;[2] but in January 1664 he was in Oxford with a man from New England seeking to persuade Thomas Gilbert, the former Shropshire minister, who now lived in St Ebbe's parish, to go to Massachusetts as the new President of Harvard College.[3] A year later Owen was prosecuted under the Conventicle Act for holding meetings in his home at Stadhampton.[4] This occasion is probably the one recorded by Anthony Wood telling how the militia raided Owen's house and found him preaching to thirty or more people.[5] The Congregational divine hoped he could avoid further raids and interruptions and wrote for help to Thomas Barlow, now Provost of Queen's, asking him to speak to the Lord Chancellor on his behalf. Barlow made a special visit to Cornbury to see his Lordship but his efforts were in vain. So Owen returned to London.

---

[1] Cf. A. J. Shirren, *The Chronicles of the Fleetwood House*, 1951, for a description of the life of the Fleetwoods and Hartopps at Stoke Newington. Shirren quotes from the local parish records on p. 81 to refer to the deaths of Judith Owen in May 1664, and Matthew Owen in April 1665.
[2] G. L. Turner, "Williamson's Spy Book," *Transactions* of the Cong. Hist. Society, V, p. 253: "Dr Owen dwells in the fields on the left hand near Moorgate where the Quarters hang and meets often with Goodwin." The Baptist, Henry Jessey, also met them in Moorgate and Stoke Newington; Ibid, p. 251.
[3] Gilbert tells of the visit in a letter to Lord Wharton. See Bodleian Rawlinson Letters, 53. f.13. He did not go to Harvard.
[4] C.S.P.D. (1664-5), p. 222.
[5] Wood, *Athenae Oxonienses*, IV, col. 100.

The note in the so-called "Spy Book" of Joseph Williamson, secretary to Lord Arlington, to the effect that "Dr Owen ... dwells near Moorgate" is probably a reference to "White's Alley," a turning out of Little Moorfields where in 1669, six years after Williamson's note, the Bishop of London reported that Owen held a conventicle.[1] It would appear that a Mrs Holmes, a widow, provided house and home for both Owen and Thomas Goodwin when they were in the City. An informer described her as "a great patronesse of the worst sort of people" and as having "a great estate and spending it among those that lie in wait to disturb the peace of the kingdom."[2] Goodwin and Owen who, in Wood's words, were "the atlases and patriarchs of Independence," also co-operated with other Congregational ministers in a regular preaching service (a lecture) in the house of Alderman Henry Ashurst, whose son of the same name was a good friend to several Presbyterian ministers.[3] During the 1665 Plague of London, which accounted for the deaths of nearly 70,000 people in a population of half a million, Owen probably spent most of his time at Stoke Newington. After the Great Fire which followed the Plague he returned with other nonconformist ministers to preach to the people in the stricken city. Baxter, who himself had left his home at Acton during the Plague to stay with Richard Hampden in Buckinghamshire, comments that Owen deliberately stayed away from the city during the Plague.[4] The reasons for Owen's absence are obvious. He had an opportunity to stay with friends away from the stricken area and he took it. Perhaps what Baxter meant is that Owen would have been a better pastor (since he had a gathered church in the city) had he stayed to suffer with his flock. Not having a congregation at Acton Baxter was in a different position. Perhaps we can admit that there is some justice in Baxter's comment.

Happily for Nonconformists, the year 1667 provided a suitable period in which to argue publicly for relief from the repressive Conventicle and Five Mile Acts. It was generally held that the Plague and the Fire were God's judgements upon the land for the harshness of the government's attitude to Nonconformity. This sentiment, or, in some cases, conviction, was given added weight by reports of the heroic work of some nonconformist preachers who had ministered to the sick and dying without thought for their own lives, as well as by news of the current trade depression. Nonconformists were also gladdened to see the impeachment of Edward Hyde, who was unjustly blamed for the successful Dutch attack on Chatham in June 1667, for financial losses in the Dutch war and for the repressive legislation that has come to bear his name. Baxter voiced the general attitude of Protestant Dissenters

[1] *Original Records of Early Nonconformity*, ed. G. L. Turner, 1911-14, III, p. 514.
[2] Ibid, III, p. 515.
[3] Ibid, II, p. 355. Cf. also Lacey, *op. cit.*, p. 375.
[4] Baxter, *Reliquiae*, III, pp. 15 and 19. For Hampden see Lacey, *op. cit.*, p. 402.

when he observed about the fall of the Earl of Clarendon that "it was a most notable providence of God that this man that . . . had dealt so cruelly with the Nonconformists should thus by his own friends be cast out."[1]

Early in September 1667 a newsletter reported that "an Act is said to be preparing, against the meeting of Parliament [on the 10th Oct.] dispensing with the Act of Uniformity and clearly against the Bishops' government."[2] This was the Bill prepared by Sir Robert Atkyns and due to be introduced into the House of Commons by John Birch, the former Colonel in the armies of Parliament. However, in view of mounting opposition, Birch desisted.[3] Meanwhile the opponents of toleration went into the attack and published several tracts to propagate their opinions. Certain of these were sent to Owen by some prominent person, possibly a member of the House of Lords, with a request that he should publish his thoughts concerning them. He did this anonymously under the title, *Indulgence and Toleration Considered*, published early in November.[4] After some remarks about the harsh language of some of the pamphleteers who were for no toleration, he briefly set out his own case. There were similarities, he suggested, between the laws of ancient Rome by which the early Christians were judged and persecuted, and the laws of England (the Clarendon Code) against Dissenters. The Jews, however, in earlier times, set a better example. They allowed Gentiles to live amongst them as long as they obeyed the seven Noachical precepts. Furthermore, the early Christian Church never "entertained thoughts of outward force against those who differed from them" for at least three hundred years after the birth of Christ. "It seems," wrote Owen, "that we are some of the first who ever anywhere in the world, from the foundation of it, thought of ruining and destroying persons of the same religion with ourselves, merely upon the choice of some peculiar ways of worship in that religion." Defining conscience as "the judgement that a man maketh of himself and his actions, with reference to the future judgement of God," he argued that liberty in such matters as worship of the Almighty should be given to people who base their worship on a faithful attempt to follow the light of sacred Scripture. "Violence," he continued, "hath been used in matters of religion to the shame and stain of Christianity, and yet it never succeeded anywhere to extinguish that persuasion and opinion which it was designed to extirpate." He concluded by expressing his deep conviction that there was "no nation under heaven wherein such an indulgence or toleration

---

[1] Ibid, III, p. 20.
[2] *C.S.P.D.* (1667), p. 437.
[3] See further Roger Thomas, "Comprehension and Indulgence," in *From Uniformity to Unity*, ed. Nuttall and Chadwick, p. 197. I found Mr Thomas' essay very helpful.
[4] *Works*, XIII, pp. 518ff. For reference to some of the tracts that Owen possibly read see John Stoughton, *History of Religion in England*, III, pp. 371ff.

as is desired would be more welcome, useful, acceptable, or more subservient to tranquility, trade, wealth and peace." Religious, social and economic arguments are here combined. Owen's use of them reflects his social class and that of his friends and acquaintances.[1]

Owen's views on the urgent need for toleration of Nonconformists were also expressed in late 1667 in another pamphlet entitled, *A Peace-Offering in an Apology and Humble Plea for Indulgence and Liberty of Conscience*.[2] Earnest in tone, yet moderate in language, it utilised common sense, human history, ancient wisdom and Biblical insights to show the essential stupidity of a policy of religious persecution. The Congregational churches believed that they were obeying Christ in their organisation and worship: thus if the government believed them to be wrong or misguided let it prove its contention by reference to the Word of God and not by unnecessary legislation. In these tracts Owen was of course restating views he had consistently held and expressed for over twenty years. Even when his party was in power during the Interregnum he spoke in favour of a controlled religious toleration. What is lacking in 1667, which was so apparent between 1646 and 1659, is the contention that religion should be guided if not controlled from the centre as it had been through the triers of the Cromwellian Settlement. The much changed circumstances after 1660 meant that Owen could no longer press for this except in so far as he wanted the King and Parliament to grant freedom to the Nonconformists. Owen had not changed his principles: he was simply applying them to a situation which in his earlier years he never thought would ever return to England.

On the 21st December 1667 the diarist, Samuel Pepys, reported that "the Nonconformists are mighty high and their meetings frequented and connived at; and they do expect to have their day now soon; for my Lord Buckingham is a declared friend of them and even of the Quakers."[3] George Villiers, the Duke of Buckingham, was married to Lord Fairfax's daughter. He was the Lord Lieutenant of Yorkshire, who had become a member of the Cabal (that is, the five men who were chief advisers to Charles II after the fall of Clarendon—Sir Thomas Clifford, Lord Arlington, Buckingham, Lord Ashley and the Earl of Lauderdale). Unfortunately for the public image of Nonconformity, Buckingham had a reputation for reckless living. In his *Life* of Oliver Heywood, a leading Northern nonconformist minister, Joseph Hunter quoted the following extract from a letter of 1667: "the Duke of Buckingham is become the most eminent convert from all the vanities

[1] Cf. J. A. W. Gunn, *Politics and the Public Interest in the Seventeenth Century*, 1969, p. 160. Gunn points out that Owen's belief that persecution only served to reduce the number of citizens working for the civic and national interest was later developed in greater detail by his former student and friend, William Penn.
[2] *Works*, XIII, pp. 542ff.
[3] Pepys, *Diary*, ed. H. B. Wheatley, 1905, VII, p. 228.

he hath been reported to have been addicted to; hath had a solemn day of prayer for the completing and confirming the great work upon him. Dr Owen and others of like persuasion were the carriers on of the work. He is said to keep correspondence with the chief of these parties."[1] Sadly this correspondence seems to be lost.

Meanwhile, a series of conferences took place between the Lord Keeper's representatives, Bishop John Wilkins and Hezekiah Burton, on the one hand, and Thomas Manton, William Bates and Richard Baxter on the other. Their purpose was to discuss proposals drawn up by Wilkins, Cromwell's brother-in-law and now the Bishop of Chester. These proposals aimed at comprehending Presbyterians in the Church of England and tolerating Independents outside. Baxter was given the task of keeping Owen informed of the progress of the discussion.[2] But it was common knowledge in London that Owen and his Congregational brethren were looking to Buckingham for help in the promotion of their toleration bill in Parliament. This Bill proposed liberty of worship in licensed premises for those who taught orthodox doctrine but the denial of any toleration to Roman Catholics and to the sects whose teaching was blasphemous or licentious. In contrast, the original proposals of Wilkins said nothing about orthodoxy and contained nothing to prohibit Roman Catholic worship.[3] Perhaps anticipating that some form of toleration would be granted, and pressed by his brethren throughout the country, Owen published a catechism for the guidance of members of gathered churches entitled, *A Brief Instruction in the Worship of God*.[4]

Such, unfortunately, were the passions of this period that when Parliament met on the 10th of February 1668 it was in no mood to make the lot of Dissenters any easier. Many members, it seems, were incensed by reports of the proposed bill to legalise conventicles and they refused even to discuss comprehension proposals from the Lord Keeper, despite the fact that the King would have favoured this discussion. Baxter blamed the prelates in the House of Lords for the failure to get the Wilkins proposals discussed but Manton regarded Owen as the villain of the piece. In a letter to Baxter dated the 26th September 1668 he complained that "the comprehension . . . endeavoured by our friends in Court was wholly frustrated by Dr Owen's proposal of a toleration

---

[1] Hunter, *The Rise of the Old Dissent exemplified in the Life of Oliver Heywood*, 1842, p. 198. The source of the letter is not given.
[2] Thomas, *op. cit.*, pp. 198ff. and Baxter, *Reliquiae*, III, p. 34.
[3] One report of the Duke of Buckingham's bill stated that he was the great favourite at Court and that "his cabal were Major Wildman, Dr Owen and the rest of that fraternity," C.S.P.D. (1667–8), p. 238. For Wildman see Maurice Ashley, *John Wildman*, 1947. The text of the proposed bill was preserved in the papers of Thomas Barlow and printed in *The Theological Works of Herbert Thorndike*, Oxford, 1854, V, p. 308. It is reprinted in *Correspondence*, p. 180.
[4] *Works*, XV, pp. 446ff.

which was entertained and carried on by other persons."[1] To defend himself, Owen visited his old friend Manton, taking with him Samuel Annesley, the emerging leader of those Presbyterians who were beginning to realise that the best they could ever achieve was adequate toleration outside the State Church.[2] Manton, however, like other older Presbyterians still held the fine ideal of the one Church containing all the Protestant Christians and ministers of the nation. Events were to prove that Owen and Annesley had rightly judged the temper of the Parliament and that Manton, Baxter and others were fighting a losing battle. So the essence of Owen's message to Manton was "comprehension will neither do the King's business nor ours;" and this was a theme which he had previously explained in his *Peace-Offering*. No doubt Manton and Owen agreed to differ on this matter.

The over-optimistic Baxter, ever ready to discuss proposals for unity, and hearing that Owen was speaking in late 1668 of the possibility of a union between Presbyterians and Congregationalists, decided to meet him. "I told him," Baxter later reported, "that I must deal freely with him; that when I thought of what he had done formerly, I was much afraid lest one that had been so great a breaker, would not be made an instrument of healing. But in other respects I thought him the fittest man in England for this work; partly because he could understand the case, and partly because his experience of the humours of men, and of the mischiefs of dividing principles and practices, had been so very great, that if experience should make any man wise and fit for a healing work it should be him."[3] Baxter admitted that he was prompted to visit Owen because he believed that in the catechism, *A Brief Instruction* (1667), the Congregational divine had given up two doctrines which he had supposedly once held. These were first, that the whole gathered church does have as a society "the keys of the kingdom of heaven" and, secondly, that the congregation gives the keys at ordination to the church officers.[4]

Baxter proceeded to draw up a series of proposals for the basis of discussion and upon these Owen made comments. Their exchange of views was virtually doomed from the start for Baxter's ideal and aim was to unite Protestant Nonconformists so that together they could present a strong front to the government and then gain entry on generous terms into the Church of England. Owen, on the other hand, believed just as firmly in the unity of Protestant Dissenters but he wanted them

[1] Quoted by Thomas, *op. cit.*, p. 204, from Dr Williams's Library MSS 59.2.273.
[2] For Annesley see *D.N.B.* and *C.R.* His daughter married Samuel Wesley and so he became the grandfather of the Wesley brothers, John and Charles.
[3] Baxter, *Reliquiae*, III, p. 61.
[4] The "keys," a word taken from Matt. 16:19, was assumed to denote the power of admission into and excommunication from the church. As Owen had not previously written on the topic, and as the *Savoy Declaration* is brief on this point, it is difficult to assess Baxter's contention that Owen had a change of mind.

united outside a Church which had too many "marks of the beast" (Revelation 13) to be an acceptable National Church. For fifteen months they exchanged letters and proposals until finally Owen remarked, "I am still a well-wisher to these mathematics," by which he presumably meant that he wanted unity but not the Baxter way.[1] Their extant letters also reveal that what separated the two men in 1654 when they were seeking to define the fundamentals of the Faith for Oliver's Parliament still divided them in 1669. Owen wanted a firm, confessional basis for any union whilst Baxter preferred and would have accepted a minimum doctrinal statement.

During the discussion between Baxter and Owen, the latter invited the former to answer a violent attack upon Nonconformists by Samuel Parker, archdeacon of Canterbury, who had been at Oxford as a student from 1657 to 1660.[2] The attack was in a book entitled, *A Discourse of Ecclesiastical Politie, wherein the Authority of the Civil Magistrate over the Consciences of Subjects in Matters of External Religion is asserted: the Mischiefs and Inconviences of Toleration are represented and all pretences in behalf of liberty of conscience are fully answered* (1669). Baxter reports that such was the confidence of the author that he confronted the Earl of Anglesey (Arthur Annesley) with the challenge, "Let us see, my Lord, whether any of your chaplains can answer it."[3] Annesley was privately a Nonconformist and publicly a Conformist in that each Sunday he went to the parish church but at the same time kept a chaplain in his home who was a nonconformist minister. This was the period when the strengthened Act against conventicles was about to become law and opponents of Nonconformity were full of confidence. Since Baxter, despite his dislike of Parker, did not regard himself as amongst those whom the archdeacon attacked, he declined Owen invitation. So Owen himself, ever ready to defend the cause to which he was totally committed, felt obliged to provide an answer wnich had the title, *Truth and Innocence Vindicated*.[4]

Encouraged in his writing by Archbishop Sheldon, Parker had maintained that numerous mischiefs ensued from allowing religious liberty. In ancient times, kingly and priestly powers were vested in one person but when they were separated as, for example, in late Judaism in Palestine or in the Roman Empire after Constantine the Great, the supremacy rested with the State. Since the civil magistrate's appointment was by the divine will (Romans 13:1), he could enjoin in morality anything that did not contradict the moral law of God; so, in religion, he could

---

[1] The two extant letters are in *Correspondence*, No's 71 and 72, pp. 136–145. In *Correspondence*, p. 136, n. 2, I asserted that Baxter's original proposals were lost. I now find that they were actually printed in his *Church Concord* (1691) between pages 62 and 76, where the date should be "Acton.Nov.21.1668".

[2] For Parker see *D.N.B.*

[3] Baxter, *Reliquiae*, III, p. 42. Cf. Lacey, *op. cit.*, pp. 459ff. One of the Earl's chaplains was Benjamin Agas for whom see *C.R.*

[4] *Works*, XIII, pp. 344ff.

require a general, national conformity of practice as long as his requirements did not debauch the conception and understanding of God provided in Holy Scripture. Citizens had the perfect right to think what they liked and believe what they wished, for their conscience was their own; but, the King and Parliament had the divine right to enforce the approved religious practice, as its worship, based on the Book of Common Prayer, did not distort the true doctrine of God. Toleration was undesirable because of its bad effects on national unity and stability. It provided opportunities for men of corrupt designs to foment trouble and work for the overthrow of the monarchy and the restoration of a republic. So, though the power of the magistrate could be abused, its abuse was less mischievous than liberty for men to worship as they pleased. The argument of Nonconformists that the Clarendon Code was an occasion of scandal to them was just nonsense. And their great cry that they had to obey God rather than man, and thus worship in illegal conventicles, was based on an inability to distinguish between basic principles and matters, which at their very best, were debatable. Their supposed tenderness of conscience was a mask for sedition and lawlessness. Obviously Parker did not understand or did not want to understand what Nonconformity was all about.

Owen's reply was based on the premise that Holy Scripture is God's only final, authoritative Word to man. Since he held that Scripture clearly taught that the Church should be pure and subject in matters of doctrine and worship only to Christ the King, the matter was not for him so simple as Parker suggested. Public morals were a different matter. Liberty to worship God according to the New Testament pattern was absolutely essential to those whose minds and hearts rejected for Christ's sake the government and liturgy of the Church of England. The worship of God was the highest duty of man and could not be placed in the realm of secondary matters. Finally, Protestant Nonconformists were not the type of people that Parker thought them to be and the powers he claimed for the magistrate were contrary to all sound reason and biblical teaching.

But Parker would not be silenced either by Owen or other anonymous writers, and in 1671 he published *A Defence and Continuation of the Ecclesiastical Politie*. Owen chose not to continue the controversy but stood aside to allow Andrew Marvell, "the liveliest droll of his age," to join in and eventually silence Parker in a torrent of caustic wit.[1] The two men were in close contact for Owen read the proofs of Marvell's *The Rehearsal Transposed* (1672-3) and Marvell kept in touch with Owen's private affairs.[2] Unfortunately, but not unexpectedly, Owen

[1] See Pierre Legouis, *Andrew Marvell*, Oxford, 1965, pp. 194ff. and C. E. Whiting, *Studies in English Puritanism, 1660-1688*, 1931, pp. 502ff for a brief description of this controversy.
[2] *Historical MSS Com. Report on Finch MSS*, II, p. 10; Marvell, *Letters*, Oxford, 1952, pp. 330-32.

also came under attack in 1670 from another source. In a pamphlet which was occasioned in part by Owen's *A Brief Instruction* and in part by Parker's attitude, and entitled *A Letter to a Friend concerning some of Dr Owen's Principles and Practices*, George Vernon accused the former Dean of Christ Church of committing various crimes and misdemenours during the 1650s and of being a "libeller of authority" after the Restoration. By implication it was an attack on all the Congregational leaders. Since Vernon, the rector of Bourton-on-the-Water in Gloucestershire, was a neighbour of Sir Thomas Overbury, a future member of his London church, Owen addressed a brief reply to Vernon in the form of a printed letter to Sir Thomas under the title, *Reflections on a Slanderous Libel*.[1] Earlier we referred to this pamphlet since in it Owen defended himself against such charges as that he abused the Lord's Prayer and worked for the overthrow of Richard Cromwell. An anonymous friend of Owen, also incensed by Vernon's accusations, defended him in *An Expostulatory Letter to the Author of the late Slanderous Libel against Dr Owen* (1671).

The Act to prevent and suppress seditious conventicles of 1670 aimed at providing "further and more speedy remedies against the growing dangerous practices of seditious sectaries," who supposedly used the plea of tender conscience as a screen behind which to plot revolution. By the terms of this Act a magistrate, acting on little more than hearsay, could impose a sentence which could materially ruin an offender. Also if the offender could not pay then others were to be compelled to pay on his behalf. Ministers were to be fined £20 for a first offence and £40 for a second, whilst the owner of the building in which a meeting was held was liable to a fine of £20 or the seizure of his property.[2] Before this notorious bill became law, Owen produced a short paper against its terms and sent it, probably via Philip, Lord Wharton, or the Earl of Anglesey, for the consideration of members of the House of Lords.[3] As we have seen with both these men Owen was well acquainted and was often their guest.

"The whole kingdom," he explained in the paper, "is at present in peace and quietness . . . and all individual men are improving their industry, according to their best skill and opportunities." Sadly he wrote that this "bill against conventicles, if passed, will introduce a disturbance into this order of things in every county, every city, every borough and town corporate, and almost every village in the nation." English trade and industry as well as the Protestant Faith would be

---

[1] For Overbury see *D.N.B.* In a letter to Lord Wharton Owen referred to an enforced stay at the home of Sir Thomas. *Correspondence*, No. 82, pp. 156–7.
[2] G. R. Cragg, *Puritanism in the Period of Great Persecution*, Cambridge, 1957.
[3] This paper was entitled "The State of the Kingdom with respect to the present Bill against Conventicles" and is in *Works*, XIII, pp. 583ff.

greatly harmed. The paper closed with a moving plea for toleration of Nonconformists. But it was all in vain. The Bill became law and when Owen saw that it was not being applied to Roman Catholics he quickly wrote another tract, *The Grounds and Reasons on which Protestant Dissenters desire their Liberty*.[1] in which he emphasised yet again that Congregationalists (and Presbyterians for that matter) were Protestants, firmly committed to the doctrinal standards of the Thirty-Nine Articles. Thus they should not be subject to pernicious laws and penalties but be given the legal right to worship God peacefully in their assemblies.

Happily the indignities were not to last long for "the King's business," as Owen had previously remarked, was best served by an indulgence. In June 1670 Charles II entered into the secret Treaty of Dover in which he pledged not only his support for the French in the war with the Dutch but also his intention to declare himself a Roman Catholic at the first favourable opportunity.[2] The nature of this treaty, one of the most discreditable instruments in the history of English diplomacy, made it imperative that Charles should do something to please both Protestant and Roman Catholic Dissenters; he knew that a war with the Dutch would be unfavourably received in the City of London by many merchants who had nonconformist sympathies, and he naturally wanted to alleviate the lot of Catholics. So it is no surprise to learn that in August 1671 "several from the King from time to time have met Dr Owen."[3] The result of these discussion, and of the more difficult ones with the Presbyterian leaders, was the famous Declaration of Indulgence issued in March 1672 on the eve of the war with the Dutch. On the 28th March two groups of Nonconformists thanked the King, whom they met in Lord Arlington's lodgings.[4] In the morning four Congregational ministers led by Owen rendered their thanks and Owen delivered a short set speech;[5] in the afternoon it was the turn of the Presbyterians led by Thomas Manton.

The preamble to the Declaration stated in cogent terms the futility of persecution. By his "supreme powers in ecclesiastical affairs" Charles would suspend all penal laws against Nonconformists. Roman Catholics were free to worship in their homes but Protestants might meet in public as long as they secured licences for both the minister and the place of worship. The licences were issued from the office of Lord Arlington. In all some 416 Congregational ministers and 642 households successfully petitioned for them.[6] Many also were granted to Presby-

[1] *Works*, XIII, pp. 576ff.
[2] Ogg, *op. cit.*, pp. 338ff.
[3] C.S.P.D. (1671), p. 264.
[4] C.S.P.D. (1671-2), p. 609.
[5] For the text of this speech see *Correspondence*, pp. 126-7. For details of the Indulgence see Frank Bate, *The Declaration of Indulgence*, Liverpool, 1908.
[6] These figures are taken from Turner, *Original Records*, III, pp. 727 and 734.

terians and Baptists. A sizeable number of Congregational ministers, however, did not make application for licences.[1] Owen, it seems, was never granted one, although an application was made on his behalf: the Society of Leathersellers gave permission for Owen, assisted by John Loder, to preach in its hall, but for reasons that are not known, Lord Arlington chose not to give a licence to this hall.[2] Loder was not discouraged for he later received a licence to preach in Cherry Tree Alley as an assistant to Philip Nye, but Owen does not appear to have made another application. He did, however, act as an intermediary for others who desired licences or who wanted changes made in the stated place of worship on licences already granted. Furthermore, he allowed his new home in Charterhouse Yard which he had recently acquired probably with the £500 left to him by his kinsman, Martyn Owen, to be used as a place where licences could be safely kept until people from country areas could collect them.[3]

The period of one year during which the Indulgence was in force was of considerable significance for churches of the Congregational way and for Protestant Dissent in general. It was like a new beginning and churches were able to survey their condition and rally their forces in an atmosphere of freedom. Licences to men or houses went to every county in England except Cornwall and Westmoreland. The main strength of Congregationalism was in the London area and in the towns of East Anglia, with strong outposts in Devon and Yorkshire. In the City of London some merchants and ministers felt that Protestant Nonconformists should provide some kind of united front. As a result they instituted a joint Presbyterian-Congregationalist Lecture, which became known as the Ancient Merchants' Lecture.[4] Six lecturers were appointed to preach in turn each Tuesday at mid-day. The original six were William Bates, William Jenkyn, Thomas Manton, Richard Baxter, John Collins and John Owen. The venue was Pinners' Hall, so named after the company, making pins and needles, who owned it. It proved to be an extremely popular Lecture and continued, even in the dark days of persecution that lay ahead, as a joint effort until 1694 when theological disagreement caused the Presbyterians to leave and set up their own Lecture.[5] The controversy in 1694 was over what were deemed to be Arminian tendencies of some of the Presbyterian lecturers. A foretaste of this was felt in 1674 when Baxter was criticised by some

[1] Cf. R. Tudur Jones, *Congregationalism in England, 1662–1962*, 1962, p. 92.
[2] Turner, *Original Records*, II, p. 980. For Loder see C.R.
[3] Turner, *Original Records*, III, p. 479.
[4] T. G. Crippen, "The Ancient Merchants' Lecture," *Transactions* of the Cong. Hist. Soc., VII, pp. 300ff.
[5] See further Peter Toon, *The Emergence of Hyper-Calvinism in English Nonconformity, 1689–1765*, 1967, pp. 49ff.

hearers for his seeming adherence to a doctrinal position that seemed nearer to Dutch Arminianism that orthodox Calvinism. Since the exchanges of 1649-50 Owen had known that Baxter was not a full-blooded Calvinist and his sympathies were therefore probably with the protesters.

Before this theological squabble took place in Pinners' Hall in 1674 the seal had been broken off the Declaration of Indulgence and its provisions ceased. When this happened in March 1673 Protestant Nonconformity had become established as a powerful and permanent part of English religious life and in this Owen had played a not inconsiderable role. Eight years later he wrote that the Congregational churches had "thankfully accepted and made use of this royal favour" although they realised that the Indulgence "was designed only as an expedient for the peace and prosperity of the kingdom until the whole matter might be settled in Parliament."[1] Such a settlement, however, had to wait until 1689, six years after Owen's death, and thus for the rest of his life he had to continue the long struggle for his cause. Unfortunately virtually nothing is known of his further activities to seek to persuade the government to grant toleration. The Duke of Buckingham was probably in close touch with him in the autumn of 1675 before he made a speech in the House of Lords on the 16th November requesting permission to bring in a bill for the ease and security of Dissenters.[2] A year earlier, when Owen had left his home to convalesce at Tunbridge Wells in Kent, he spent several hours with the Duke of York, who was also taking the waters, and explained to him, even though he was a Roman Catholic, his own position with regard to Protestant Nonconformity and its need for freedom.[3] Some little time later, when Owen had returned to London, the King himself sent for the Congregational divine and gave him one thousand guineas to use for the relief of suffering Dissenters, who were writing to Owen and his colleagues for help and advice.[4] When news of the gift became public, Owen had to justify his acceptance of the money against the criticism that his taking of it implied that he agreed with the toleration of Roman Catholic worship. That Owen was totally opposed to the Roman Catholic system of doctrine and worship was widely known since he had written against it and in his proposals for toleration he had specifically outlawed it. Furthermore in 1674 and for several years afterwards, he was actively engaged in giving a series of lectures known as "The Morning Exercises

---

[1] "To the Reader" in *An Inquiry* . . . in *Works*, XV, p. 190.
[2] This bill would have allowed two or more J.P's so license any place for worship as long as certain regulations were obeyed. Cf. Thomas, *op. cit.*, p. 222, and Lacey, *op. cit.*, p. 80.
[3] Asty, p. xxix.
[4] Cf. Stoughton, *op. cit.*, III, p. 401.

against Popery" in the Meeting House in Farthing Alley, Southwark.[1]

Like many of his contemporaries Owen was extremely sensitive to the threat of Popery because of, amongst other things, the Roman Catholic sympathies of the House of Stuart. In 1678, and in the years immediately following, when Titus Oates had supposedly exposed an alleged Popish Plot to assassinate the King, massacre Protestants and invade Ireland with a French army, Owen believed most of the rumours he heard. "Half the talk of the world," he remarked in 1680, "is upon this subject." A year later he referred to the discovery of the Plot and the subsequent punishment of Roman Catholic conspirators as a proof that England was not yet "utterly forsaken of the Lord its God."[2] Apart from sermons (at which we shall look in chapter seven) on this topic preached to his church, Owen felt moved to publish a short work entitled *The Church of Rome no safe Guide* (1679) and three years later *A Brief and Impartial Account of the Nature of the Protestant Religion* (1682).[3] These clearly reveal that the general range of Owen's eschatological thought had remained constant since the mid-1640s. He still saw in Revelation and II Thessalonians the prophecy of the rise, apostasy and then ultimate destruction of the Church of Rome as well as God's promise that Biblical religion would finally triumph in the latter days. Since, therefore, the imperfectly reformed Church of England had only a limited life, the saints of God should continue to look to God as their Deliverer.

The three Exclusion Parliaments which met between 1679 and 1681 in the aftermath of the disclosure of the Plot were assemblies in which not only Owen but Nonconformists in general took a lively interest. One Lancashire minister writing to a friend in Massachusetts expressed himself cautiously but hopefully: "Some more hopeful members are chosen unto our Parliament (that of March 1679) and it seems as if there might be some lifting of the yoke. The danger is lest the Parliament be too good to sit long."[4] One of the forty or more Presbyterian and Congregationalist members of the three Parliaments was Sir John Hartopp, by now an intimate friend of Owen. We may presume that from Sir John and from the Earl of Anglesey, who was both in the Lords and the Privy Council, as well as from others (e.g. Lord Wharton), Owen was kept well informed as to what transpired in both Whitehall and Westminster. He must have been fairly pleased with the work of the first Parliament, even though he probably shared Anglesey's vehement conviction that the King should never have dissolved it.[5] The passing

---

[1] Three of his sermons were printed in collections of the sermons edited by Nathaniel Vincent and Samuel Annesley. See *Works*, VIII, pp. 473ff.
[2] *Works*, IX, pp. 13 and 505. For the Plot see Ogg, *op. cit.*, pp. 559ff.
[3] *Works*, XIV, pp. 482ff and 530ff.
[4] Thomas Jollie to Increase Mather, *Collections* of the Massachusetts Historical Society, 4th series, Boston, 1868, VIII, p. 325.
[5] Lacey, *op. cit.*, p. 134.

of the Habeas Corpus Amendment Act, which provided that a prisoner could demand that his case be examined before the courts, may possibly have given him some satisfaction, while the decision not to renew the Licensing Act of 1662 must certainly have pleased him. On account of this Act Owen had encountered troubles in publishing several of his books. Yet the failure to pass the Bill which would have excluded the Duke of York from the throne must have been a real disappointment to him, dedicated as he was to the removal of all traces of popery. However, the substantial victory won by the Earl of Shaftesbury and his political associates in the new elections of the summer of 1679 came as a relief to the Nonconformists. In no small way they had contributed to the success of the Whig Party and they were naturally disappointed when the King prorogued Parliament immediately after its first meeting on the 7th October. When it seemed that the new Parliament would never be requested to return to Westminster, certain Whig and Nonconformist leaders organised petitions. Among the latter were John Owen, Richard Baxter, John Howe and Thomas Jacombe.[1] Little is known of these petitions but the fact that Owen and his brethren were involved with them reveals to what extent they were involved in active politics. In their view the propagation of the Gospel included necessary participation in political action.

Eventually Parliament returned to Westminster on the 26th October 1680. The Commons proceeded to pass a new and more stringent Exclusion Bill which was only rejected in the House of Lords by the brilliant advocacy of the Earl of Halifax. Shaftesbury, bold as ever, tried to indict the Duke of York as a popish recusant; he wanted to ensure that Charles was succeeded by the Duke of Monmouth, his illegitimate but Protestant son. Others wanted to see one of the Duke's Protestant daughters become heir to the throne. Despite the differences of opinion concerning the Protestant succession, most Whigs and Nonconformists were gratified to see the impeachment and execution of Lord Stafford, an elderly Roman Catholic, for his supposed part in the Popish Plot. With reference to this and earlier executions, Owen maintained that God had "stirred up some . . . of the nobles and our rulers . . . to pursue them to condign punishment who were the contrivers, authors, abettors and carriers on of that bloody design."[2] Nevertheless the Exclusion Bill was never passed either in this or the third brief Exclusion Parliament. The "Whig frenzy" was succeeded by the "Royalist reaction." The humiliated King regained much of his popularity and the Court party prepared to make the law courts the instrument of its revenge. In May 1682 the Duke of York was allowed to return from exile. The immediate future for Nonconformists seemed, and in fact turned out to be, bleak.

[1] Ibid, p. 138.   [2] *Works*, IX, p. 13.

In the period during which the second Exclusion Parliament was prorogued, Nonconformity found a formidable opponent in the person of Edward Stillingfleet, the Dean of St Paul's, London. Compared with the controversy the Dean caused, that which Parker had initiated a decade earlier was unimportant. Even Richard Baxter felt obliged to join in this time. Early in May 1680 the Dean preached before the Lord Mayor, Sir Robert Clayton, and other dignitaries in the Guildhall Chapel.[1] The sermon was later published as *The Mischief of Separation* (1680) and within twelve months had gone through at least four printings. According to its preface it was not designed to stir up a further persecution of Dissenters but rather to lay "a certain foundation for a lasting union" amongst English Protestants, that is between Conformists and Nonconformists. After deploring the sad divisions in English Christianity, Stillingfleet proceeded to an examination of his text (Philippians 3:16 "by that same rule let us walk") which he believed contained an apostolic rule—uniformity of worship and practice in the one Church in the one country. He went on to apply this supposed rule to the ecclesiastical situation in England with special reference to the practice of "lay communion" (i.e. attendance as laymen at the service of Holy Communion, etc.) by nonconformist ministers at parish churches. Protestant Dissenters agreed with the doctrinal articles of the Church of England; they conceded that many parish churches, if not all, contained congregations professing the true Faith of Christ, but yet they still stayed away from them. Their claim was that they were using the New Testament as their model; but if they were, he continued, why did they not have family churches like that of Aquila (Romans 16:3) or why did not they return to the community of goods (Acts 2:44) or to the washing of each other's feet (John 13)?

One of Stillingfleet's most subtle arguments was his use of the declaration of the majority of the divines of the Westminster Assembly against the request of the Dissenting Brethren for toleration of their congregationally-governed churches. He even supplied a quotation from the *Papers and Answers for . . . Accomodation* (1648),[2] to show that Nonconformists even fell under the condemnation of the Westminster divines! Then he continued by ridiculing the notion of "tender conscience" pleaded by many. In conclusion, he called for a realisation that no Church can be wholly pure on earth, that great men of the past (e.g. John Hooper and Nicholas Ridley)[3] had stayed within the Church, that the threat

[1] For Stillingfleet and Clayton see *D.N.B.*
[2] The full title was *The Papers and Answers of the Dissenting Brethren and the Committee of the Assembly of Divines. Given in to the Honorable Committee of Lords and Commons and Assembly of Divines with the Scotch Commissioners, for Accomodation at the Reviving of the Committee in 1645.*
[3] They were both martyrs under Mary Tudor. See A. G. Dickens, *The English Reformation*, 1967, pp. 362ff.

of Roman Catholicism demanded unity amongst Protestants, and that Nonconformists should not be always complaining of the suffering they underwent for their principles.

The publication of the sermon soon caused many men to write replies. Baxter wrote a private letter to the Dean and, not being satisfied with the answer he received, wrote "with so much anger and unbecoming passion," *Richard Baxter's Answer to Dr. E.S.'s Charge of Separation* (1680). Like "a well disposed gentleman" John Howe wrote *A Letter written out of the Country to a Person of Quality in the City* (1680). Vincent Alsop produced "with more than ordinary briskness" *The Mischief of Impositions* (1680). John Barret recalled Stillingfleet's earlier moderate views in his *The Rector of Sutton committed with the Dean of St Paul's: or, A Defence of Stillingfleet's "Irenicum" . . . against his late Sermon* (1680). With "civility and decent language" John Owen penned *A Brief Vindication of the Nonconformists from the Charge of Schism* (1680).[1] It was these five replies that Stillingfleet singled out for reply in his defence of the first book under the title, *The Unreasonableness of Separation* (1681).[2]

Owen decided that the purpose of *The Mischief of Separation* was threefold. First, it aimed at proving all Nonconformists guilty of schism and separation from the Church of England. Second, it sought to aggravate their supposed guilt and its consequences. Third, it charged them, and especially their ministers, with a lack of sincerity in the management and conduct of their dissent, especially in relation to "lay communion" with the Church of England. Neither did he agree with the Dean's explanation of Philippians 3:16. In his opinion the rule there stated required forbearance and charity amongst Christians of different backgrounds and attainments (e.g. between Jewish and Gentile Christians) not uniformity. So the verse had a very different application to Nonconformists than that envisaged by the Dean. As Owen explained:

> We deny that the apostles made or gave any such rules to the churches present in their days, or for the use of the churches in future ages, as should appoint and determine outward modes of worship, with ceremonies in their observation, stated feasts and fasts, beyond what is of divine institution, liturgies, or forms of prayer, or discipline to be exercised in law courts, subservient unto a national ecclesiastical government.[3]

The disputes in the Church of the second and third centuries over the date of Easter, with some claiming Johannine and others Petrine authority, prove that the apostles laid down no laws of uniformity.

With regard to lay communion Owen had some pertinent comments to make:

---
[1] *Works*, XIII, pp. 304ff.
[2] The descriptions of the men in this paragraph are those of Stillingfleet in his preface.
[3] *Works*, XIII, p. 323.

The question about lay communion is concerning that which is absolute and total, according unto all that is enjoined by the laws of the land and by the canons, constitutions, and orders of the Church. Hereby are they obliged to bring their children to be baptised with the use of the aerial sign of the cross; to kneel at Communion; to the religious observance of holidays; to the constant use of the Liturgy in all the public offices of the Church, unto the exclusion of the exercise of those gifts which Christ continues to communicate for its edification; to forego all means of public edification besides that in their parish churches, where, to speak with modesty, it is of times scanty and wanting; to renounce all other assemblies wherein they have had great experience of spiritual advantage unto their souls; to desert the observation of many useful Gospel duties, in their mutual watch that believers of the same church ought to have one over another; to divest themselves of all interest of a voluntary consent in the discipline of the Church, and choice of their pastors; and to submit unto an ecclesiastical rule and discipline which not one in a thousand of them can apprehend to have anything in it of the authority of Christ or rule of the Gospel.[1]

As far as he knew not more than six nonconformist ministers in the nation held the practice of "lay communion" to be lawful.

Owen was particularly sensitive to the claims made on behalf of a National Church to have the rights and power through the supreme magistrate of imposing rites and ceremonies as well as a particular form of church government. "Our sole enquiry," he emphasised, "is with what our Lord Jesus Christ hath ordained." He went on to admit that Stillingfleet's point about the views of the majority of divines in the Westminster Assembly seemed valid, but he refused to agree that it had any reference to the situation in 1680 when the issues were different.

> Those who pleaded then for a kind of conformity or agreement in total communion did not propose one of those things, as the condition of it, which are now pleaded as the only reasons of witholding the same kind of conformity from the Church of England, and the non-imposition of any such things that made the foundation of their plea for the compliance of others with them; and those on the other side, who pleaded for liberty and forbearance in such a case as wherein there were no impositions, did it mostly on the common liberty which, as they judged, they had with their other brethren to abide by the way which they had declared and practised long before any rule was established unto its prejudice.[2]

In other words, the uniformity proposed by Presbyterians in 1645 did not include those things (e.g. compulsory liturgy, prelacy, diocesan ecclesiastical courts, ceremonies, and the sign of the cross in baptism) which were required by the Act of Uniformity of 1662. Owen ended

[1] *Works*, XIII, p. 313.
[2] *Works*, XIII, p. 338.

his tract with a moving defence of those whom the Dean had been pleased to accuse of chronic complaining.

Following Stillingfleet's answer, *The Unreasonableness of Separation* which first appeared in print in the London bookshops in December 1680 when Parliament was discussing two further bills which related to Comprehension and Toleration, more replies appeared and the controversy dragged on for several more years.[1] Owen himself briefly replied to Stillingfleet's second tract in an appendix to his *An Inquiry into the Original Nature . . . and Communion of Evangelical Churches* (1681).[2] One point that he made exceedingly clear was that Nonconformists were in no way guilty of encouraging Popery through their separation from the Established Church. For, as he pointed out, if the Jesuits did take over England it would be the staunch opponents of Roman Catholicism, mostly Nonconformists, who would first drink the "cup of their fury."

A most interesting fact about the discussions in the second Exclusion Parliament was that it was Churchmen alone who took any interest in comprehension of Dissenters within the State Church. The Nonconformists in the Commons worked only for an Act allowing legal conventicles. Outside Parliament London merchants had drawn up proposals for an agreement between Presbyterians and Congregationalists. These were sent for study by ministers in Bristol and then returned for revision by London ministers.[3] Owen himself studied this document, and told Thomas Jollie, the minister at Wymondhouses in Lancashire, of his agreement with it and of his great desire to see some form of unity amongst Nonconformists.[4] Unfortunately we have little or no information about the progress of discussions in London concerning the document. Possibly they were kept secret in order not to cause resentment in government circles. And the same fear may have been the reason why they were never implemented. Hopefully waiting for the toleration Bill to become law, it was probably the intention of the ministers and merchants to publicise it after the Bill was on the Statute Book, but, when the Bill failed to become law and when persecution was intensified, the contents of the document became for the time being impractical and it was shelved until after the Revolution of 1688. However, one fact is clear from a study of the document. The unity aimed at was to strengthen Nonconformity as a force permanently outside the Church of England. Gone was the idealism of Baxter which hoped to see most Dissenters back into the National Church.

As we have seen, the renewal of persecution in 1681 came about

[1] Thomas, *op. cit.*, pp. 225ff.
[2] *Works*, XV, pp. 188ff.
[3] This document has been edited by Roger Thomas and printed as a pamphlet by Dr Williams's Library as Occasional Paper, No. 6.
[4] See Dr Will.Lib. Occasional Paper No. 6, p. 16 for details.

because Shaftesbury and the Whigs, by their demands and their attempts to exclude the Duke of York from the succession to the throne, had over-reached themselves and allowed the humiliated King to invoke the sympathy of his subjects.[1] Royalist reaction and general fear of another period of civil unrest like that of the 1640s caused magistrates to implement the law against Nonconformists with zeal. Protestant Dissenters suffered the penalty for their support of the Whig programme. Though a sick man Owen was incensed by what was happening around him and he proceeded to write at least two pamphlets in defence of his brethren who were being roughly treated. In *The Case of Present Distresses on Nonconformists Examined*[2] he argued that the trial practised under the Conventicle Act was contrary to the basic law of nations (cf. Acts 25:16), to common sense, and to the very purpose of penal laws, which were to enquire into offences for the good of the public peace, not to function for the advantage of informers. Laws ought not to be turned into snares and neither should they be construed to the gain of some other person than the one accused. It was probably the strong measures taken against conventicles during 1681-2 by magistrates in London (who were urged to act by the Privy Council) which led to the writing of *A Word of Advice to the Citizens of London*.[3] In this he protested against the equation in law of such crimes as murder and theft with the harmless activity of worshipping God in a conventicle. This was a monstrous situation and ought to be remedied.

The same persecution against which he vehemently protested Owen also personally experienced in mild form. On one occasion, for example, when travelling into the City of London from Kensington, where he lived in the late 1670s, his horse and carriage was stopped in the Strand by two government informers and he was required to get out. Happily for Owen, Sir Edmund Berry Godfrey, a Justice of the Peace who figured prominently in the early history of the disclosure of the Popish Plot, was passing at the time and he stopped his carriage to ascertain what was happening. He ordered both Owen and the informers to meet him in his rooms at Bloomsbury where he satisfied himself that there was no case against the divine.[4] A few years later, in November 1681, Owen was prosecuted under the Five Mile Act along with other notable Congregational ministers, John Collins, Samuel Slater, Matthew Mead and Robert Ferguson.[5] In 1682 further summonses were issued against George Griffith and Owen and government spies reported that he did not pray for either the King or government in his prayers within his

[1] Lacey, *op. cit.*, pp. 150ff.
[2] *Works*, XIII, pp. 578ff. "Distresses" is the equivalent of the modern word "distraints" and is a legal term relating to the seizure of goods. Stoughton, *op. cit.*, IV, pp. 54ff.
[3] *Works*, XIII, pp. 587ff.
[4] Asty, p. xxxii. For Godfrey see *D.N.B.*
[5] *C.S.P.D.* (1680-81), pp. 592 and 613.

PROTESTANT NONCONFORMIST 149

gathered church which met in Leadenhall Street.[1] He was arrested once more in 1683, suspected of complicity in the Rye House Plot to assassinate Charles II and place the Duke of Monmouth on the throne.[2] Owen had no part in this plot but his former assistant minister, Robert Ferguson (whom we shall notice in the next chapter) had, and it was probably this connexion which was used to justify suspicion being cast on Owen. This, however, was the last time that the authorities were able to arrest or persecute him, for he died at Ealing in August 1683.

In comparison with some of his fellow nonconformist ministers Owen had not experienced great personal difficulties under the effects of the Clarendon Code. He had not been in prison, but his friend Thomas Jollie had been in prison five times.[3] Richard Baxter and John Bunyan had also seen the inside of a gaol for considerable periods. Owen's comparative freedom from persecution and privation was in part due to the fact that during his days as Dean of Christ Church he had accumulated a large group of friends, many of them wealthy, and these stood by him and supported him with their hospitality and help. Even if, like Sir William Morice, they did not wholly agree with his Congregational viewpoint, they still admired and respected him. His financial position was secured by the possession of lands and property which he had bought during the 1650s, the legacy of Martyn Owen in 1668 of £500 and by his second marriage in June 1677 to the wealthy young widow of Thomas D'Oyley.[4] Yet, despite his affluence, Owen was not ignorant of the suffering of his brethren under the severity of the penal laws. Utilising his friendship with members of both Houses of Parliament he gave much of his time after 1660 to the search for a legal toleration of Protestant Nonconformists. Regrettably, he did not live long enough to see his efforts come to fruition.

---

[1] C.S.P.D. (1682), pp. 86-7, and 104.
[2] C.S.P.D. (Jan-June, 1683), p. 356. His brother, Henry Owen, was arrested for alleged support of a proposed rebellion. Ibid, pp. 349 and 367-8.
[3] Cf. Jones, *Congregationalism in England*, p. 76.
[4] Owen's possession of lands is seen in his will, *Correspondence*, p. 181. His wife was the niece of John D'Oyley of Stadhampton. The marriage is recorded in *Calendar of Marriage Licences issued by the Faculty Office, 1632-1714*, 1905, p. 68.

CHAPTER VII

## PASTOR AND THEOLOGIAN

"IF A MAN ASPIRES TO THE OFFICE OF AN OVERSEER," WROTE THE APOSTLE Paul to Timothy, "he desires a noble task." Since Owen was a pastor for most, if not all, of the years from the Restoration to his death, he did indeed have a noble task as his primary calling. To be a pastor of a gathered church, or, as it was often called, a conventicle, in the reign of Charles II involved a rather different attitude towards the State and the law than it did, for example, in the reign of William and Mary or than it does today. From 1662 to 1689 Nonconformists lived under the dark cloud of repressive legislation and of this the pastor and his flock had to take careful notice. Owen and most of the ejected ministers who became nonconformists seem to have regarded both the Five Mile Act and Conventicle Act as legislation they should not necessarily obey. They had no feelings of guilt when prosecuted under these laws.[1] Their disobedience brought suffering and financial loss but it meant they were obeying Christ which to them was far better. Nevertheless, as we have seen, their disobedience was accompanied by a reasonable attempt to persuade both King and Parliament that persecution of Protestant Dissenters was not in either the national or Protestant interest. In this chapter we shall be particularly concerned with Owen's work as a pastor, Congregational leader and theologian. This will involve, first of all, an attempt to establish the identity of the churches to which he regularly preached and the type of people who belonged to them. Secondly, we shall note what kind of sermons he preached to his hearers. Then thirdly, since Owen was a staunch advocate of fellowship amongst churches, we shall look at his relationship with other men of the Congregational way. Finally, we shall examine the great devotional and theological books that came from his pen in the last twenty years of his life, when, relieved of direct academic and political responsibility, his mind was relatively free to study those things he loved most of all.

In previous chapters we have made reference to the Congregational church which Owen gathered at Coggeshall in 1646, to the problem of his church affiliation from 1651 to 1658, to the church to which he preached in Wallingford House in 1659, and to the conventicles at Stadhampton and in the City of London in which he ministered after 1660. It may well be that the small church of which he was pastor in

[1] Cf. Cragg, *Puritanism in the Period of Great Persecution, 1660–1688*, pp. 31ff.

1673 and which joined that same year with the larger church whose pastor, Joseph Caryl, had recently died, was the continuation of the church which had met until 1660 in Wallingford House, and then afterwards in various places in and around the home of Mrs Holmes near Moorgate. Though, as we shall see, certain members of the church in Wallingford House were also members of the church which took part in the union in 1673, this in itself is not conclusive evidence of the direct continuity of the church founded in 1659 into the 1670s. Since no church book or other similar evidence has been forthcoming to throw light on this matter, one cannot speak with any certainty about this continuity.

From a list preserved in the Congregational Library, London,[1] we know that Owen's small pre-1673 church had fewer than forty members, though we may presume that more than this number would have attended to hear his sermons. To the contemporary onlooker it must have seemed that this church was as much a society of old friends and former associates of Oliver Cromwell as a gathered church. Indeed, it could have appeared to some that it was a group of discontented former army officers and their friends enjoying the comforts offered by the ministrations of a former chaplain of Oliver. Such a view, whilst containing more than a grain of truth, is far from being the whole truth, as will be seen in the examination of the membership and its relationship to Owen. First of all there were at least five former soldiers, their wives, relatives and servants connected with the church. They were Charles Fleetwood, John Desborough, James Berry, Jeffrey Ellaston and Griffith Lloyd.

Charles Fleetwood, the former general who now lived at Stoke Newington with his third wife, the former Lady Hartopp, was among twenty named in the Act of Indemnity (1660) as incapacitated for ever from holding public appointment.[2] Despite this incapacitation he seems to have lived peacefully in the Fleetwood House, as it was called. Perhaps he fulfilled some of his political ambitions through advising his son-in-law, Sir John Hartopp, who was a member of the three Exclusion Parliaments. John Desborough, with whom Owen co-operated in the moves to persuade Oliver not to become King of England, was likewise legally incapacitated from public office. Suspected of plotting, he was imprisoned. Escaping, he fled to Holland but returned to England in 1666 only to be cast into Dover Castle and then the Tower of London before being released. He finally settled down at Hackney, a village not

---

[1] This List containing the names of members of Owen's church, Caryl's church, and all admitted to the united church is described and printed in part by T. G. Crippen, "Dr Watts's Church Book," *Transactions* of the Cong. Hist. Soc., I, April, 1901, pp. 26ff.

[2] The Bill of Indemnity received the royal assent on 29 August 1660. It bestowed a general pardon for all treasons, felonies and many other offences committed since 1 January 1637. Thirty men were excluded by name from the benefits of the Bill and some of these were executed.

too far from Stoke Newington, and within easy reach of Moorgate. Like Desborough, James Berry, who had been Comwell's Major-General in charge of Wales and the border counties, was also arrested after the Restoration. He spent time in the Tower of London as well as in the castle at Scarborough, where one of his fellow prisoners was George Fox, the Quaker. Eventually he was set free in 1672 and then, through the help of Fleetwood, he found a house in Stoke Newington. So the three men, all of whom had been members of the church in Wallingford House, were able to meet frequently and discuss both former and current times.[1] The two other former soldiers were Lieutenant-Colonel Jeffrey Ellaston and Captain Griffith Lloyd. Ellaston became a Major in 1658 and a year later the Lieutenant-Colonel of the Foot Regiment. In his will Owen left him £10. Lloyd, who died in 1682, was made a captain in the New Model Army in 1647 and in 1659 he had the honour of negotiating for Fleetwood and Lambert with Monck. Both Ellaston and Lloyd probably had been members of the church in Wallingford House.[2]

Other members included Mrs Bridget Bendish, the daughter of Henry Ireton and thus granddaughter of Oliver. Born in 1649 she lived with her step-father, Charles Fleetwood, at Stoke Newington until her marriage in 1669 to Thomas Bendish of Yarmouth, the son of the Ambassador to Turkey of the same name. It was said that her features closely resembled those of her grandfather. Then there were Mr and Mrs Thomas D'Oyley, relatives of the D'Oyleys of Stadhampton; Mrs Polhill, wife of Edward Polhill of Burwash, Sussex; William Steele, a serjeant-at-law and former Lord Chancellor of Ireland from 1656 to 1659; Dr William Staines, a physician; Sir John and Lady Elizabeth Hartopp and Smith Fleetwood, son of Charles.[3] Another interesting member who eventually left in 1677 to become a pastor himself was Samuel Lee, the former Dean of Wadham College, Oxford. He had a very strong belief in the doctrine of the restoration of the Jewish nation to Palestine and published a widely read book, *Israel Redux* (1677), which was several times reprinted. Naturally there would have been an element of nostalgia amongst many of the members as they looked back to former times when they were in positions of authority. But that

[1] For the careers of Fleetwood and Desborough see Maurice Ashley, *Cromwell's Generals*, 1954, and for Berry, Sir James Berry and S. G. Lee, *A Cromwellian Major-General*, Oxford, 1938.
[2] For reference to Ellaston and Lloyd see C. Firth and G. Davies, *The Regimental History of Cromwell's Army*, Oxford, 1940, pp. 93-9 and 485-7. See *Correspondence*, p. 185 for Owen's bequest to Ellaston.
[3] For Edward Polhill see *D.N.B.* as also for William Steele. When the latter died in 1680 Owen had the following to say about him: "As far as I know by thirty years' acquaintance and friendship, and half that time in church fellowship, it may be the age wherein he lived did not produce many more wise, more holy more useful than he in his station, if any." *Works*, IX, p. 341. Incidentally, this suggests that in 1665 Owen's church, which eventually joined with Caryl's, was in existence.

the church was basically a spiritual institution, gathered to the glory of God, is seen in the letters which Owen wrote to some of them.[1] After the death in July 1673 of Mrs Griffith Lloyd, Owen wrote a moving letter to her sister Mrs Polhill, who was probably at her Burwash home. "It adds to my trouble," he told her, "that I cannot possibly come down to you this week. . . . Christ is your Pilot; and however the vessel is tossed whilst He seems to sleep, He will arise and rebuke these winds and waves in His own time. . . . Sorrow not too much for the dead; she is entered into her rest and is taken away from the evil to come." Writing to Lady Hartopp in 1674 after the death of her baby, Anne, he advised her to remember God's faithfulness to His elect: "your dear infant is in the eternal enjoyment of the fruits of all our prayers; for the covenant of God is ordered in all things and sure. We shall go to her; she shall not return to us." Owen had in mind the statement of the Apostle Peter in Acts 2:42, "The promise (of salvation) is unto you and your children." Also in 1674 he shared with Charles Fleetwood his feelings about his recurring illness and of the future of the churches, asking, him "to contend (with God) yet more earnestly . . . after spiritual revivals." "Christ is our best friend," he told Sir John Hartopp as he lay ill, "and ere long will be our only friend. I pray God with all my heart that I may be weary of everything else but converse and communion with Him."

If the charge could be levelled against Owen's church that it was a society of discontented republicans then it could also be levelled, but with even less justice, against the church of which Joseph Caryl was pastor until 1673. Caryl had been a member of the Westminster Assembly of divines and a prominent Independent during the Interregnum. After 1662 he became a leading Nonconformist. In 1663 he was reported as meeting frequently with a congregation in Soper Lane and of preaching in his own house. In 1672 he was licensed as a Congregational pastor to preach in Leadenhall Street with William Beerman, the ejected chaplain of St Thomas's Hospital, Southwark, as his assistant.[2] The church to which they preached had about one hundred and thirty-six members. It is impossible to identify most of these people now, but amongst those who may be identified were Benjamin and Mary Shute, the parents of the first Viscount Barrington; Lady Vere Wilkinson, wife of the former Canon of Christ Church, Henry Wilkinson; Mrs Sarah Abney, who owned the house at Theobalds where Owen stayed, and Mrs Frances Thompson, daughter of the Earl of Anglesey and wife of John Thompson, who was created Baron Haversham in December 1673.[3] The membership of Caryl's church gives the impression of being rather more broadly

---

[1] *Correspondence*, No's 83–87 and 93, pp. 157ff.
[2] For both Caryl's and Beerman's movements after 1662 see *C.R.*
[3] For John Shute Barrington and John Thompson see *D.N.B.*

based than was Owen's. Be that as it may, following the death of Caryl the church realised that there was no better man available to be its guide than John Owen.

The union of the two churches took place on the 5th June 1673 in the Meeting House in Leadenhall Street. For his text Owen took Colossians 3:14, "And above all things put on charity, which is the bond of perfection."[1] His theme was mutual love amongst the members, especially at this time when persecution was likely to return since the seal had been broken off the Declaration of Indulgence a few weeks earlier. "Let none," he proclaimed, "pretend that they love the brethren in general, and love the people of God and love the saints, while their love is not fervently exercised towards those who are in the same church-society with them." Since the new church contained rich people as well as their servants and others of little material wealth, he closed his sermon with a few words of advice to those who enjoyed the benefits of this world's goods.

> I would speak to them who have the advantage of riches, wealth, honour, reputation in the world; which encompass them with so many circumstances that they know not how to break through them to that familiarity of love with the meanest member of the church which is required of them. Brethren, know the gospel leaves all your providential advantages entirely to you; whatever you have by birth, education, inheritance, estate, titles, places, it leaves the entire enjoyment of them. But in things which purely concern your communion together, the gospel lays all level: there is neither rich nor poor, free nor bond in Christ, but the new creature . . . And let me beg of you that are rich to remember this common Lord and Master; and let not your outward advantages, therefore, keep you at a distance from the meanest, the poorest saint that belongs unto the congregation.

Obviously believing that the class structure of society was within God's permissible will for mankind, Owen was true to his gospel in emphasising that the church should be the place where there is true equality in Christ. Unfortunately we have no information as to how the church exercised the virtue of charity either towards poor members or towards suffering, penniless Nonconformists in country areas. That the church did help is suggested by the contents of the will of William Beerman who left £200 for the relief of ministers and their widows.[2]

Between 1673 and 1683 one hundred and eleven people from all walks of life were received into the membership of the new church. Amongst those who can be identified with certainty were a daughter of Dr Owen named Mrs Kennington who died in April 1682 and a son of

---

[1] The sermon is in *Works*, IX, pp. 256ff.
[2] The reference to the will is in *C.R.* s.v. Beerman. In the united church Beerman does not seem to have held office and therefore done no regular preaching.

Charles Fleetwood by his second wife, Cromwell Fleetwood. Two of the wealthier new members were the Countess of Anglesey (Mrs Arthur Annesley) and Sir Thomas Overbury. Though her daughter, Frances Thompson, had been a member for over seven years, the Countess did not feel able to join for one reason or another until October 1680. Before that time, the Countess had often entertained both the first and second Mrs Owen with their husband. Indeed, so great was the attachment of the Countess to Owen, her spiritual director, that she requested permission from Mrs Dorothy Owen to be buried near him in Bunhill Fields. And in January 1684, a few months after his decease, she was arrested for attending the conventicle in Leadenhall Street to hear Owen's successor, David Clarkson, preach.[1] Sir Thomas Overbury, nephew of the poet of the same name, was knighted by Charles II in June 1660.[2] He settled at Bourton-on-the-Hill in 1663. Soon afterwards he became convinced of the justice of the Protestant Nonconformist position and on at least one occasion he had Owen as a guest. However, being often in London, he joined the Leadenhall Street church in 1675. A few years later he sold his property at Bourton and moved to a new house at Quinton in Northamptonshire. But before he left Gloucestershire he was involved in a sharp controversy with a neighbour and former opponent of his pastor, George Vernon, the rector of Bourton-on-the-Water. The issue was whether human rulers had the right to impose forms of religious worship upon their people and persecute those who for conscience-sake refused to obey. Overbury answered in the negative, Vernon in the affirmative.

To help with the preaching and pastoral responsibilities in the enlarged church, three ministers were chosen to share the burden of the work with Owen during the last ten years of his life. The first was Isaac Loeffs who was ordained or set apart as teacher of the church on December 26 1673. A graduate of Cambridge and former Fellow of Peterhouse, he had been rector of Shenley in Hertfordshire and had attended the Savoy Assembly in 1658. After his ejection in 1662 he remained in Hertfordshire and preached at such places as Shenley, St Albans, Elstree, Codicote and Ridge. He probably remained as teacher of the London church for nine years, preaching regularly both on the Lord's Day and at mid-week services. In 1682 David Clarkson succeeded him.[3] Like Loeffs, Clarkson was a Cambridge graduate. He was ejected from the curacy of Mortlake, near London, but was licensed to preach near his former parish church in 1672. Richard Baxter considered him to be "a divine of extraordinary worth." Owen must have had a similar estimation of him and found in him a great source of help in the last

[1] Asty, p. xxix and Lacey, op. cit., p. 460.
[2] For Overbury and his uncle see D.N.B.
[3] Both Loeffs and Clarkson are in C.R.

year of his life. It would have been a comfort for the dying pastor to know that in Clarkson the church had a teacher who was eminently suited to take over the leadership when he died.

The most controversial of Owen's ministerial colleagures was Robert Ferguson who was appointed as Owen's personal assistant in November 1674.[1] Educated in Scotland, Ferguson moved to England and became vicar of Godmersham in Kent. After his ejection he was imprisoned for four months in 1663 for illegal activities as a Nonconformist. But it was his book on the Protestant doctrine of justification by faith, *Justification only upon a Satisfaction* (1668), which brought him to the attention of Owen and which led on to his work with him. During 1675 in the first year of his assistantship Ferguson joined with Edward Polhill and others to defend Owen from the attack by William Sherlock, a London Anglican rector, on his views concerning the believer's communion with God. It was not these two books, however, which brought Ferguson a national reputation. The latter came out of his involvement in the politics of the period. He enthusiastically joined with the Earl of Shaftesbury in efforts to ensure the Protestant succession to the throne. In 1680 he published his first political pamphlet *A Letter to a Person of Honour concerning the "Black Box."* The box, if there was one, was supposed to contain proof that Charles II was legally married to Lucy Walters, the mother of the Duke of Monmouth. Ferguson believed that the story about the box was false and that it had been invented to divert attention from the treasonable activity of the Duke of York. So he sought to turn popular prejudice against the Duke. The King replied to the demands in this and other pamphlets by disavowing any true marriage to Lucy Walters. This action induced Ferguson to produce another pamphlet which promised that evidence of the marriage would be forthcoming soon. Further pamphlets flowed from his pen as controversy raged around the Exclusion Bill. When, a little later, the Tory reaction had set in against the Whigs and Shaftesbury's life was in danger Ferguson sought to show that there never had been a Protestant Plot and that the very idea of one was the invention of the Papists. In 1683 he was involved in the Rye House Plot and after its failure he found it expedient to make his escape with Shaftesbury and return to Holland where he had sought refuge in 1682. But this was not the end of his activities. For twenty more years he was involved in efforts of various kinds either to prevent James succeeding to the throne, or, strangely, at a later date, to support the Jacobites! Since it is not known when Ferguson ceased to be a member of the Leadenhall Street church (although it was probably not until 1682), it is difficult to assess to what extent, if

---

[1] For Ferguson see both *C.R.*, and *D.N.B.*, and James Ferguson, *Robert Ferguson the Plotter*, Edinburgh, 1887. For Ferguson and Monmouth see W. R. Emerson, *Monmouth's Rebellion*, New Haven, 1951, pp. 10ff.

any, Owen supported his more extreme political activities. There must have been something particularly attractive about Ferguson, apart from his obvious Calvinistic orthodoxy, to have caused Owen to like him and stand by him. When he fled to Holland in 1682, Owen wrote to him there and in his will he left his former assistant the sum of five pounds (the same amount which he left to Loeffs and Clarkson).[1] Perhaps Owen, irenical in nature, was glad to have by his side a man who was so militantly anti-Catholic. Maybe he had a psychological need to be complemented by an aggressive personality.

Whatever were the reasons that bound Ferguson to Owen, the latter's concern for the spiritual welfare of the church and the church-officers, of whom Ferguson was one, is seen in the moving letter he wrote to his church from Wooburn, where he was the guest of Lord Wharton. The date of the letter is not known but its contents reflect a period of impending persecution, probably 1681 or 1682.[2] "Although I am absent from you in body," he wrote, "I am in mind, affection and spirit present with you, and in your assemblies; for I hope you will be found my crown and rejoicing in the day of the Lord." He prayed that any shame and financial loss they might undergo for the sake of Christ they would regard as a great honour. He hoped that any season of difficulty would be a means of causing the increase of mutual love amongst the church members. And in particular he counselled:

> I could wish that because you have no ruling elders, and your teachers cannot walk about publicly with safety, that you would appoint some among yourselves, who may continually as their occasions will admit, go up and down from house to house and apply themselves peculiarly to the weak, the tempted, the fearful, those who are ready to despond, or to halt, and to encourage them in the Lord. Choose out those unto this end who are endued with a spirit of courage and fortitude; and let them know that they are happy whom Christ will honour with His blessed work.

Finally, he requested that they see whatever happened to them as from the Lord and to be used for the blessing of their souls.

Only a small proportion of the many sermons that Owen preached to the Congregational church in Leadenhall Street between 1673 and 1683 were ever printed.[3] From these it is clear that he regarded his principal task as a preacher to be that of carefully expounding and explaining the nature of the biblical view of the Christian life and witness, exhorting his hearers zealously to obey and seek after God and to cultivate the

---

[1] For Owen's will see *Correspondence*, pp. 181ff. Our knowledge of Owen's letters to Ferguson comes from letters written by Ferguson to his wife. In these he mentioned receiving letters from Owen. Cf. *C.S.P.D.* (1682), pp. 554, 575 etc. and J. Ferguson, *op. cit.*, pp. 93ff.
[2] *Correspondence*, No. 94, p. 110.
[3] What were printed are in *Works*, VIII and IX.

grace of God in their hearts. He placed great stress not only upon sound doctrine but also upon the actual experience of God in Christian worship and in the soul of the believer. The extant sermons cover such topics as the excellency of Christ, personal holiness, the nature of the church, cases of conscience, reaction to persecution and the proper approach to the Lord's Supper. As we shall be briefly examining both his views on Christ, the church and personal holiness later in this chapter it will perhaps be in order here to notice what approach to the Lord's Supper he advocated and just how he, as a leading Nonconformist, counselled his hearers to face difficulties and opposition.

At least eleven sermons of contemporary interest were preached during 1680 and 1681 when, despite the sitting of Whig Parliaments, there was still a grave fear that Charles II might die and be succeeded by James, Duke of York, who was expected to encourage popery. All eleven sermons recommend the saints to trust in God and to have faith in His grace and providence, but, two in particular, one preached in May 1680 and the other in December 1681, may be used to illustrate Owen's interpretation of how the believer should respond to the contemporary threat of Roman Catholicism.[1] Beginning from the proposition that "the just shall live by faith" (Habakkuk 2:4), Owen raised the question on the 7th May 1680 as to how one lived by faith in the prospect of the danger of the return of popery to England. He regarded this as an important question, for, as he said: "I verily believe that those who have the conduct of the papal, antichristian affairs throughout the world are endeavouring to bring Popery in upon us." His answer was in the form of the enunciation of various themes and propositions for the comfort and strengthening of faith in his hearers. The first was "that there is a fixed, determinate time in the counsel of God when Antichrist and Babylon, and idolatry and superstition, together with the profaneness of life they have brought in, shall be destroyed." The future destruction of Roman Catholicism was assured in divine prophecy. Following from this, his second theme was that "it is no less glorious to suffer under the beast and the false prophet than it was to suffer under the dragon." The early Christians were persecuted by the Roman Empire and for this they had been universally praised. Likewise those who suffered under Roman Catholicism would be as widely acclaimed. Recalling the example of the martyrs of the sixteenth century, he counselled that "if a time of going unto Smithfield should come again—if God shall call us to that fiery trial or any other whatever it be—remember that to suffer against Antichrist is as great and glorious as to suffer against Paganism." Yet, come what may, the Protestant cause would "be as truly, certainly, and infallibly victorious, as that Christ sits at the right hand of God." He closed by issuing a warning, based

[1] *Works*, IX, pp. 505ff and pp. 3ff.

upon his experiences over the years, especially perhaps in the 1650s. "Take heed of computations. How wofully and wretchedly we have been mistaken by this! We know the time is determined—its beginning and ending is known to God; and we must live by faith till the accomplishment."

The sermon preached on the 22nd December 1681 was on the occasion of a day of prayer and fasting, and it found Owen in a most serious and solemn mood. He was convinced that England was filled with open sin and rebellion against God. "Oh, poor England," he exclaimed, "among all thy lovers thou hast not one to plead for thee this day! From the height of profaneness and atheism, through the filthiness of sensuality and uncleanness, down to the lowest oppression and cheating, the land is filled with all sorts of sin." He went on to maintain that God had given repeated warnings to the land since 1662. There was the "desolating Plague" of 1665, the "raging Fire" of 1666, the "bloody war" with the Dutch, and the "prodigious appearances in the heaven."[1] Not paying heed to these divine warnings, the King and his government had continued to compromise the Protestant faith in their dealings with France and the Papacy. Happily, however, England was not utterly forsaken by God even though judgement was near. The disclosure of the Plot, the determination to punish those implicated in it and the fact that the nation was still one and not torn by war were all sure signs of divine blessing. But the question was: what could be done to avert God's future judgement? There must be, he answered, national repentance and universal reformation. Means must quickly be provided for the *free* propagation of the Word of God throughout the land and magistrates must work from better principles. In other words, the restrictions on, and persecution of, Protestants must cease in order that the gospel could be freely heard in the whole land and the people could be given the opportunity to repent. When Owen died two years later he still expected judgement from God to descend upon England and the churches to pass through a time of severe trial. Had he lived, as did Richard Baxter, to see the arrival of William of Orange and experience the freedom after the passing of the Toleration Act of 1689, perhaps he would have felt that God's immediate threat of judgement had been lifted.

Of Owen's sacramental discourses it may be said with truth that they have not become obsolete with the passing of time. They contain no contemporary references; rather they reveal a profound understanding of what may be termed the Calvinistic view of the Lord's Supper. The meal for him was a thanksgiving, a memorial and a communion. In it he thanked God for the benefits of redemption, remembered the body and blood of Christ whereby that redemption was won, and communed

[1] Owen probably refers to Halley's Comet of 1680. See J. M. Robinson, *The Great Comet of 1680*, Northfield, Minnesota, 1916.

in his soul through the Holy Spirit with the risen Lord. "Christ is present in this ordinance," he stated, "in an especial manner in three ways: by representation, by exhibition and by obsignation."[1] By representation Owen meant that Christ presented Himself at the Supper through the symbols of bread and wine as the food for the believers' souls and as the One who suffered for their sins. By exhibition, he understood that Christ manifested Himself through the elements revealing "His flesh as meat indeed and his blood as drink indeed" (John 6:56). Finally, by obsignation he meant that the Lord's Supper was the form of a seal from God, a confirmation of the new testament, the new relationship between the believer and his Saviour. Though he believed that the Lord's Supper should be commemorated every Lord's Day, his own church probably held the service less frequently than this in the difficult years between 1662 and 1683. As to the other ordinance, baptism, no records of child baptisms have been preserved but we must presume that he performed this rite on some occasions since Lady Hartopp, at least, had several children during the years of his pastorate.

Having looked at Owen's work in the church in Leadenhall Street, we must now turn to his larger rôle within Congregationalism. Several years ago Geoffrey F. Nuttall expressed the view that "after the Restoration his position as a Congregational leader and thus a link between the now scattered and persecuted churches, became, if it were possible, yet more striking" than his leadership in the 1650s.[2] George Vernon, who, as we have seen, had no particular love for Owen, unwittingly supplied confirmation of this when he informed his readers in 1670 that the Congregational churches maintained contact and passed news by means of lines of communication established originally at the Savoy Assembly in 1658. News of what happened in London and Westminster was conveyed to Owen and his "under-officers" (Goodwin, Nye, Griffith etc.) and by them and their contacts to all parts of the country.[3] To Vernon, Owen was "the Prince, the Oracle, the Metropolitan of Independency." Further evidence for Owen's leadership is seen in his dealings with the King and government on behalf of the churches and at this we looked in the last chapter. Now we must notice the advice he gave in person or by letter to men who either came to see him or sought his help in writing.

Between 1675 and 1679, for example, he corresponded with and met Robert Asty, once a member of the Congregational church at Coggeshall.[4] The young man's first problem was whether or not he should accept the call of the Norwich church to be its teacher. Following the decease

---

[1] *Works*, IX, p. 573.
[2] Nuttall, *Visible Saints*, p. 39.
[3] Vernon, *Letter to a Friend*, p. 34.
[4] For the letters see *Correspondence*, No's 88-90, pp. 161-3. Owen to Asty.

of Thomas Allen, the former pastor and (before 1662) rector of St George, Tombland, the Norwich church decided to call both a pastor and a teacher. This was a common practice even though the rôles of the two were far from clearly defined in Congregational thinking. Even Owen admitted to Asty that he knew "no difference between a pastor and a teacher but what follows (from) their different gifts." Owen's advice to Asty was that he should accept the call. "I do not see how you can waive or decline the call of the church," he wrote, "either in conscience or reputation." Before accepting it, however, Asty ought to sit down and consider what it would cost him in view of the demands of the ministry and the difficulties faced by Dissenters. Asty finally decided to accept the call of the church as also did John Cromwell, the ejected minister of Clayworth, Nottinghamshire, who became the pastor.[1] Unfortunately, the two men did not always see eye to eye and both sought the wisdom of Owen on how to heal their relationship. We only have his reply to Asty to whom his advice was to beware of "earnestness of spirit and aggravation of things in our own concerns" and to suffer injustice quietly. What impact Owen's letters had on Asty and Cromwell we do not know; what is certain is that Cromwell suffered much: he "was pursued with indictments at Sessions and Assizes and then with citations out of the Ecclesiastical Courts." So apart from the internal problems of his church he, and no doubt Asty as well, faced much persecution.

Other people whom Owen helped were Thomas Jollie and John Bunyan. After Jollie had come from the north to visit Owen in London he wrote: "I may not deny that special guidance and assistance which I had both privately and publicly (whilst in London). I must own the grace of God in Dr Owen especially and in others also."[2] This visit was in 1675; five years later Owen discussed with Jollie the plans for unity of Congregationalists and Presbyterians and, as we noticed in the last chapter, he was wholly in favour of the scheme. During 1675-6 Owen was also able to be of some help to the pastor of the Bedford Congregational church, the famous John Bunyan. The former tinker was often in prison because of his nonconformist principles and practice and to assist in the task of getting him released someone wrote to Owen for his help. Owen contacted his former tutor, Thomas Barlow, now the Bishop of Lincoln, but Barlow could not effect the release. So in this undertaking Owen's help proved of no avail. When, however, Bunyan was released in 1676, he brought out of prison a manuscript, the worth and importance of which he could hardly have comprehended.

[1] For the details of the Norwich church see J. Browne, *History of Congregationalism in Norfolk and Suffolk*, 1877, pp. 252ff. For Cromwell see C.R. It was John Asty, son of Robert, who wrote the *Memoir* of Owen in 1721.
[2] *The Note Book of the Rev. Thomas Jolly*, ed. Henry Fishwick, Manchester, 1895, pp. 24-5, 136 and 49.

He took it to London in order to find a publisher and printer and took the opportunity of calling upon Owen. After long conversation (the text of which every historian of Nonconformity would dearly love to be able to read!) Owen recommended Bunyan to take the manuscript to his own publisher, Nathaniel Ponder. A few years later when *The Pilgrim's Progress* was beginning to be acknowledged as a literary and spiritual masterpiece, London printers jokingly referred to Ponder as "Bunyan Ponder": such was the success of the book. But not only did Owen admire the writing of Bunyan; he also admired his ability as a preacher. When asked by the King, whom, as we have seen, he met occasionally, why he listened to an uneducated tinker, Owen is said to have replied, "Could I possess the tinker's abilities for preaching, please your majesty, I would gladly relinquish all my learning."[1]

From time to time the Congregational ministers in and around London seem to have met in order to enjoy Christian fellowship, agree on advice to be sent to their brethren in country areas, and raise financial help for those in distress. Included in this group of ministers were such veteran Congregationalists as Thomas Goodwin, Philip Nye, Joseph Caryl, William Greenhill, and Thomas Brooks, with such younger men as John Collins, John Loder and George Griffith. Though Nye, Caryl and Greenhill all died between 1671 and 1673, Goodwin, who preached to the church in Fetter Lane, and Brooks, who preached to the church in Lime Street, continued to serve the cause of Nonconformity until 1680. Collins, a gifted speaker and constant correspondent with New England, served his church in Paved Alley until 1687 when he died of dropsy. Loder died at the age of forty-seven in 1673, but Griffith, who lived to see the Toleration Act of 1689, continued to serve Congregationalists until the dawn of the eighteenth century.

At a meeting in March 1669 they felt constrained to write a letter to the Governor of Massachusetts, whom some of them knew personally, to request the cessation of the persecution of Baptists in the colony.[2] In Old England, Nonconformists of all types were fighting a single battle for freedom to worship God according to their consciences, and their cause was not helped by news from New England (of which opponents of Nonconformity made much use) that Baptists were not given basic freedoms by the Congregational ministers and magistrates. Unfortunately their letter had little or no immediate effect since the Congregational brethren in Massachusetts believed that in giving Baptists freedom they would be opening up the flood gates to all kinds of sectarianism. A second letter sent by the group in 1669 likewise had no immediate effect.[3] This was sent not to New England but to the Independent

---

[1] Asty, p. xxx, and J. Ivimey, *Life of Mr John Bunyan*, 1809, p. 294.
[2] *Correspondence*, No. 74, pp. 145–6, London ministers to the Governor of Massachusetts.
[3] *Correspondence*, No. 75, pp. 146–8: London ministers to the church at Hitchin.

Church at Hitchin in Hertfordshire, where there was a schism which led ultimately to the formation of a separate Baptist church. But before this happened the London ministers counselled that those who were not part of the schismatic group should pray for their brethren and win them back into a unified church through love and tenderness.

From Massachusetts in 1671 came a letter signed by nine ministers and seven magistrates and addressed to Owen and his colleagues.[1] It requested help for Harvard College. There was need, the London men were told, to rebuild the College, find a new President and persuade English students to pursue studies in the College. In reply, the ministers stated that they would very much like to help but, due to the effects of the Clarendon Code, they were "entangled in many straits."[2] The "daily relief" of many Nonconformists in "many counties" was dependent on the generosity of the people of London. Thus there was little hope of doing much for New England. However, they promised to do all they could. One practical thing they were able to do was to recommend Leonard Hoar to them as President of Harvard.[3]

Owen took a leading part in the discussions which lay behind these letters and his signature appeared on all of them. He also took part, whenever possible, in services of ordination. Though the calling and actual ordination of a pastor or teacher was the prerogative of the local church, he was sometimes asked to be a guest preacher. On the 14th December 1671, for example, he travelled to Stepney, east of London, to share in the ordination service for Matthew Mead.[4] Others taking part were Caryl, Griffith and Collins. In that same year a young Congregationalist named Thomas Hardcastle went from London to Bristol with a view to becoming pastor of the church worshipping at Broadmead, and he took with him a letter of commendation "signed with ten ministers' hands . . . whereof Dr Owen was one." Hardcastle looked upon Owen as one of the two "most loving friends" that he had in London.[5]

Whilst taking a lively interest in the state of the Congregational churches, Owen also wrote several books which rank amongst the classic statements of Congregational church polity. Reference has already been made to the catechism, *A Brief Instruction in the Worship of God*. Apart from this there were three other major works: *A Discourse concerning Envangelical Love, Church-Peace and Unity* (1672), *An Inquiry*

[1] *Correspondence*, No. 77, pp. 149–51: Magistrates and Ministers of Massachusetts to London ministers.
[2] *Correspondence*, No. 78, pp. 151–3: London ministers to Magistrates and Ministers of Massachusetts.
[3] For Hoar see C.R. He was President from 1672 to 1675.
[4] A. T. Jones, *Notes on the Early Days of Stepney Meeting*, 1887, p. 50. In *Works*, IX, there are several sermons preached at unspecified ordination services.
[5] *The Records of a Church of Christ meeting at Broadmead, Bristol, 1640–1687*, ed. E. B. Underhill, II, pp. 148 and 382.

*into the Original, Nature . . . and Communion of Evangelical Churches* (1681) and the posthumously published *True Nature of a Gospel Church* (1689).[1] Of these the latter has been regarded as a "text-book" for the doctrine of Congregational church government and organisation.[2] The doctrine expounded in them is essentially the same as that in the *Declaration of . . . Order* (1658) which we noticed in chapter five; but there is one major difference. The *Declaration* allowed a man to be a parish incumbent and also hold office within a gathered church; but after 1662 this was not possible any longer and so the church which was in the mind of Owen in these books was only the gathered church, and the minister was only the man who held office in such a church.

Dr Nuttall has expounded in his book, *Visible Saints*, the Congregational way in terms of the principles of separation, fellowship, freedom and holiness. That is, the separation of the true church from worldliness and the State, the mutual edification of the members in the love of Christ by the Word of God, the voluntary nature of membership, and the pursuit of individual sanctification towards a conformity to the mind of Christ. All these themes are to be found in Owen's writings. His doctrine of the church was based on the New Testament alone. He defined the church as "a society of persons called out of the world, or their natural wordly state, by the administration of the Word and Spirit, unto the obedience of the faith, or the knowledge and worship of God in Christ, joined together in a holy band, or by special agreement, for the exercise of the communion of the saints, in the due observation of all the ordinances of the gospel." A group of Christian people became a gospel church "upon their own voluntary consent and engagement to walk together in the due subjection of their souls and consciences unto Christ's authority, as their King, Priest and Prophet."[3]

If this was the divine pattern which Congregational people must follow, what, many of them asked, should be their attitude towards the services and people of the State Church? First of all, Owen replied, members of a semi-reformed National Church were to be treated with respect and love for they might belong "to the church catholic mystical," that universal company of the regenerate who made up the Body of Christ. Certainly there were true Christians in the Church of England.

> We believe that among the visible professors in this nation, there is as great a number of sincere believers as in any nation under heaven; so that in it are treasured up a considerable portion of the invisible mystical church of Christ. We believe that the generality of the inhabitants of this nation are by their profession constituted an eminent part of the kingdom of Christ in this world.[4]

[1] These four treatises are in *Works*, XV and XVI.
[2] Cf. for example the reprint in 1947 edited by John Huxtable.
[3] *Works*, XV, pp. 479 and 486.
[4] *Works*, XVI, p. 253.

To admit there were Christians in the parish churches was one thing; to worship in these "public places" was another. Though a few nonconformist ministers did attend the parish services, the majority resolutely refused to do this. To attend was to deprive the gathered churches of "the principal plea for the justification of their separation from the Church of England"[1] in its contemporary state. In this matter Owen would not compromise; to have gone to take part in a liturgy would have been to do no less than flout the authority of Christ and His Word.

Apart from producing many pamphlets and books defending Nonconformity or expounding the Congregational way, he also wrote in the last twenty years of his life a series of works which rank amongst the greatest theological books of seventeenth-century European Protestantism. They may be divided for convenience into three basic types—doctrinal divinity, practical divinity and Biblical commentaries—although in making this division it must be remembered that those books which are basically doctrinal have practical application, that the practical divinity is based on Biblical exegesis, and that the commentaries contain both doctrine and practice. It is these books, much prized in Britain, Holland and North America, and reprinted many times, that have given Owen a lasting reputation in evangelical Protestantism.

Central to the appreciation and understanding of these books is Owen's conception of authority in religion. G. R. Cragg writes that "for any thoughtful person in the seventeenth century the problem of authority was urgent. It was involved, directly or indirectly, in every controversy of the age."[2] Owen had no doubts. For him Holy Scripture, God's written Word, was the sole authority for Christian faith, hope and conduct. Creeds, confessions of faith and systems of doctrine were useful as summaries of the common faith as well as aids to the memorizing and understanding of the faith, but they could never take the place of the Bible. Theirs was only a human authority, whereas the concepts and words of the Bible were divinely inspired because the human authors had been as "pens" in the hands of the Holy Spirit. Thus, being a spiritual book, its divine truth and authority was self-evidencing to those who were regenerate and spiritually-minded. Rational arguments for the veracity of Scripture (e.g. that the Old Testament prophecies were fulfilled in the N.T.) were helpful, but secondary, for in and of themselves they could never convince anyone of the truth of Scripture. Without the presence of the Holy Spirit in the heart of the hearer or reader the Bible was as a dead letter. He who inspired the authors must likewise inspire the readers.

Further, Owen maintained, the Bible is God's Word in another

[1] *Works*, XVI, p. 253.
[2] G. R. Cragg, *The Church and the Age of Reason*, 1966, p. 71.

important sense. The sum, substance and centre of the Old and New Testaments is Jesus Christ, the Son of God and the Eternal Word (John 1:1). This was a conviction to which he adhered more strongly as he grew the older. "So much as we know of Christ, his sufferings and glory," he wrote in 1683, "so much do we understand the Scriptures." This, however, is not to say that in his early polemical writings against Arminianism he proposed that the substance of the Christian religion was intellectual assent to propositional, orthodox divinity. He had, as we shall see, too high a doctrine of the Holy Spirit to fall into this error which has unfortunately sometimes engulfed those who over-emphasise orthodoxy.[1] What is true is that in both his early and later works he makes free use of the conceptual apparatus of academic, reformed divinity (e.g. federal theology). The difference between his early writing (e.g. *A Display of Arminianism*) and later writing (e.g. *A Discourse concerning the Holy Spirit*) is that the former is primarily polemical whilst the latter aims to be expository and devotional as well.

Indeed, it is significant that Owen dealt in some detail with the relationship of the Holy Spirit to Scripture in his greatest contribution to the discipline of systematic theology (doctrinal divinity), his five-volume exposition of the doctrine of the Person and Work of the Holy Spirit, the third Person of the Holy Trinity.[2] The first of the five, published in 1674, is the longest and bears the title, *Pneumatologia, or, A Discourse concerning the Holy Spirit: wherein an Account is given of His Name, Nature, Personality, Dispensation, Operations and Effects*. Subsequent volumes dealt with the relationship of the Holy Spirit to the understanding of Scripture, to His helping of the believer in prayer and to His work as the Advocate and Comforter of the Church and as the Author of spiritual gifts.

Although the Protestant Reformation had brought a new emphasis to the role of the Spirit in the Church, it was left to divines of the seventeenth century to develop this emphasis. Amongst these Owen stands supreme. In the preface to *Pneumatologia* he declared, "I know not of any who ever went before me in this design of representing the whole economy of the Holy Spirit." He was not repudiating the work of those early Fathers who had sought to define the doctrine of the Spirit; neither was he repudiating the work of Calvin or Bucer. Rather he combined "the suffrage of the Ancient Church" with "the plain testimonies of the Scripture" and "the experience of them who do sincerely believe." The new element here is the place given to experience, the account of the reception of divine grace through the Holy Spirit

---

[1] Cf. G. W. Bromiley, "The Church Doctrine of Inspiration," in *Revelation and the Bible*, ed. C. F. H. Henry, Grand Rapids, 1969, for a discussion of this question of changes in the Protestant doctrine of Scripture.

[2] These are in *Works*, III and IV.

in the hearts of believers. As Dr Nuttall remarks, this stress on experience was not confined to Puritans and Nonconformists in the seventeenth century.[1] This was the century which had Hamlet as its prototype and exemplar and which produced a philosophical system which began with "*cogito, ergo sum.*"[2] This fact in no way invalidates Owen's Biblical emphasis on personal experience; it merely sets it in context.

In his thinking and preaching Owen closely linked the gift of Christ to the world with the gift of the Holy Spirit to the Church.

> For when God designed the great and glorious work of recovering fallen man and the saving of sinners, to the praise of the glory of his grace, he appointed, in his infinite wisdom, two great means thereof. The one was *the giving of his Son for them*, and the other was *the giving of his Spirit unto them*. And hereby was way made for the manifestation of the glory of the whole blessed Trinity; which is the utmost end of all the works of God.

He held that "the great promise of the Old Testament, the principal object of the faith, hope and expectation of believers, was that concerning the coming of the Son of God in the flesh." This being so "the Holy Ghost, the doctrine concerning his person, his work, his grace, is the most peculiar and principal subject of the Scriptures of the New Testament." He believed that "no doctrine ... is more fully and plainly declared in the Gospel than this of our regeneration by the effectual and ineffable operation of the Holy Spirit."[3] So naturally many pages are spent in the elucidation of this doctrine and of the subsequent doctrine of santification, the making of the heart and life of the believer holy.

The principal aim of the five volumes was thoroughly to expound an important doctrine. Owen also sought to confute three contemporary erroneous views of the Holy Spirit and His work. The two most obvious of these were the Quaker notion of the inner light and secret revelations and the Socinian denial of the deity of the Spirit. The third, though less obvious, was much more common both amongst Churchmen and Dissenters. Many people admitted the truth of the deity of the Holy Spirit but they paid no attention to His work of regeneration and sanctification in their hearts and lives. Thus their living denied their doctrine. In both his principal aim and his subsidiary tasks Owen more than succeeded. His work was attacked by William Clagett, a chaplain to Charles II;[4] nevertheless, it remains to this day the most exhaustive exposition of the doctrine of the Holy Spirit in the English language.

Amongst Owen's practical writings, which were designed to help

---

[1] Nuttall, *The Holy Spirit in Puritan Faith and Experience*, Oxford, 1947, p. 7.
[2] That of Descartes. ("I think, therefore I exist.")
[3] *Works*, III, p. 23 and 29.
[4] Clagett's study was entitled *A Discourse Concerning the Operations of the Holy Spirit*. John Humfrey defended Owen's views and Clagett replied to Humfrey. See Orme, p. 297.

he reader practise love to God and man, were studies on *The Nature of . . . Indwelling Sin* (1668) *and The Grace and Duty of being Spiritually-Minded* (1681).[1] The former was based on a series of sermons preached either at Stadhampton or in London from Romans 7:21 ("I find then a law that when I would do good evil is present with me"). By modern standards it contains a rather pessimistic view of human nature and its susceptibility to sin and temptation, but it is thoroughly in the Augustinian and Calvinist tradition. It begins with the following statement by Owen: "That the doctrine of original sin is one of the fundamental truths of our Christian profession hath been always owned in the Church of God." The whole treatise then expounds what original sin really means in terms of the evil impulses, desires, affections and actions that proceed from the human heart. Owen clearly believed that the mortification of sin in the life of the believer could not truly begin until he was conscious of the power of indwelling sin in his old, Adamic nature. The latter treatise with a more positive theme was the result of his meditations as he lay ill in his home at Ealing. When partially recovered he put his thoughts into sermon-form and addressed them to his church in Leadenhall Street. Later he prepared the sermons for the press. As with the letters he wrote to Sir John and Lady Hartopp and Charles Fleetwood which were briefly considered above, this book (and others of this period) reveal that Owen's mind during his last few years of life were much taken up with meditation upon the Person of Christ, and of heaven. To some this may appear as a form of escapism but to the Christian it is the goal of all theology. Owen defined being spiritually-minded as the exercise of the mind in its thoughts and the inclination of the mind in its affections upon God, His omnipotence and omnipresence and upon His Son, Jesus Christ. Whilst the doctrinal content is always there, this treatise rises above doctrine in the sense that its aim is to achieve a living relationship between the believer and his Saviour, a relationship which Owen himself must certainly have enjoyed to produce such sermons and books.

Owen's greatest work of Biblical exposition was, without any doubt, his study of the Epistle to the Hebrews, published in four folio-volumes between 1668 and 1684.[2] When he finished it he is reported by one who was very close to him to have said: "Now my work is done: it is time for me to die." Unlike most modern commentators, but in harmony with the majority of his contemporaries, Owen believed that the author of the Epistle was the Apostle Paul. The first of the folio-volumes contained preliminary "exercitations" (Owen's word) on questions of authorship, original language, and other topics. In the second volume he considered two basic doctrines of the Epistle, namely the doctrines

[1] *Works*, VII.
[2] *Works*, XVIII-XXIV.

of the Sabbath and the Priesthood of Christ. To the former topic, which had often been studied by earlier Puritans, he added little if anything that was new. In dealing with the second theme he justly claimed that his treatment was more extensive and thorough than any other published study. The Epistle to the Hebrews, of course, demonstrates that Jesus Christ is superior both to angels and to Moses; more importantly, it shows that He is the great High Priest (4:14) after the order not of Aaron but of Melchizedec, and His Priesthood is eternal. At one and the same time He offered, and was Himself, the final sacrifice. To the rich Old Testament background of this theme and to its relevance to Christian theology Owen did full justice.

The two other volumes contained the Commentary itself, into which Owen put the wealth of his knowledge of Hebrew, Aramaic, Greek, Rabbinical learning, Protestant theology and human nature. He had three aims: to explain the actual meaning of the text; to attack any heresies or errors (especially in Judaism, Roman Catholicism and Socinianism) based on a false understanding or neglect of the text; and to apply any truths he found within the text to the practical needs of Christians who wished to grow in grace and knowledge. He went, as it were, through the length and breadth of his subject leaving no stone unturned and no dark corner without light. As with the exposition of the doctrine of the Holy Spirit, this Commentary is exhaustive. Indeed for most students of the Epistle it is too exhaustive. They prefer to consult Delitzsch, Wescott or more modern writers.

A word or concept that often occurs in this Epistle to the Hebrews is "covenant." The new covenant, inaugurated by Christ's death and resurrection, is described, for example, as "a better covenant," better, that is, than the covenant God made with Moses (cf. 8:6). So we find an extensive treatment of covenant (federal) theology by Owen in this Commentary. As no previous reference has been made to this important ingredient of seventeenth-century Puritan and Reformed theology, which was obviously a central idea in Owen's thought, it will be appropriate to describe in brief his interpretation of it.[1] He held that there were two basic covenants between God and man.

> There were never absolutely any more than two covenants: wherein all persons indefinitely are concerned. The first was the covenant of works made with Adam and with all in him. And what he did as the head of that covenant, as our representative therein, is imputed unto us as if we had done it, Romans 5:12. The other is that of grace, made originally with Christ and through him with all the elect.[2]

[1] There does not yet exist a satisfactory study of the origins and early development of Federal Theology. Cf. the articles listed in P. Toon, *Emergence of Hyper-Calvinism*, pp. 29–30.
[2] *Works*, XXII, p. 391.

He admitted that the relationship between Jehovah and Adam was "not expressly called a covenant." Nevertheless, he held that it contained "the express nature of a covenant for it was the agreement of God and man concerning obedience and disobedience, rewards and punishments." If the covenant of works was made in the Garden of Eden the covenant of grace was made in heaven. It had "its beginning in God's love from all eternity." "All the elect of God were, in his eternal purpose and design, and in the everlasting covenant between the Father and the Son, committed unto him, to be delivered from sin, the law, and death, and to be brought into the enjoyment of God."

It may be asked, what relationship did Owen conceive to exist between these two covenants and the Abrahamic, Mosaic, and New covenants? First, we may note that he believed that the Mosaic covenant (Exodus 20ff.) "revived, declared and expressed all the commands" of the covenant of works in its decalogue. Further, it revived the sanction, curse and sentence of death for transgressors and the promise of eternal life as a reward for perfect obedience. So the Mosaic covenant was related in essence to the original covenant of works.[1] On the other hand, the Abrahamic covenant (Genesis 12ff) and the New covenant (Matthew 26:28 etc.) were the publication, at the human level, in two related forms of the eternal covenant of grace. In eternity God the Father, Son and Holy Spirit covenanted to redeem the elect (Owen sometimes called this the covenant of redemption), but putting this into operation on earth meant the publication and ratification of the Abrahamic and New Covenants.

This summary is of course inadequate, but before we leave this topic we may ask whether Perry Miller's widely accepted thesis that Puritan federal theology was a device to take the sting out of the "harsh" doctrine of God's sovereignty applies in the case of Owen's teaching.[2] The answer would seem to be clearly in the negative since Owen uses covenant theology both in his Commentary as well as in his *The Doctrine of Justification by Faith* (1677)[3] in order to emphasise the sovereignty and predestination of God. And all human response to the covenant of grace is seen by him in the light of God's gracious assistance and empowering of individual believers. Covenant Theology provided both for Owen and many of his colleagues the intellectual framework for their views of God's relationship with man, and man's place and role in the world. In the covenant of redemption they found the key to the meaning of creation and of salvation; in the larger term of reference, the covenant of grace, they could understand the reason for the choice

---

[1] *Works*, XXIII, pp. 77-8.
[2] E.g., P. Miller, *Errand into the Wilderness*, Cambridge, Mass., 1956, pp. 48ff. Cf. The critique of Miller's views in J. S. Coolidge, *The Pauline Renaissance in England*, Oxford, 1970.
[3] *Works*, V.

of Abraham and his descendants as an elect nàtion, for the Incarnation, Death, Resurrection and Ascension of Jesus Christ, for the Church, the gift of the Holy Spirit, the Last Judgement and heaven and hell. Within the covenant of works they found the key to the nature and responsibilities of man, his place in the universe, his suffering and the presence of evil in the world. It was certainly a comprehensive concept and was in the background of Owen's thoughts from 1643 onwards.

The final volume of the Commentary on Hebrews was completed whilst Owen was living at Ealing. He was constantly ill and his physicians were often in attendance. His friends in both Old and New England waited for the expected news of his death whilst Owen himself suffered in quiet confidence.[1] Writing to Charles Fleetwood he expressed his delight that he was going to the One whom his soul loved.[2] "I am leaving the ship of the Church in a storm," he continued, "but while the great Pilot is in it the loss of a poor under-rower will be inconsiderable." On the morning of 24th of August 1683 he was visited by William Payne, a minister from Saffron Walden in Essex who was supervising the printing and proof-reading of Owen's recently completed *Meditations on the Glory of Christ*. Seeing his friend, Owen exclaimed, "O, brother Payne, the long-wished-for day is come at last, in which I shall see the glory in another manner than I have ever done or was capable of doing in this world."[3] This sentiment is often found in the book that Payne was proof-reading.

> The revelation made of Christ in the blessed Gospel is far more excellent, more glorious, and more filled with rays of divine wisdom and goodness, than the whole creation and the just comprehension of it, if attainable, can contain or afford. Without the knowledge hereof, the mind of man, however priding itself in other inventions and discoveries, is wrapped up in darkness and confusion. This, therefore, deserves the severest of our thoughts, the best of our meditations and our utmost diligence in them. For if our future blessedness shall consist in being where He is, and beholding of His glory, what better preparation can there be for it than in a constant previous contemplation of that glory in the revelation that is made in the Gospel, unto this very end, that by a view of it we may be gradually transformed into the same glory.[4]

So it was that on the twenty-first anniversary of the Great Ejection of 1662, another sad day came upon English Protestant Dissent. Its greatest theologian and most ardent advocate of religious toleration was no more on earth, but with his Lord. From Ealing Owen's body was conveyed to a house in St James, Westminster, and from here, on the

[1] Cf. the letters to Increase Mather in *Collections* of the Mass. Hist. Soc. 4th Series, 1852, VIII, pp. 496 and 500.
[2] *Correspondence*, No. 98, p. 174.
[3] Orme, p. 342.
[4] *Works*, I, p. 275.

4th September, it was taken to Bunhill Fields for burial, attended by the carriages of sixty-seven noblemen and gentlemen, as well as by a great crowd of ordinary people. With no natural children or grandchildren to survive him, Owen left behind, as Calvin had done a century earlier, many "spiritual" sons and daughters to preserve his name and teaching.

CHAPTER VIII

# EPILOGUE

JOHN OWEN HAS BEEN DESCRIBED IN A VARIETY OF WAYS BY HIS ADMIRERS and friends. In the seventeenth century he was "the Calvin of England" to Ambrose Barnes, a Congregationalist from Newcastle,[1] while to Anthony Wood, the Oxford Anglican, he was an "Atlas and Patriarch of Independency."[2] For a modern Congregationalist, Dr Erik Routley, he was "the greatest of the Puritan scholastics,"[3] while he is described on the jacket of the 1965 reprint of Vols. I-XVI of his *Works* by the Banner of Truth Trust as "the greatest Britain theologian of all time." All four descriptions contain one or more aspects of the whole truth. Certainly Owen was the kind of man whom his contemporaries as well as his later readers seem either to have loved or to have despised. If the intransigent Anglicans, Samuel Parker and George Vernon found both Owen and his principles distasteful, David Clarkson found them to be exemplary. In his funeral sermon for Owen in 1683, Clarkson expressed the opinion that the account of the life of Owen "due to the world required a volume," not merely a few words in an oration. For, he stated, "a great light is fallen; one of eminency for holiness, learning, parts and abilities; a pastor, a scholar, a divine of the first magnitude; holiness gave a divine lustre to his other accomplishments, it shined in his whole course, and was diffused through his whole conversation . . . He had extraordinary intellectuals, a vast memory, a quick apprehension, a clear and piercing judgement; he was a passionate lover of light and truth, of divine truth especially, he pursued it unweariedly, through painful and wasting studies, such as impaired his health and strength, such as exposed him to those distempers with which he conflicted many years."[4] A similar estimate of Owen written by Thomas Gilbert appears on his tombstone in Bunhill Fields.[5] It describes the dead Nonconformist as "furnished with human literature in all its kinds and in all its degrees" and using it all "to serve the interests of Religion and to serve in the Sanctuary of God." Owen was "a scribe

[1] *Memoirs of Ambrose Barnes*, ed. W. H. D. Longstaffe, 1867, p. 16.
[2] Wood, *History of the University of Oxford*, ed. Gutch, II, p. 650.
[3] Routley, *English Religious Dissent*, Cambridge, 1960, p. 10.
[4] The sermon is printed in Orme, pp. 411ff.
[5] The Latin inscription is translated in Orme, p. 346, and reproduced in Appendix II below.

every way instructed in the mysteries of the kingdom of God" and "the effulgent lamp of evangelical truth."[1]

In these descriptions we see the beginning of the "nonconformist view of Owen" that was to be dominant in the eighteenth and nineteenth centuries. It was a view of Owen which arose from his writings, preaching and pastoral work after the Restoration. His involvement in the political and ecclesiastical affairs of the Commonwealth and Protectorate was virtually forgotten or pushed into the background, despite the critical comments of Baxter in his *Reliquiae*.[2] Thus in the twó *Memoirs* which were published in 1720–21 Owen is portrayed as pre-eminently the Calvinist divine, the writer on theological, devotional and practical themes, and the Biblical commentator.[3] This is perhaps to be expected in that in 1721 a large portion of Protestant Dissent was quickly moving in the direction of Arminianism and Socinianism. A few years earlier Cotton Mather, the American writer, had declared that "the Church of God was wronged in that the life of the great John Owen was not written."[4] Unfortunately, these two brief *Memoirs* did not wholly right the wrong that Mather had sensed. If one removes from them the descriptions of the contents of Owen's books there is very little biographical information left.

It was not until 1820 that a full-scale attempt was made to write the life of Owen. Entitled *Memoirs of the Life and Writings of John Owen*, it came from the pen of William Orme (1787–1830), a Congregational minister. It was reprinted in 1826 as Volume I of Thomas Russell's edition of *The Works of John Owen*. This biography added much factual information to the knowledge of Owen's life and connexions. Orme, however, had been much influenced by the evangelical Calvinism of Robert Haldane and his view of Owen was necessarily coloured by this. Though he had no basic disagreement with his subject's theology, he did express criticism of Owen's manner of style and writing. More importantly, he found it difficult to believe that Owen, the great devotional writer, could have been closely involved in the "shadowy" activities of the Independents between 1649 and 1660. So he chose either to deny Owen's part in them or to minimise it. Further, he simply grouped together all the material on Owen that he could find without employing any basic, unifying themes.

---

[1] Owen's wide reading is confirmed both by the references to other authors in his own books and by the size of his library. This was sold by public auction in 1684 and according to the Catalogue, *Bibliotheca Oweniana sive Catalogus Librorum*, it contained 1418 Latin treatises, 32 bound volumes of Greek and Latin manuscirpts, and 1454 English books. They included works by every major theological and classical author as well as books on history, travel and geography.
[2] Baxter, *Reliquiae*, I, p. 101.
[3] I.e. the anonymous *Life* (1720) and that by Asty in 1721.
[4] Quoted by Orme, p. 2.

The next influential biography to appear, written by Andrew Thomson of Edinburgh, was printed as part of the contents of Volume I of *The Works of John Owen* edited by W. H. Goold in 1850-53. This was brief and took its information from the previous *Memoirs* but it was concise and easily read. It provides an excellent picture of what has previously been described as the "nonconformist view of Owen," a view that was shared by the evangelical Calvinists of the Scottish Kirk. Thomson had little desire to investigate Owen's political involvement; rather, he made a deliberate attempt to see him primarily as the theologian. And he allowed himself to criticise Owen on one point only—his unfortunate controversy with Brian Walton over the various readings of ancient manuscripts of the Bible which were printed in the *London Polyglot* (1657) edited by Walton.

If Thomson was hesitant to criticise him, Owen's next biographer, James Moffatt, who became a noted Scottish theologian, was ready to bring his youthful and critical theological mind to bear upon his subject.[1] Unfortunately Moffatt seems to have done little original research and thus to have made use only of the previous biographies and the new secondary sources that had appeared since 1850. This fact tends to make his evaluation of Owen less effective. He was ready to admit that Owen's relationship to the officers at Wallingford House in 1659 tarnished his reputation. He was also quite free in his criticism of both the content and style of Owen's book. "Owen's mind," he stated, "was essentially abstract . . . He failed to allow for the wind, and thus his sheer powers of ratiocination often played him false, when he had to deal with less logical but equally acute and earnest minds."[2] Here Moffatt allowed his rhetoric to run away with him. However, he did consider that Owen's writings on toleration and schism were important; further, he allowed that "the two subjects which may be said to have moved him to his highest reach of power" were "first, the infirmity of the human heart, as it aspired and twists in the moral passage and discipline of this life, and secondly, the splendour, the bliss, the pre-eminence of Jesus."[3] Here again the "nonconformist view of Owen" has come through. Indeed it must come through, for some of Owen's theological writings after 1660 continue to rank among vitally important theological books.

Without, it is hoped, neglecting this "nonconformist view" of Owen, the present study has aimed to portray the total Owen, the pastor, the chaplain, the educator, the ecclesiastical statesman, the politician and the theologian. Nevertheless, it must be admitted that despite the many new facts about his career and connexions which have come to light

---

[1] The biography is in the "Introductory Sketch" in *The Golden Book of John Owen*, ed. J. Moffatt, 1904, pp. 1-96.
[2] Ibid, p. 46.
[3] Ibid, pp. 87-8.

in this study, Owen as a man, as a human being, still remains an elusive character. After reading the *Reliquiae* or Dr Nuttall's biography[1] one feels that one knows Owen's contemporary, Richard Baxter, as a real, living person, but the same cannot be said of Owen after reading this or previous "Memoirs."

To a certain extent we still cannot get nearer to Owen than did Asty when he wrote:

> As to his person his stature was tall, his visage grave and majestic and withal comely: he had the aspect and deportment of a gentleman, suitable to his birth. He had a very large capacity of mind, a ready invention, a good judgement, a great natural wit which being improved by education, rendered him a person of incomparable abilities. As to his temper he was very affable and courteous, familiar and sociable; the meanest persons found an easy access to his converse and friendship. He was facetious and pleasant in his common discourse, jesting with his acquaintance but with sobriety and measure; a great master of his passions especially that of anger; he was of a serene and even temper, neither elated with honour, credit, friends, or estate, nor depressed with troubles and difficulties.[2]

The majestic deportment of Owen is partially confirmed by the portraits of him that still may be seen.[3] Of his natural wit, tinged perhaps at times with a little sarcasm, we have an example in one of his letters to John Thornton. Referring to the scientific activity of Henry Oldenburgh and his friends Owen wrote: "I hope that they are upon some serious consultations for the benefit of mankind, how a hen may sit on her eggs and addle none, how oysters may be so geometrically layd that instead of 200 or 300 an oyster wench may lay 8 or 900 in her basket at once and sell them all without tearing her throat or tiring her head."[4] That Owen was "a great master of his passions" is evident from the way he conducted theological controversy. As Stillingfleet remarked, Owen's writings were coloured "by civility and decent language." Finally, to illustrate Owen's affectionate nature, we may quote from the postscript of the letter to Thornton mentioned above. "Our musk melons are ripe," he wrote, "witness that I have sent you some; I would have sent more, but you know Matthew!" Matthew was his young son.

As viewed in terms of both the seventeenth century and Christian

---

[1] Nuttall, *Richard Baxter*, 1965.
[2] Asty, p. xxxiii.
[3] As far as I know the extant portraits of Owen are as follows:
   1. The portrait in the National Gallery, London.
   2. The portraits in the Congregational College, Manchester, Baptist College, Bristol, and Mansfield College, Oxford.
The N.P.G. portrait is of the younger Owen whilst those in the denominational Colleges are of the older Owen.
   3. The *Radio Times* Hulton Picture Library. Here the portrait is of Owen in academic dress.
[4] *Correspondence*, No. 70, p. 132.

history as a whole, Owen obviously stands out as a great theologian. This fact has been readily admitted throughout this book. However, let it not be forgotten that he was a theologian of the seventeenth century! We may briefly illustrate this point. First, his methodology was based on an Aristotelian education and is not in common use today. Secondly, like so many of his contemporaries, he dealt with most topics in such detail (meandering "ad nauseam" through that which many would now regard as trivialities) that he obscured the main principles in a plethora of words. Thirdly, he defended positions (e.g. the antiquity of Hebrew vowel-points and the Pauline authorship of Hebrews) which informed evangelical scholarship has long since abandoned. Finally, he used and interpreted the Old Testament in a way which few would do today. For example, he deduced the duties of the Christian magistrate (i.e. the English Parliament) directly from the duties laid down in the Old Testament for the King of Israel; the compilers of the Westminster Confession of Faith also did this but it is significant that modern Presbyterian Churches have changed the chapter on the civil magistrate. These things being so it surely behoves modern readers of Owen's writings to approach them with care if they are to gain from them the maximum benefit.

Taking into account he was a man of the seventeenth century the one real criticism that may fairly be levelled against Owen, and which has already been raised, concerns his literary style. The words of John Stoughton written a century ago are still apt:[1]

> It is to be feared Owen will never gain that position in literature to which his learning and abilities fairly entitle him; and the comparative neglect which encircles one of the greatest names in English theological literature is a confirmation of the great critical maxim, that no writer, however able, can secure for his works abiding popularity if he be heedless of the style and dress in which he arrays his thought.

And today Owen's long, involved sentences and many digressions of thought seem even more removed from contemporary style and idiom.

It is greatly to be regretted that none of Owen's diaries were preserved. Perhaps in Puritan fashion he destroyed them before his death. From them we could perhaps have entered into the secrets of his heart and mind and learned much more of his inner life. As it is, we have to rely on a few letters and a few remarks of others to seek to understand him as a man. And these are insufficient to probe the depths of his character. So Owen must remain hidden as it were behind a veil. His actions, his concerns and his theology we have gleaned from his letters, his books, and contemporary sources but his secret thoughts remain his own. However,

---

[1] Stoughton, *British Heroes and Worthies*, London, n.d., p. 174.

this much can be said: Owen shines through the available information as a truly great man, whose one basic concern in word and deed, book and action, was the proclamation of Jesus Christ and His gospel.

*Additional Note:*

Since this book was written a further brief study of Owen has appeared. It covers only the years 1616–1660, and is entitled, *John Owen, Commonwealth Puritan* (1972). The author, Dr R. G. Lloyd, died in 1968, leaving behind an unfinished manuscript, which is why the book stops at 1660. The treatment is at a popular level and no attempt was made by the author to consult manuscript sources or recent studies of Puritanism and Protestant Nonconformity.

Appendix I

# THE WORKS OF DR JOHN OWEN

1. A Display of Arminianism (1643)
2. The Duty of Pastors and People Distinguished (1643)
3. Two Short Catechisms, wherein the Doctrines of Christ are explained (1645)
4. A Vision of Unchangeable Free Mercy, a Sermon (1646)
5. Eshcol; or Rules of Direction for the Walking of the Saints (1647)
6. Salus Electorum, Sanguis Jesu; or the Death of Death (1647)
7. Ebenezer; a Memorial of the deliverance in Essex: two sermons (1648)
8. Righteous Zeal: a sermon with an Essay on Toleration (1649)
9. The Shaking of Heaven and Earth: a sermon (1649)
10. Of the Death of Christ, the Price He Paid (1650)
11. The Steadfastness of the Promises: a sermon (1650)
12. The Branch of the Lord: two sermons (1650)
13. The Advantage of the Kingdom of Christ: a sermon (1651)
14. The Labouring Saint's Dismission to Rest: a sermon (1652)
15. Christ's Kingdom and the Magistrate's Power: a sermon (1652)
16. Humble Proposals for the Propagation of the Gospel [with others] (1652)
17. Proposals for the Propagation of the Gospel . . . also some principles of Christian religion [with others] (1653)
18. De Divina Justitia Diatriba (1653)
19. The Doctrine of the Saints' Perseverance (1654)
20. Vindiciae Evangelicae: or the Mystery of the Gospel Vindicated (1655)
21. Of the Mortification of Sin in Believers (1656)
22. A Review of the Annotations of Grotius (1656)
23. God's Work in Founding Zion: a sermon (1656)
24. God's Presence with His People: a sermon (1656)
25. Of Communion with God the Father, Son and Holy Ghost (1657)
26. Of Schism (1657)
27. A Review of the True Nature of Schism (1657)
28. An Answer to a later Treatise of Daniel Cawdry about . . . Schism (1658) in *A Defence of Mr John Cotton* (1658)
29. Of Temptation: the Nature and Power of it (1658)
30. Pro Sacris Scripturis Exercitationes adversus Fanaticos (1658)
31. Of the Divine Original . . . of the Scriptures (1659)
32. A Vindication of the Hebrew and Greek Texts (1659)
33. The Glory and Interest of Nations: a sermon (1659)
34. Two Questions concerning the Power of the Supreme Magistrate about Religion (1659)
35. *Theologovmena Pantodapa* (1661)
36. Animadversions on a Treatise entitled Fiat Lux (1662)

37. A Discourse concerning Liturgies (1662)
38. A Vindication of the Animadversions on Fiat Lux (1664)
39. Indulgence and Toleration Considered (1667)
40. A Peace-Offering, in an Apology and Humble Plea for Indulgence (1667)
41. A Brief Instruction in the Worship of God (1667)
42. The Nature, Power, Deceit and Prevalency of Indwelling Sin (1667)
43. A Practical Exposition of Psalm cxxx. (1668)
44. Exercitations on the Epistle to the Hebrews, I (1668)
45. Truth and Innocence Vindicated (1669)
46. A Brief Declaration and Vindication of the Doctrine of the Trinity (1669)
47. An Account of the Grounds and Reasons on which Protestant Dissenters desire Liberty (1670)
48. Reflections on a Slanderous Libel (1670)
49. Exercitations concerning the . . . Day of Sacred Rest (1671)
50. A Discourse concerning Evangelical Love, Church-Peace and Unity (1672)
51. A Vindication of some passages in a Discourse concerning Communion with God (1674)
52. A Discourse on the Holy Spirit (1674)
53. An Exposition of the Epistle to the Hebrews, II (1674)
54. The Testimony of the Church is not the chief reason for our belieivng the Scripture to be the Word of God (printed in N. Vincent, *The Morning-xercises against Popery*) (1675)
55. How we may bring our hearts to bear reproofs (printed in S. Annesley, *A Supplement to the Morning-Exercises*) (1676)
56. The Nature of Apostasy from the Profession of the Gospel (1676)
57. The Reason of Faith (1677)
58. The Doctrine of Justification by Faith (1677)
59. The Causes, Ways and Means of understanding the Mind of God (1678)
60. A Declaration of the Glorious Mystery of the Person of Christ (1678)
61. The Church of Rome no Safe Guide (1679)
62. Some Considerations of Union among Protestants (1680)
63. A Brief Vindication of the Nonconformists from the charge of Schism (1680)
64. A Continuation of the Exposition of the Epistle to the Hebrews, III (1680)
65. An Inquiry into the Original, Nature . . . and Communion of Evangelical Churches (1681)
66. An Humble Testimony unto the Goodness and Severity of God (1681)
67. The Grace and Duty of being Spiritually-minded (1681)
68. A Discourse of the Work of the Holy Spirit in Prayer (1682)
69. A Brief and Impartial Account of the Protestant Religion (1682)
70. The Chamber of Imagery in the Church of Rome Laid Open (in *The Morning Exercises against Popery*) (1683)
71. A Letter concerning the Matter of the Present Excommunications (1683)
72. Meditations and Discourses on the Glory of Christ (1684)
73. A Continuation of the Exposition of the Epistle to the Hebrews, IV (1684)
74. Of the Dominion of Sin and Grace (1688)
75. True Nature of the Gospel Church (1689)
76. Seasonable Words for English Protestants: a sermon (1690)
77. Meditations and Discourses on the Glory of Christ Applied (1691)

## APPENDIX I

78. A Guide to Church-Fellowship and Order (1692)
79. Two Discourses, of the Holy Spirit as Comforter . . . and Author of Spiritual Gifts (1693)
80. Gospel Grounds and Evidences of the Faith of God's Elect (1695)
81. An Answer unto Two Questions . . . with Twelve Arguments against any Conformity to Worship not of Divine Institution (1720)
82. A Complete Collection of the Sermons of . . . J. Owen . . . also several tracts . . . to which are added his Latin Orations (1721)
83. Three Discourses delivered at the Lord's Table (1750)
84. Thirteen Sermons preached on various occasions (1756)
85. Twenty-five Discourses suitable to the Lord's Supper (1760)
86. Posthumous Sermons (in Goold, *Works*, Vol. XVI) (1850)

## APPENDIX II

## EPITAPH BY THOMAS GILBERT

*On Owen's tombstone in Bunhill Fields, London*

JOHANNES OWEN, S.T.P.
Agro Oxoniensi Oriundus;
Patre insigni Theologo Theologus ipse Insignior;
Et seculi hujus Insignissimis annumerandus:
Communibus Humaniorum Literarum Suppetiis,
Mensura parum Communi, Instructus;
Omnibus, quasi bene Ordinata Ancillarum Serie,
Ab illo jussis suæ Famulari Theologiæ:
Theologiæ Polemicæ, Practicæ, et quam vocant Casuum
(Harum enim Omnium, quæ magis sua habenda erat, ambigitur)
In illa, Viribus plusquam Herculeis, serpentibus tribus,
Arminio, Socino, Cano, Venenosa Strinxit guttura:
In ista suo prior, ad verbi Amussim, Expertus Pectore,
Universam Sp. Scti. Œconomiam Aliis tradidit:
Et, missis Cæteris, Coluit ipse, Sensitque,
Beatam quam scripsit, cum Deo Communionem,
In terris Viator comprehensori in cælis proximus:
In Casuum Theologia, Singulis Oraculi instar habitus;
Quibus Opus erat, et copia, Consulendi;
Scriba ad Regnum Cælorum usquequoque institutus;
Multis privatos intra Parietes, a Suggesto Pluribus,
A Prelo omnibus, ad eundem scopum collineantibus,
Pura Doctrinæ Evangelicæ Lampas Præluxit;
Et sensim, non sine aliorum, suoque sensu,
Sic prælucendo Periit,
Assiduis Infirmitatibus Obsiti,
Morbis Creberrimis Impetiti,
Durisque Laboribus potissimum Attriti, Corporis,
(Fabricæ, donec ita Quassatæ, Spectabilis) Ruinas,
Deo ultra Fruendi Cupida, Deseruit;
Die, a Terrenis Potestatibus, Plurimis facto Fatali;
Illi, A Coelesti Numine, felici reddito;
Mensis Scilicet Augusti XXIV° Anno a Partu Virgineo.
M.DC.LXXXIIIo Ætat. LXVIIo.x

Translation:—JOHN OWEN, D.D. born in the county of Oxford, the son of an eminent Minister, himself more eminent, and worthy to be enrolled among the first Divines of the age. Furnished with human literature in all its kinds, and in all its degrees, he called forth all his knowledge in an orderly train to serve the interests of Religion, and minister in the Sanctuary of his God. In Divinity, practical, polemical, and casuistical, he excelled others, and was in all equal to himself. The Arminian, Socinian, and Popish errors, those Hydras, whose contaminated breath, and deadly poison infested the church, he, with more than Herculean labour, repulsed, vanquished, and destroyed. The whole economy of redeeming grace, revealed and applied by the Holy Spirit, he deeply investigated and communicated to others; having first felt its divine energy, according to its draught in the Holy Scriptures, transfused into his own bosom. Superior to all terrene pursuits, he constantly cherished, and largely experienced, that blissful communion with Deity, he so admirably describes in his writings. While on the road to Heaven his elevated mind almost comprehended its full glories and joys. When he was consulted on cases of conscience his resolutions contained the wisdom of an Oracle. He was a scribe every way instructed in the mysteries of the kingdom of God. In conversation, he held up to *many*, in his public discourses, to *more*, in his publications from the press, to *all*, who were set out for the celestial *Zion*, the effulgent lamp of evangelical truth to guide their steps to immortal glory. While he was thus diffusing his divine light, with his own inward sensations, and the observations of his afflicted friends, his earthly tabernacle gradually decayed, till at length his deeply sanctified soul longing for the fruition of its God, quitted the body. In younger age a most comely and majestic form; but in the latter stages of life, depressed by constant infirmities, emaciated with frequent diseases, and above all crushed under the weight of intense and unremitting studies, it became an incommodious mansion for the vigorous exertions of the spirit in the service of its God. He left the world on a day, dreadful to the Church by the cruelties of men, but blissful to himself by the plaudits of his God, August 24, 1683, aged 67.

## ABBREVIATIONS

| | |
|---|---|
| Asty | John Asty, "Memoir of Dr John Owen," in *A Complete Collection of the Sermons of Dr John Owen*, 1721. |
| C.J. | *The Journals of the House of Commons.* |
| Correspondence | *The Correspondence of John Owen (1616–1683)*, ed. Peter Toon, 1970. |
| C.R. | *Calamy Revised*, ed. A. G. Matthews, Oxford, 1934. |
| C.S.P.D. | *Calendar of State Papers* (Domestic Series). |
| D.N.B. | *Dictionary of National Biography.* |
| L.J. | *The Journals of the House of Lords.* |
| Orme | *The Works of John Owen*, ed. Thomas Russell, 1826, Volume I, "Memoirs of the Life and Writings of Dr John Owen" by William Orme. |
| Oxford Orations | *The Oxford Orations of Dr John Owen*, ed. Peter Toon, Linkinhorne House, Linkinhorne (Cornwall), 1971. |
| Works | *The Works of John Owen*, ed. W. H. Goold, Edinburgh, 1850–53, 24 vols. |

COMPARATIVE CHRONOLOGICAL TABLE OF EVENTS 185

|  | *National* |  | *Personal: John Owen* |
|---|---|---|---|
| 1616 | William Shakespeare dies | 1616 | Born. |
| 1617 | Raleigh's expedition to Guiana | | |
| 1620 | Pilgrim Fathers sail to New England | | |
| 1625 | Charles I becomes King and marries Henrietta Maria | | |
| | | 1628 | Enters Oxford University. |
| 1630 | Laud becomes Chancellor of Oxford. | | |
| | | 1632 | Graduates B.A. |
| 1633 | Laud becomes Archbishop of Canterbury. Samuel Pepys, the diarist, is born | | |
| | | 1635 | Graduates M.A. |
| 1637 | Charles I introduces new Prayer Book in Scotland | 1637 | Becomes a private tutor |
| 1640 | Short Parliament meets. Long Parliament (1640–53) begins to sit. | | |
| 1641 | Irish Rebellion. Grand Remonstrance | | |
| 1642 | Civil War begins | 1642 | Moves to London and experiences assurance of salvation |
| 1643 | Westminster Assembly meets. Solemn League and Covenant signed | 1643 | Publishes his first book, *A Display of Arminianism*, and becomes minister at Fordham |
| 1644 | Battles of Marston Moor and Newbury | 1644 | Marries Mary Rooke |
| 1645 | Laud executed. Formation of New Model Army | | |
| 1646 | End of first civil war | 1646 | Preaches before Parliament and moves to Coggeshall as minister. He becomes a Congregationalist |
| 1648 | Siege of Colchester in the second brief civil war. Pride's purge of Parliament | 1648 | Chaplain at the siege of Colchester |
| 1649 | Charles I executed. Cromwell's expedition to Ireland | 1649 | Accompanies Cromwell to Ireland |

| | |
|---|---|
| 1650 Cromwell invades Scotland | 1650 Appointed preacher to the Council of State and a chaplain to Cromwell with the expedition to Scotland |
| 1651 Battle of Worcester | 1651 Appointed Dean of Christ Church |
| 1652 War with the Dutch | 1652 Appointed Vice-Chancellor |
| 1653 Rump of Long Parliament expelled. Barebone's Parliament. Cromwell becomes Protector | 1653 Created D.D. |
| 1654 Cromwell's first Parliament | 1654 Appointed a "Trier" in the "Cromwellian" State Church |
| 1655 The rule of the major-generals. Penruddock's rising | 1655 Prepares the defence of Oxford |
| 1656 Cromwell's second Parliament | |
| | 1657 Opposes moves to make Cromwell the King. Ceases to be Vice-Chancellor |
| 1658 Cromwell dies and his son, Richard, becomes Protector | 1658 Takes prominent part in the Savoy Assembly |
| 1659 Richard Cromwell abdicates. General Monck marches from Scotland | 1659 Forms a gathered church of officers in London |
| 1660 Convention Parliament. Charles II returns. Act of Indemnity | 1660 Removed from Christ Church Deanery and so lives quietly at Stadhampton |
| 1661 Cavalier Parliament begins its long sitting. Corporation Act | |
| 1662 Act of Uniformity | |
| | 1663-4 Family move to Hartopp's home in Stoke Newington |
| 1664 Conventicle Act | |
| 1665 Five Mile Act. The Plague in London | |
| 1666 Fire of London | |
| 1667 Fall of Clarendon Milton publishes *Paradise Lost* | 1667 Active in seeking to persuade Parliament pass a Toleration Act |
| | 1669-70 Discusses Nonconformist Unity with Richard Baxter |
| 1670 Secret treaty of Dover concluded by Charles II | |
| 1672 Declaration of Indulgence | 1672 Personally thanks the King for the Indulgence |
| 1673 Test Act | 1673 Union of Caryl's church with that of Owen's under the latter's ministry |

1674 Death of John Milton

1678 Popish Plot
1679 Cavalier Parliament dissolved. First Exclusion Parliament
1680 Second Exclusion Parliament

1681 Third Exclusion (i.e. Oxford) Parliament
1683 Rye House Plot
1688 "Glorious Revolution"
1689 Toleration Act

1674 First volumes on Doctrine of Holy Spirit and Epistle to Hebrews appear
1675 First wife, Mary, dies
1676 Marries Dorothy D'Oyley


1680 Controversy with Dean Stillingfleet


1683 Dies at Ealing

# SELECT BIBLIOGRAPHY

## PRIMARY SOURCES

### A. MANUSCRIPT

1. *Bodleian Library, Oxford.*
   Correspondence of Philip, Lord Wharton, Rawlinson MSS 49–54.
   Register of Congregation, 1647–1658.
   Register of Convocation, 1647–1658.
   Note-Books of Students. Rawlinson MSS 233, 254 and 258.
2. *British Museum, London.*
   Correspondence of Henry Cromwell. Lansdowne MSS 821–3.
   Diary of Arthur Annesley. Additional MSS 18730 (1667–1675) and 40860 (1675–1684).*
   Note-Book of Oxford Student. Sloane MS 1472.
   Correspondence of Henry Hammond etc. Harleian MSS 6942.
3. *Christ Church, Oxford.*
   Chapter Book, 1647–1660.
   Disbursements Book, 1647–1660.
4. *Dr Williams's Library, London.*
   Correspondence of Richard Baxter. D.W.L. MSS 59.
   'The Entering Book, 1677–1691' of Roger Morrice. D.W.L. MSS P.Q.R.*
5. *Essex Record Office, Chelmsford.*
   Parish Registers of Coggeshall for 17th Century.
6. *Fordham Parish Church, Essex.*
   Parish Registers of Fordham for 17th Century.
7. *Lambeth Palace, London.*
   Admission Books of the Triers. MSS L.996–999.
   List of Ministers who supplied testimonials to the Triers, Jenkins MSS 1662.
8. *New College, London.*
   Owen MS Letters.
   Yarmouth Congregational Church Book.

*Parts of these are written in Shorthand.

## B. Printed

*Acts and Ordinances of the Interregnum, 1642–1660*, ed. C. H. Firth and R. S. Rait, 3 vols, 1911.
Asty, John: "Memoirs of the Life of John Owen," in *A Complete Collection of the Sermons of John Owen*, 1721.
Baillie, Robert: *Letters and Journals*, ed. David Laing, 3 vols, Edinburgh, 1842.
Barnes, Ambrose: *Memoirs of Ambrose Barnes*, ed. W. H. D. Longstaffe, (Surtees Society, L), 1867.
Baxter, Richard: *Reliquiae Baxterianae*, ed. Matthew Sylvester, 1696.
*Calendar of State Papers* (Domestic Series for years 1646–1683).
Canne, John: *Time of the End*, 1657.
*Constitutional Documents of the Puritan Revolution*, ed. S. R. Gardiner, 3rd ed., 1906.
Cotton, John: *The Keyes of the Kingdom of Heaven*, 1644.
*Creeds and Platforms of Congregationalism*, ed. W. Walker, with a new introduction by D. Horton, Philadelphia, 1960.
Cromwell, Oliver: *The Writings and Speeches of Oliver Cromwell*, ed. W. C. Abbott, 4 vols, Camb. Mass., 1937–47.
Crosfield, Thomas: *The Diary of Thomas Crosfield*, ed. F. S. Boas, 1935.
*Declaration of the Faith and Order . . . of the Congregational Churches (1658)*, ed. A. G. Matthews, 1958.
*Desiderata Curiosa*, ed. Francis Peck, 2 vols, 1779.
*Essay of Acomodation (1680)*, ed. Roger Thomas (Dr Williams's Library Occasional Paper No. 6.), 1957.
Evelyn, John: *The Diary of John Evelyn*, ed. E. S. De Beer, 1959.
*Flemings in Oxford*, ed. J. R. Magrath, Vol. I, Oxford, 1904.
Goodwin, Thomas: *The Works of Thomas Goodwin*, ed. J. C. Miller, IX Vols, Edinburgh, 1861.
*Here followeth a true Relation of some of the Sufferings inflicted upon . . . the Quakers*, 1654.
Henry, Philip: *Diaries and Letters*, ed. M. H. Lee, 1882.
Hubberthorne, Richard: *A True Testimony of the Zeal of Oxford-Professors*, 1654.
Hull, John: "Diary of John Hull" in *Archaeologia Americana*, Vol. 3, Boston, 1865.
Jaffray, Alexander: *The Diary of Alexander Jaffray*, ed. J. Barclay, 1833.
Johnston, Archibald: *The Diary of Sir Archibald Johnston*, ed. J. D. Ogilvie, Vol. III (1655–1660), Edinburgh, 1940.
Jolly, Thomas: *The Note Book of the Rev. Thomas Jolly*, ed. Henry Fishwick, Manchester, 1895.
Josselin, Ralph: *The Diary of Ralph Josselin, 1616–1683*, ed. E. Hockliffe, 1908.

*Journals of the House of Commons.*
*Journals of the House of Lords.*
*Life of John Owen,* 1720.
Ludlow, Edmund: *The Memoirs of Edmund Ludlow,* ed. C. H. Firth, 1894.
Marvell, Andrew: *The Poems and Letters,* ed. H. M. Margoliouth, 2 vols, Oxford, 1952.
Milton, John: *The Poetical Works,* ed. Helen Darbishire, 2 vols, Oxford, 1955.
*Musarum Oxoniensum,* 1654.
*Nicholas Papers,* ed. G. F. Farmer, 4 vols, 1886–1920.
*Original Records of Early Nonconformity,* ed. G. Lyon Turner, 3 vols, 1911–14.
*Original Memoirs written during the Civil War,* ed. Sir W. Scott, Edinburgh, 1806.
Owen, John: *The Correspondence of John Owen,* ed. Peter Toon, 1970.
Owen, John: *The Oxford Orations of John Owen,* ed. Peter Toon, Linkinhorne House, Linkinhorne, Cornwall, 1971.
Owen, John: *The Works of John Owen,* ed. W. H. Goold, 24 vols, Edinburgh, 1850–53.
Owen, John (and others): *Humble Proposals,* 1652.
Owen, John (and others): *Proposals,* 1653.
*Oxford University Statutes,* trans. G. R. M. Ward, 1854. Vol. I "The Caroline Code."
Pepys, Samuel: *The Diary of Samuel Pepys,* ed. H. B. Wheatley, 10 vols, 1893–99.
Pope, Walter: *The Life of Seth, Lord Bishop of Salisbury,* ed. J. M. Bamborough, Oxford, 1961.
*Records of the First Church of Boston, 1630–1868,* ed. R. D. Pierce, Boston, 1961.
*Register of the Visitors of the University of Oxford, 1647–1658,* ed. Montagu Burrows, 1881.
*Register of the Consultations of the Ministers of Edinburgh,* ed. William Stephen, Vols I and II (1652–1660), Edinburgh, 1921–30.
Rogers, John: *Ohel or Beth-shemesh,* 1653.
(Terrill, Edward): *The Records of a Church of Christ meeting in Broadmead, Bristol, 1640–1687,* ed. E. B. Underhill, 1847.
Thurloe, John: *A Collection of the State Papers of John Thurloe,* ed. Thomas Birch, 7 vols, 1742.
Vernon, George: *Letter to a Friend concerning some of Dr Owens Principles and Practices,* 1670.
*Westminster Confession of Faith,* 1648.
Wood, Anthony: *Athenae Oxonienses,* ed. Philip Bliss, 4 vols, Oxford, 1813–18.
Wood, Anthony: *History and Antiquities of the University of Oxford,* ed. John Gutch, 2 vols, Oxford, 1791.

SELECT BIBLIOGRAPHY 191
SECONDARY SOURCES

A. WORKS OF REFERENCE

*Alumni Cantabrigienses*, ed. J. and J. A. Venn, 4 vols, 1922–7.
*Alumni Oxonienses*, ed. J. Foster, 4 vols, 1891–2.
*Bibliography of Printed Works relating to the University of Oxford*, ed. E. H. Cordeaux and D. H. Merry, Oxford, 1968.
*Calamy Revised: being a revision of Edmund Calamy's "Account" of the ... Ejected*, ed. A. G. Matthews, Oxford, 1934.
*Catalogue of Ecclesiastical Records of the Commonwealth, 1643–1660, in the Lambeth Palace Library*, ed. Jane Houston, 1968.
*Dictionary of National Biography.*
*Dictionary of Welsh Biography down to 1940*, ed. Sir John Lloyd and R. T. Jenkins, 1959.
*Oxford Books, a Bibliography*, ed. F. Madan, Vol. 3. 1651–1660, Oxford, 1931.
Thomason, George: *Catalogue of the Pamphlets. Books, Newspapers, collected by George Thomason, 1640–1661*, 2 vols, 1908.


B. BOOKS AND PAMPHLETS

Abernathy, G. R.: *The English Presbyterians and the Stuart Restoration, 1648–1663*, Philadelphia, 1965.
Allen, J. W.: *English Political Thought, 1603–1660*, 2 vols, 1938.
Ashley, Maurice: *England in the Seventeenth Century*, 1952.
Ashley, Maurice: *Cromwell's Generals*, 1954.
Ashley, Maurice: *John Wildman*, 1947.
Bangs, Carl: *Arminius. A Study in the Dutch Reformation*, Nashville, 1971.
Barbour, Hugh: *The Quakers in Puritan England*, New Haven, 1964.
Bate, Frank: *The Declaration of Indulgence, 1672*, Liverpool, 1908.
Bayley, W. D'Oyley: *A Biographical Account ... of the House of D'Oyley*, 1845.
Berry, Sir J. (with S. G. Lee): *A Cromwellian Major-General: the Career of James Berry*, Oxford, 1938.
Bolam, C. G. (with others): *The English Presbyterians*, 1968.
Bosher, R. S.: *The Making of the Restoration Settlement*, 1951.
Brown, L. F.: *The Political Activities of the Baptists and Fifth Monarchy Men*, New York, 1965.
Browne, John: *History of Congregationalism in Norfolk and Suffolk* 1877.
Bruce, F. F.: *Tradition Old and New*, Exeter, 1970.
Brunton, D. (with D. M. Pennington): *Members of the Long Parliament*, 1954.

Buxton, L. H. D. (with S. Gibson): *Oxford University Ceremonies*, Oxford, 1935.
Carleton, J. D.: *Westminster School*, 1965.
Carruthers, S. W.: *The Everyday Work of the Westminster Assembly*, Philadelphia, 1943.
Clark, G. N.: *The Later Stuarts, 1660–1714*, Oxford, 1947.
Costin, W. C.: *The History of St John's College, Oxford, 1598–1860*, Oxford, 1958.
Cragg, G. R.: *The Church and the Age of Reason, 1648–1789*, 1966.
Cragg, G. R.: *Puritanism in the Period of the great persecution, 1660–1688*, Cambridge, 1957.
Cranston, Maurice: *John Locke*, 1957.
Curtis, M. H.: *Oxford and Cambridge in Transition*, Oxford, 1959.
Davids, T. W.: *Annals of Evangelical Nonconformity in Essex*, 1863.
Davies, Godfrey: *The Early Stuarts, 1603–1660*, Oxford, 1949.
Davies, Godfrey: *The Restoration of Charles II*, San Marino, 1955.
Davies, Horton: *The Worship of the English Puritans*, 1948.
Debus, A. G.: *The English Paracelsians*, 1965.
Dunlop, R.: *Ireland under the Commonwealth*, 2 vols, Manchester, 1913.
Douglas, J. D.: *Light in the North: the Story of the Scottish Covenanters*, Exeter, 1964.
Emerson, W. R.: *Monmouth's Rebellion*, New Haven, 1951.
Everitt, A. M.: *The Community of Kent and the Great Rebellion, 1640–1660*, Leicester, 1966.
Ferguson, James: *Robert Ferguson the Plotter*, Edinburgh, 1887.
Firth, C. H.: *The Last Years of the Protectorate*, 2 vols, 1909.
Firth, C. H. (with Godfrey Davies): *The Regimental History of Cromwell's Army*, Oxford, 1940.
Gardiner, S. R.: *History of the Great Civil War*, 3 vols, 1888–1891.
Gardiner, S. R.: *History of the Commonwealth and Protectorate*, 4 vols, 1903.
Greaves, R. L.: *The Puritan Revolution and Educational Thought*, New Brunswick, 1969.
Gunn, J. A. W.: *Politics and the Public Interest in the Seventeenth Century*, 1969.
Haller, William: *The Rise of Puritanism*, New York, 1957.
Haller, William: *Foxe's Book of Martyrs and the Elect Nation*, 1963.
Henderson, G. D.: *Religious Life in Seventeenth-Century Scotland*, Cambridge, 1937.
Henderson, R. W.: *The Teaching Office in the Reformed Tradition*, Philadelphia, 1962.
Hill, Christopher: *God's Englishman, Oliver Cromwell and the English Revolution*, 1970.
Hill, Christopher: *Puritanism and Revolution*, 1965.

## SELECT BIBLIOGRAPHY

Hyde, Edward: *The History of the Rebellion*, 7 vols, Oxford, 1849.
Jones, A. T.: *Notes on the Early Days of Stepney Meeting, 1614–1689*, 1887.
Jones, R. Tudur: *Congregationalism in England, 1662–1962*, 1962.
Jordan, W. K.: *The Development of Religious Toleration in England, 1640–1660*, 1938.
Kearney, Hugh: *Scholars and Gentlemen: Universities and Society in pre-industrial Britain, 1500–1700*, 1970.
Lacey, D. R.: *Dissent and Parliamentary Politics in England, 1661–1689*, New Brunswick, 1969.
Mahaffy, J. P.: *An Epoch in Irish History: Trinity College, Dublin, 1591–1660*, 1903.
Mallet, C. E.: *A History of the University of Oxford*, 3 vols, 1924–27.
Masson, D. H.: *The Life of John Milton*, 7 vols, 1877.
McLachlan, H. J.: *Socinianism in Seventeenth-Century England*, 1951.
Miller, Perry: *Orthodoxy in Massachusetts, 1630–1650*, Cambridge, Mass., 1933.
Miller, Perry: *Errand into the Wilderness*, Cambridge, Mass., 1956.
Moffatt, James: "Introductory Sketch: The Life of Owen" in *The Golden Book of John Owen*, 1904.
Mullinger, J. B.: *The University of Cambridge*, 3 vols, 1873–1911.
Neal, Daniel: *History of the Puritans*, 4 vols, 1732–38.
Nuttall, G. F.: *The Holy Spirit in Puritan Faith and Experience*, Oxford, 1946.
Nuttall, G. F.: *Visible Saints, The Congregational Way, 1640–1660*, Oxford, 1957.
Nuttall, G. F. (with Owen Chadwick) (ed's): *From Uniformity to Unity, 1662–1962*, 1962.
Ogg, David: *England in the reign of Charles II*, 1956.
Orme, William: "Memoirs of the Life and Writings of Dr John Owen" in *Works of John Owen*, ed. T. Russell, Vol. I, 1826.
Packer, J. W.: *The Transformation of Anglicanism, 1643–1660, with special reference to Henry Hammond*, Manchester, 1969.
Paul, R. S.: *The Lord Protector*, 1955.
Purver, Marjery: *The Royal Society, Concept and Creation*, 1967.
Rex, M. B.: *University Representation in England, 1604–1690*, 1954.
Richards, Thomas: *A History of the Puritan Movement in Wales*, 1920.
Richards, Thomas: *Religious Developments in Wales, 1654–1662*, 1923.
Richards, Thomas: *The Puritan Visitation of Jesus College, Oxford*, 1925.
Roots, Ivan: *The Great Rebellion, 1642–1660*, 1966.
Shaw, W. A.: *A History of the English Church, 1640–1660*, 2 vols, 1900.
Shirren, A. J.: *Chronicles of the Fleetwood House*, 1951.
Smith, Harold: *The Ecclesiastical History of Essex*, Colchester, 1932.
Stoughton, John: *History of Religion in England*, 4 vols, 1881.
Thomas, Keith: *Religion and the Rise of Magic*, 1970.

Thompson, H. L.: *Christ Church*, 1900.
Trevor-Roper, H. R.: *Archbishop Laud, 1573–1645*, 1965.
Toon, Peter (ed.): *Puritans, the Millennium and the Future of Israel, Puritan Eschatology, 1600–1660*, 1970.
Whiting, C. E.: *Studies in English Puritanism, 1660–1688*, 1931.
Wilson, J. F.: *Pulpit in Parliament*, Princeton, 1969.
Woolrych, A. H.: *Penruddock's Rising, 1655*, 1955.
Zagorin, Perez: *A History of Political Thought in the English Revolution*, 1954.

C. ARTICLES

Crippen, T. G.: "Dr Watt's Church Book," *Transactions* of the Cong. Historical Society, Vol. I, 1901.
Liu Tai: "The Calling of the Barebone's Parliament Reconsidered," *Journal of Ecclesiastical History*, Vol. XXII, 1971.
Mayor, Stephen: "The Teaching of John Owen concerning the Lord's Supper," *Scottish Journal of Theology*, Vol. XVIII, 1965.
Nuttall, G. F.: "Presbyterians and Independents," *Journal* of the Presbyterian Historical Society, Vol. X, 1952.
Pocock, N.: "Illustrations of the State of the Church during the Rebellion," *Theologian and Ecclesiastic*, Vols VI–XV, 1848–53.
Powicke, F. J.: "The Independents of 1652," *Transactions* of the Cong. Hist. Society, Vol. IX, 1924.
Turner, G. L.: "Williamson's Spy-Book," *Transactions* of the Cong. Hist. Society, Vol. V, 1907.
Woolrych, A. H.: "The Calling of the Barebone's Parliament," *English Historical Review*, LXXX, 1965.

D. UNPUBLISHED THESES

Davis, J. C. W.: "John Owen D.D. Puritan Preacher and Ecclesiastical Statesman," Liverpool University, M.A., 1949.
Gundry, S. N.: "John Owen's Doctrine of the Scriptures," Union College of British Columbia, S.T.M., 1967.
Liu, Tai: "Saints in Power: The Barebone's Parliament," University of Indiana, Ph.D., 1969.
Lloyd, R. G.: "The Life and Work of John Owen with special reference to the Socinian Controversies of the 17th Century," Edinburgh University, Ph.D., 1942.
Pytches, Peter: "The Doctrine of the Holy Spirit in the thought of John Owen," Bristol University, M.Litt., 1965.

Vose, G. N.: "Profile of a Puritan: John Owen and his theology," University of Iowa, Ph.D., 1963.
Wallace, D. B.: "The Life and Thought of John Owen to 1660: A Study of the Significance of Calvinist Theology in English Puritanism," Princeton University, Ph.D., 1965.

*Note:* These theses on Owen are all primarily theological except the first by Mr Davis which is very brief. None of them covers the large area dealt with in this book. That by the late R. G. Lloyd is possibly the best.

# INDEX OF SUBJECTS AND PLACES

ACT, The (*Comitia*), 4, 65, 74–5, 79
Acts of Parliament: Advancement of Gospel in Ireland, 42; Clerical Disabilities, 68, 95; Conventicle, 125–6, 130–1, 138, 150; Corporation, 125; Five-Mile, 125, 131, 148, 150; Habeus Corpus Amendment, 142; Indemnity, 151–2; Licensing, 143; Oblivion, 126; Uniformity, 125, 132
Accomodation Order, 106
Amyraldism, 27, 40
Antichrist, 9, 12, 26, 81, 158
Arminianism, 6–7, 12, 13–15, 25, 26–7, 40, 95, 140, 174
Arts, Liberal, 5–6, 52
Ascot, Hamlet of, 10
Astrology, 52, 84
Atonement, doctrine of, 13, 26–7, 40
Attacks on the Universities, 69–73

BAPTISTS, 10, 85, 91, 140, 162
Barebone's Assembly, 69–70, 87–89, 91, 93, 95
Bible: authority of, 23, 28, 34, 59–60, 87, 120, 123, 137, 165. Polyglot, 59, 175

CABAL, 133
Calvinism, 3, 8, 12, 26–7, 49, 56, 104
Cambridge University, 51–2, 70
Catechisms: by Owen, 17–18; Racovian, 83; Twofold, 95
Cause, the good old, 109–110, 121
Christ Church, London, 37
Christ Church, Oxford, 6–7, 47–8, 53–63
Christ, the glory of, 168–171
Code, the Clarendon, 125, 132, 137, 149
Coggeshall, the parish of, 25–9
Colchester, the siege of, 31
Communion, Holy, 4, 8, 28, 159–160
Communion, Lay, 145–6
Congregational churches, 102, 116, 117, 118, 133, 160ff; Bedford, 161; Coggeshall, 28, 150, 160; Leadenhall Street, London, 149, 153–160; Magdalen College, 57; Newcastle, 43; Norwich, 161; Wallingford House, 109–115, 150; Yarmouth, 105, 114–119
Congregational Way, 18, 23, 27–30, 44, 46, 57–8, 104–7, 124–5, 129, 150, 163–5
Conventicles: in Moorgate, 130–1, 150–53; in Stadhampton, 57, 123, 130, 150
Covenant, Sacred Vow and, 16

DECLARATION OF THE ARMY, 43
*Declaration of Faith and Order*, 81, 104–6
Diggers, 69
Directory for Public Worship, 26–8, 52
Discipline: in parishes, 22–3; in Oxford, 60, 75–7
Dissenting Brethren, 18, 20, 29, 144
Distresses, 148
Dover, Secret Treaty of, 139
Dress, academic, 73–4, 79
Drogheda, massacre at, 39
Dunbar, battle of, 45

EDGEHILL, BATTLE OF, 12
Ejectors, 93
Engagement, the, 48, 53, 99
Epistles, dedicatory (by Owen), 14, 16, 21, 26, 34, 46, 59, 78, 98, 127
Essex, religion in, 20–22, 29
Eschatology, doctrine of, 34–6, 49, 81–2, 88, 120, 142 (See Millennium)

FEDERAL THEOLOGY, 169–70
Fifth Monarchists, 36, 91
Fordham, parish of, 17–19

GOSPEL, the need for propagation of, 1, 20–2, 38, 40, 41–2, 66, 79–80, 83, 104, 120, 123, 143; *Proposals* for propagation of, 84–5, 86–7, 89, 94–5
Grand Remonstrance, 11

HARVARD COLLEGE, 130, 163
Hebrews, Epistle to, 127, 168, 171, 177
Holy Spirit, doctrine of, 13, 83, 166–7
Hurley, 10–11
*Humble Petition and Advice*, 90, 100–101
*Humble Remonstrance*, 32

196

# INDEX OF SUBJECTS AND PLACES 197

INDEPENDENTS (Independency), 20, 30, 31, 33, 35, 37, 53, 58, 64, 82, 92, 110, 126, 129, 131, 162
Indulgence(s): 129, 132-5, 139, 141
*Instrument of Government*, 90, 92, 95
Ireland, expedition to, 36-42, 48

JEWS: entry into England, 97; conversion of, 80, 83, 96, 152; conference concerning, 96-7
Justification by faith, 156, 170

KENTISH REBELLION, 16
Keys of the Kingdom, 18, 27, 105, 135
Kirk, the Scottish, 45, 97-8

LAUDIANISM, 6-10, 15, 21, 25
League, Solemn League and Covenant, 19, 22, 43-4, 48
Lecture, the Ancient Merchants, 140-1
Levellers, 37, 69
London, City of, 22, 37, 130, 139, 148
Lord's Prayer, 58

MAGDALEN COLLEGE, Oxford, 38, 57
Magistrate, the Christian, 34, 38, 87, 90, 119, 125, 136-8, 148, 155
Massachusetts, 2, 29, 30, 124, 162-3
Millennium, doctrine of, 12, 30, 36, 85, 91 (see Eschatology)

NASEBY, BATTLE OF, 20
Nobility, 59, 125-6
Nonconformists, 61, 79, 131, 133ff., 142ff
Nonconformist Unity, 135, 147

OXFORD UNIVERSITY, 4-9, 12, 47, 50ff; Congregation of, 52; Convocation of, 52-3, 63-5; Statutes of, 9-10, 79; Visitation of (1647), 51-2; Visitors of, 65-8

PELAGIANISM, 14
Perseverance of the saints, doctrine of, 13, 95
Penruddock's Rising, 68, 96
Plague; at Oxford, 2, 63; in London, 131, 159
Plots: Popish, 142, 158-9; Protestant, 156; Rye House, 149, 156
Prayer Book, 3, 16, 26, 94, 123
Preaching, the importance of, 55-7, 80

Predestination, doctrine 15, of, 7, 13, 107
Presbyterianism, 18, 23, 29-30, 35, 42, 82, 106-7, 119
Providence, doctrine of, 13, 19, 32, 40, 46, 120
Puritanism, 2-3, 12, 16, 17, 22, 40

QUAKERS, 47, 76-7, 101, 119
Queen's College, Oxford, 3-7

RADICALS, 88-9, 91
Religion, Settlement of, 1, 83ff, 90ff
Remonstrance (Dutch Arminian), 13
Remonstrants (Scottish Protestors), 97-8
Resolutioners (Scottish), 97-8
Restoration of Charles II, 123-4
Revelation, Book of, 12, 34, 35, 49, 82, 136, 142
Roman Catholicism, 11, 12, 26, 35, 38, 82, 128, 134, 141-2, 147, 158
*Root and Branch Petition*, 18
Royal Society, 71

SABBATH (Sabbatarianism), 2-3, 169
Savoy Assembly (1658), 103-7
Savoy Conference (1661), 129
Schism, 94, 175
Scotland, invasion of, 43-7
Scot's Hall, 15-16
Sermons (by Owen), 20, 25, 31-4, 35, 37-8, 41, 43, 46, 47, 81-3, 88, 96, 108, 157-160
Socinianism, 40, 58, 95, 174
Stadhampton, parish of, 2-3, 10, 57, 130

TERRAE FILIUS, 4, 75
Temptation, doctrine of, 55
Toleration; pleas for, 20, 24, 30, 34-5, 62, 129, 132-5, 137-9, 147, 175; bills for, 134
Triers, 22, 91-3, 98
Trinity College, Dublin, 36, 39-40, 42

WALLINGFORD HOUSE, 109-112, 118, 151, 175
Westminster Assembly, 18, 22, 25, 29, 104, 106
Westminster Confession of Faith, 15, 104, 177
Westminster School, 54-5, 61
Whigs, 143-4, 148, 156
Worcester, battle of, 81

# INDEX OF PERSONAL NAMES

(*modern authors are not given if their names appear only in the footnotes and bibliography.*)

ABELL, William, 19
Abney, Sir Edward, 129
Abney Lady Sarah, 129, 153
Adolphus, King Gustavus, 44
Airay, Henry, 4
Alsop, John, 17
Alsop, Vincent, 145
Alsted, Henry, 12
Ames, William, 15
Amyraut Moise, 27
Andrewes, Lancelot, 6
Angier, Samuel, 61, 123
Anglesey, Countess of, 126, 155
Anglesey, Earl of (Arthur Annesley), 109, 111, 125, 136, 138, 142, 153
Annesley, Samuel, 135, 142
Arlington, Lord, 131, 139
Arminius, Jacobus, 14
Arrowsmith, John, 69, 91
Ashfield, Colonel, 109
Ashley, Lord (Earl of Shaftesbury), 133, 143, 148, 156
Ashurst, Henry, 131
Asty, John, 5, 12, 13, 26, 36, 60, 75, 77, 114, 126-7, 148, 155, 161-2, 174, 176
Asty, Robert, 160, 161
Atkyns, Sir Robert, 132
Augustine of Hippo, 14, 15
BAGSHAW, Edward, 61
Baillie, Robert, 121
Bancroft, John, 6
Barker, Matthew, 84, 116
Barlow, Thomas, 6, 48, 71, 130, 134, 161
Barnes, Ambrose, 43, 173
Baron, James, 67, 74
Barret, John, 145
Barrow, Henry, 69
Bartlet, William, 18
Basnet, Samuel, 65
Bates, William, 134, 140
Baxter, Richard, 40, 85, 91-2, 95-6, 113, 131, 134-136, 140-143, 145, 147, 149, 155, 174, 176
Baylie, Richard, 8
Bedford, Duke of 129
Beerman, William, 153, 154
Bendish, Mrs Bridget, 152
Berkeley, Earl of, 125, 127
Berry, Benjamin, 61
Berry, James, 96, 110, 112, 115, 151-152

Beverley, John, 57, 94
Beza, Theodore, 15
Bidle, John, 95
Birch, John, 132
Bishop, Samuel, 60
Blower, Samuel, 57
Blackwell, Charles, 60
Bold, Henry, 60
Booth, Sir George, 115-116
Bowles, Edward, 45
Brett, Anthony, 60
Bridge, William, 18, 84, 103, 115, 118
Brightman, Thomas, 12
Brockman, Sir William, 16
Brooks, Thomas, 162
Browne, Robert, 69
Bruce, Andrew, 61
Bruce, Thomas, 92
Buckingham, Duke of (George Villiers), 133-134
Bunyan, John, 149, 161-2
Burgess, Benjamin, 62
Burnet, Gilbert, 103
Burnet, William, 92
Burton, Hezekiah, 134
Burroughs, Jeremiah, 18
Butler, William, 85, 86
Button, Ralph, 54, 84, 93
Busby, John, 60
Busby, Richard, 61
Byfield, Adoniram, 84
Byfield, Richard, 27
CALAMY, Edmund, 13, 108
Calvin, John, 14, 15
Cameron, James, 27
Canes, Vincent, 128
Canne, John, 36, 91
Cardell, John, 33
Caryl, Joseph, 45, 46, 48, 56, 92, 98, 101, 103, 115-116, 129, 151, 153, 162, 163
Casaubon, Meric, 58
Cawdry, Daniel, 94
Chaundler, Walter, 2
Charles I, 1, 7, 11, 16, 20, 30, 32, 33, 37, 43, 82
Charles II, 42, 44, 45, 47, 82, 122-123, 125, 129, 139, 142, 149, 156, 158
Charnock, Stephen, 57
Cheynell, Francis, 51, 53, 95
Chillingworth, William, 3
Clagett, William, 167
Clarkson, David, 155, 157, 173

Clayton, Sir Robert, 144
Clifford, Thomas, 133
Cock, Samuel, 18
Cole, Thomas, 60, 62
Collins, John, 140, 148, 162-3
Conant, John, 65, 67, 77-8
Cope, Sir Anthony, 2
Cornish, Henry, 54, 93
Cosin, John, 6, 9
Cotton, John, 18, 27, 30, 36, 94, 105, 124
Cox, Richard, 53
Cragg, G. R., 138, 150, 165
Crompton, William, 62
Croke, Unton, 103
Cromwell, Henry, 9, 42, 99, 109
Cromwell, John, 161
Cromwell, Oliver, 30, 36, 37, 38, 39, 40ff, 43ff, 50, 52, 54, 77, 80-1, 85, 87-8, 89-90, 91, 94-102, 151-2
Cromwell, Richard, 77, 99, 103, 107, 111-113, 138
Crosfield, Thomas, 4
Cudworth, Ralph, 25
Curl, Thomas, 62
Curtis, Mark, 6
DAILLÉ, Jean, 27
Desborough, John, 89, 96, 99-100, 110, 111, 115, 117, 151-2
Dell, William, 70
Dscartes, René, 167
Dodd, John (the elder), 25
Dodd, John, 25, 60
Dodd, Nehemiah, 25
Dodd, Robert, 25
Dolben, John, 77
Dormer, Sir Robert, 10
D'Oyley, Dorothy, 149, 152
D'Oyley, John, 2, 149
D'Oyley, Thomas, 149, 152
D'Oyley, Ursula, 2
Duppa, Brian, 7, 8, 53
Durie, John, 69, 83-4, 91, 102
Dye, Abraham, 92
Dyer, Richard, 62
EDWARDS, Jonathan, 63
Elizabeth, Queen, 53, 61
Ellaston, John, 151-2
Erbery, William, 51
Evelyn, John, 72
FAIRFAX, Thomas, Lord, 20, 30, 31, 32, 36, 37, 42, 43, 50, 52, 80, 133

198

## INDEX OF PERSONAL NAMES

Fell, John, 51, 77
Fell, Samuel, 48, 53
Ferguson, Robert, 148–149, 156, 157
Fisher, Samuel, 119
Fitch, Colonel, 109
Fleetwood, Charles, 43, 96, 110, 111–112, 113, 115–116, 117–118, 130, 151, 153, 155, 168, 171
Fleetwood, Cromwell, 155
Fleetwood, Smith, 130
Fletcher, Elizabeth, 76
Forbes, James, 114
Ford, Stephen, 92
Francis, John, 92
French, Peter, 50, 54, 65, 67, 68, 73, 93
French, Samuel, 62
Frewen, Accepted, 8
GALE, Theophilus, 57
Gardiner, S. R., 30, 42, 68, 73, 86, 90, 92, 94, 100
Gilbert, Thomas, 130, 173
Gillespie, Patrick, 98
Godfrey, Sir E. B., 148
Goddard, Jonathan, 42, 50, 65, 67, 68
Godolphin, William, 62
Goffe, William, 38, 89, 109–110, 116
Good, William, 43
Goodwin, John, 67, 95
Goodwin, Thomas, 18, 37, 38, 42, 50, 55, 56, 57, 65, 67, 73, 74, 84, 90, 91, 93, 95, 103–5, 107, 131, 160
Goold, W. H., 28, 175
Gower, Stanley, 27
Greenhill, William, 84, 103, 116, 162
Greenwood, Daniel, 63
Griffith, George, 84, 98, 103, 112, 148, 160, 162, 163
Grotius, Hugo, 58
HAMPDEN, Richard, 131
Hammond, Henry, 58–9, 79
Hardcastle, Thomas, 163
Hartcliffe, Mrs Hester, 2
Hartcliffe, John, 2
Harris, Robert, 2, 67, 93
Harrison, Colonel, 39
Harrison, Thomas, 84
Hartlib, Samuel, 69
Hartopp, Sir Edward, 130
Hartopp, Lady Elizabeth, 130, 153, 168
Hartopp, Sir John, 130, 142, 151, 153, 168
Hartopp, Lady Mary, 130

Hawkins, William, 60
Henry VIII, 2, 53
Henry, Matthew, 57, 79
Henry, Philip, 57, 62, 79
Herbert, Henry, 59
Herbert, Lord, 59
Hewson, John, 51
Heywood, Oliver, 133
Hibbert, John, 61
Hill, Christopher, 20–21 35, 37, 38, 88
Hill, Thomas, 8
Hoar, Leonard, 163
Hodges, Nathaniel, 62
Holmes, Mrs, 131
Homes, Elizabeth, 76
Honeywood, Sir Thomas, 31
Hooper, John, 144
Horton, Thomas, 92
How, Samuel, 69
Howe, John, 143, 145
Howell, Francis, 57, 65, 67, 74, 93
Hoyle, Joshua, 51
Hughes, Obadiah, 62
Hunter, Joseph, 133–134
Hyde, Edward (Earl of Clarendon), 78, 128–9, 130–131, 133
IGNATIUS, 58–9
Ingoldsby, Colonel, 109
Ireton, Henry, 31, 33, 39, 42, 83
JACKSON, Arthur, 13
Jaffray, Alexander, 46, 47
Jacombe, Thomas, 143
James I (VI of Scotland), 1, 73
James II, 141, 143, 148, 158
Janeway, James, 62
Jenkyn, William, 140
Jennings, John, 62
Jessey, Constantine, 38
Jessey, Henry, 88, 92, 130
Johnston, Archibald, 91, 95, 99, 112
Johnson, John, 92
Johnson, Thomas, 60
Jollie, Thomas, 142, 147, 149, 161
Josselin, Ralph, 29, 31, 48, 74
KEARNEY, Hugh, 69–71
Kempster, John, 62, 92
Kennington, Mrs, 154
Kiffin, William, 69
LAMBERT, John, 30, 43, 71, 89, 110, 112, 115–116, 117–118
Langley, Henry, 54
Laud, William, 4, 6, 7, 8, 9, 10, 17, 21, 42, 51, 53

Lauderdale, Earl of, 133
Lee, Richard, 84
Lee, Samuel, 152
Leslie, David, 44
Lightfoot, John, 69
Lilburne, Robert, 44, 47, 109
Lisle, Sir George, 31
Lisle, John, 44
Lloyd, Griffith, 151-2
Lloyd, Jenkin, 42, 84
Locke, John, 60, 62
Lockyer, Nicholas, 115, 121
Loder, John, 126, 140, 162
Loeffs, Isaac, 155, 157
Long, Thomas, 58
Lovelace, John Lord, 10–12
Lovelace, Lady Anne, 10
Lucas, Sir Charles, 19, 31
Lucas, Sir John, 19
Ludlow, Edmund, 99, 106, 110, 115, 117
Luther, Martin, 73, 112
MADDOCKS, William, 62
Malbon, Samuel, 92
Manduit, John, 62
Manton, Thomas, 95, 108, 111, 129, 134–5, 139–140
Mary Tudor, Queen, 53, 144
Marvell, Andrew, 137
Marshall, George, 84
Marshall, Stephen, 48, 88, 95
Martyr, Peter, 53
Mather, Cotton, 174
Matthews, A. G., 105–6
Mead, Matthew, 148, 163
Mede, Joseph, 12
Menasseh, ben Israel, 97
Meadows, John, 92
Mildmay, Sir Henry, 33
Miller, Perry, 2, 170
Mills, John, 53-4
Milton, John, 85, 101, 121
Moffatt, James, 175
Monck, George, 116–120
Monmouth, Duke of, 143, 149, 156
Montague, Richard, 6, 8
Montgomery, Maj. Gen., 44, 45
Morice, Sir Wm., 127, 149
Moulin, Lewis Du, 51
NALTON, James, 21
Naylor, James, 101
Neile, Richard, 6
Newham, Thomas, 62
Nicholas, Sir Edward, 128
Norwich, Earl of, 30, 32
Norwood, Robert, 85
Nuttall, G. F., 40, 73, 113, 115, 132, 160, 164, 167
Nye, Philip, 18, 48, 83-4,

Nye, Philip, *contd.*
  88, 90, 92, 95, 99, 101,
  103–5, 116, 119, 140, 160,
OATES, Titus, 142
Oliver, William, 127
Orrery, Earl of, 125–6
Orme, William, 34, 103,
  126, 167, 173, 174
Overbury, Sir Thomas, 1,
  138, 155
Owen, Mrs Dorothy, 155
Owen, Henry (Rev), 1–4
Owen, Henry, 2, 99, 149
Owen, Mrs Mary, 63, 130
Owen, Philemon, 2
Owen, Matthew, 176
Owen, Martyn, 140, 149
Owen, Thankful, 57, 65, 74,
  91, 93, 123
Owen, William, 2, 3, 5, 93
PARKER, Samuel, 136–138,
  173
Payne, Robert, 48
Payne, William, 171
Pelagius, 14
Pembroke, Earl of, 47
Penn, William, 123, 133
Pepys, Samuel, 133
Perkins, William, 15, 56
Peter, Hugh, 20, 111
Philippa, Queen, 4
Pickering, Charles, 60, 89
Plumsted, Augustine, 84
Pococke, Edward, 51, 53–4,
  93
Polhill, Edward, 152, 156
Polhill, Mrs, 152–153
Ponder, Nathaniel, 162
Pope, Walter, 74
Potter, Christopher, 4, 7
Powell, Vavasor, 91
Pride, Colonel, 33, 99
Prideaux, John, 8
Prynne, William, 8
Puleston, Lady Elizabeth, 63
Puleston, Sir John (Judge), 63
Puleston, Roger, 63
RATCLIFFE, Anthony, 60
Reynolds, Edward, 48, 51,
  53–4, 108, 120
Reynolds, Sir John, 101
Rich, Robert (Earl of
  Warwick), 25–26
Ridley, Nicholas, 144
Rogers, Christopher, 8, 54,
  67, 68, 93, 99
Rogers, John, 36, 40, 91
Rooke, Mary, 17
Rooke, Thomas, 16, 17
Rooke, William, 17
Routley, Erik, 173

Russell, Thomas, 174
SADLER, Anthony, 92
Samson, Thomas, 53
Sayer, John, 62
Scobell, Henry, 116
Scott, Sir Edward, 15, 16,
  17
Scott, Lady Mary, 15
Sedgwick, Joseph, 70, 72
Sedgwick, Obadiah, 25, 92
Segary, William, 62
Shakespeare, William, 1
Sharp, James, 98, 104, 110
Sheldon, Gilbert, 48, 136
Shute, Benjamin, 153
Shute, Mary, 153
Singleton, John, 2, 60, 62–3
Simpson, Sidrach, 18, 70,
  72, 83–4, 95
Slater, Samuel, 148
Smyth, William, 8
South, Robert, 62
Stafford, Lord, 143
Staines, William, 152
Staunton, Edmund, 65,
  75–6, 93
Stephens, Philip, 67, 68
Steele, William, 152
Sterry, Peter, 121
Strachan, Colonel, 45
Stubb, Henry,
Stillingfleet, Edward,
  144–147, 176
Stoughton, John, 115, 118,
  132, 141, 148, 177
Stoughton, Thomas, 25
Sydenham, Colonel, 110, 112
Sylvester, Edward, 3
TABBAL, 82
Taylor, Thomas, 56
Terry, Edward, 57
Thanet, Earl of, 16
Thomson, Andrew, 175
Thompson, Mrs Frances, 153
Thompson, John, 62, 153
Thornton, John, 129, 176
Thorndike, Herbert, 134
Thurm, Henry, 60
Travers, Walter, 40
Trevor, Sir John, 125, 127
Trosse, George, 79
Tuckney, Anthony, 91
Twisse, William, 8, 30
Tyrell, Lady, 129
UPTON, Ambrose, 54, 93
Ussher, James, 40
VANE, Sir Henry, 106, 112,
  115, 117
Veal, Edward, 60, 62
Venner, Thomas, 123
Vernon, George, 58,

113–4, 138, 155, 160, 173
Vincent, Nathaniel, 62, 142
Vincent, Thomas, 60, 62
Vivien, Daniel, 66
WALL, John, 51, 54
Waller, Edmund, 30
Wallis, John, 51, 93
Walters, Lucy, 156
Walton, Brian, 59, 175
Ward, John, 61
Ward, Seth, 51, 71, 72, 74, 93
Washbourne, Richard, 61
Waterhouse, Thomas, 92
Watson, Thomas, 33
Watts, Isaac, 129, 151
Webster, John, 71, 79
Wentworth, Sir Peter, 19
Wesley, Charles, 61, 135
West, Edward, 62, 92
Westrow, Thomas, 15, 19
Whalley, Edmund, 89,
  109–110, 116
Wharton, Philip Lord,
  125–7, 130, 138, 142, 157
Whitelocke, Bulstrode, 38,
  111, 116, 128
Whitfield, Henry, 82
Wildman, John, 134
William of Orange, 150
Williamson, Sir Joseph, 123,
  131
Willis, Dr, 76–7
Willoughby, Francis Lord
  125–6
Willoughby, William Lord
  125–6
Wilkins, John, 50, 71, 72,
  93, 98, 134
Wilkinson, Henry (of Christ
  Church), 3, 53–4, 67–8, 93
Wilkinson, Henry (of
  Magdalen Hall), 51
Wilkinson, John, 8
Wilkinson, Lady Vere, 153
Wilson, Thomas, 6
Winter, Samuel, 42
Wood, Anthony, 1, 3, 7, 8,
  52, 53, 55, 60, 65, 67, 68,
  73, 74, 102–3, 110, 124,
  126, 130, 131, 173
Wren, Christopher,
Wren, Matthew, 9
Wyche, Cyril, 62
Wyclif, John, 4

www.ingramcontent.com/pod-product-compliance
Lightning Source LLC
Chambersburg PA
CBHW070742160426
43192CB00009B/1544